Flagstad

FLAGSTAD

Singer of the Century

HOWARD VOGT

Secker & Warburg
London

First published in England 1987 by
Martin Secker & Warburg Ltd
54 Poland Street, London W1V 3DF

Copyright © 1987 by Howard Vogt

British Cataloguing in Publication Data

Vogt, Howard
    Flagstad : singer of the century.
    1. Flagstad, Kirsten   2. Singers ——
    Biography
    I. Title
    782.1'092'4   ML420.F55

ISBN 0–436–55800–9

Photoset by Deltatype, Ellesmere Port
Printed by Redwood Burn Ltd., Trowbridge, Wiltshire

In memory of
my mother and father
whose love of music
found expression in their
children

I see the singer's mission, in this world of too much unrest, misery and hatred, as one of qualifying himself as an artist and as a human being to the point where he is able to bring to his listeners a message of beauty, humanity and poetry. It is a great task, one whose goal reaches far beyond psychological and geographical barriers, and one which in the achievement shows that spiritaul values can unite the divided.

Aksel Schiøtz
Danish tenor
1906–75

Contents

Contents

Illustrations

Illustrations

Between pages 108 and 109

Between pages 172 and 173

Illustrations

29 Victor de Sabata lectures Flagstad at La Scala, Milan, 1949. Kirsten Flagstad Memorial Collection, San Francisco.
30 Flagstad's first post-war appearance in London, 1947. Kirsten Flagstad Memorial Collection, San Francisco.
31 Pickets outside Carnegie Hall, New York, 1947. Kirsten Flagstad Memorial Collection, San Francisco.

Between pages 204 and 205

32 Flagstad and Hans Hotter in *Die Walküre*, Covent Garden, 1948. Kirsten Flagstad Memorial Collection, San Francisco.
33 A *Fidelio* rehearsal at the Metropolitan Opera, 1951. Courtesy of Metropolitan Opera Archives.
34 Karl Böhm, Constance Shacklock, Kirsten Flagstad and Set Svanholm, London, 1949. Courtesy of Norsk Musikksamling.
35 Four generations at Amalienborg, Kristiansand, Norway, 1952. Photo Sturlason; courtesy of Aslaug Rein.
36 Flagstad at rehearsal for recording of *Das Rheingold*, with Set Svanholm and George London, Vienna, 1958. Photo Hans Wild, London.
37 The music room at Amalienborg, 1957. Photo Kjell Mardon Olsen; courtesy of Berit Stabben.
38 Flagstad at the Grieg memorial concert, Albert Hall, London, 1957. Courtesy of Norsk Musikksamling.
39 The Flagstad family at the dedication of the Kirsten Flagstad statue, Oslo, 1982. Photo Tor T. Gulliksrud; courtesy of Aslaug Rein.

Note: in regard to photographs from the various archives, an effort has always been made to identify the photographer and/or agency.

Foreword

The Grand Canyon, that amazing two-hundred-mile stretch of Arizona, is like nothing else in the world. To see it is to be taken immediately by its grandeur and welcoming serenity. The voice of Kirsten Flagstad was no less awe-inspiring: it was a grand and glorious monument to nature.

In her stillness, in her minimal use of gesture, the natural expressiveness of her voice with its myriad of textures and colours flowed freely. Just as subtle changes in the relative positions of sun and earth cast different colours over the Canyon, so Flagstad's slightest movement was at once telling and just enough. The splendid vocal line, the ability to fill up every space in the bar and phrase with wonderfully sustained and focused sound made her, quite simply, a marvel.

Howard Vogt has written a loving account of Flagstad the voice and Flagstad the person. Here we see her natural development as a musician growing up in a household where music-making was the family industry. And it is clear how these early experiences enhanced and sustained her later life.

The grace with which Kirsten Flagstad lived her life and, through her art, enriched the lives of countless others reminds me of the words of still another natural wonder – Leonardo da Vinci, who said: 'Why not let your work be such that after death you become an image of immortality?' And so she did.

Jessye Norman
April 1987

Preface

After I turned fifty, in 1974, I found myself looking back over the years and reliving experiences that had shaped my life. My most vivid memory was both aural and visual: the voice and presence of the Norwegian soprano, Kirsten Flagstad. This book has its origin in that memory.

Of all musical instruments, the human singing voice is the one that most readily engages the mind and most deeply moves the heart. Once in a lifetime a voice is heard that transcends time and place. Through its unique beauty and communicative power, it stills the worldly hubbub of our lives and lifts us to that higher realm of peace and harmony that we know, intuitively, is our real home. Such was the voice of Kirsten Flagstad. She belonged, as Susan Jacoby wrote in 1976 about another musician, 'to the rare class of performing artists who redefine the boundaries of their art in ways that can alter our vision of life'.

Today, in the last quarter of the twentieth century, when the mediocre and the spurious are often mistaken for the great and the genuine, we need to be reminded of the time-honoured standards in the light of which sound aesthetic judgements are made. There is no substitute for learning, and there is no road to learning but hard work. This book is the story of one gifted person who recognized that fact, and who worked unceasingly to acquire and refine the learning that enabled her to adhere throughout her life to the highest standards of her chosen profession. I think it is an inspiring story, and I offer it to the public, especially to those who love great music, in the hope that it will serve as an inspiration to them.

In addition to telling the story of Kirsten Flagstad, this book is partly autobiographical. It grew out of my experiences as a child and as a young man, my training and development as a musician and singer, and my gratitude for having heard and seen the singer who, to quote the late Lanfranco Rasponi, author of *The Last Prima Donnas*, 'was way over and above any other singer I have ever heard'. Inevitably, along the way, I have revealed my own character, my beliefs, and my love of singing. I hope that this does not intrude upon my theme – indeed, that it may even sometimes illuminate it.

I began collecting photographs for a projected pictorial biography of Kirsten Flagstad in 1975. I was interested primarily in action shots: those taken of her in rehearsal or performance. During a trip to Europe in July 1976, I met the late John Culshaw, record producer, writer and Metropolitan Opera radio commentator, who had worked with Flagstad during the last years of her life. He expressed interest in my plans, and suggested that some sort of accompanying text – perhaps letters – would add an element of human interest to the book and make it a more satisfying and significant work.

When I was in Oslo that October I met Aslaug Rein, whose biography of Flagstad, in Norwegian, I had first seen in the Library of Congress, Washington, DC, the previous April. She showed me the draft of an English translation of the book by herself, Anna Erichsen and Agnete Larson, and the sections I read convinced me that it contained pertinent information not hitherto available in English. I obtained her permission to make a complete translation and to incorporate the parts I chose into my own book, which by this time I had decided to expand into a full-length narrative with pictures. Some time later I met Arthur V. Dusenberry, Flagstad's son-in-law, of Phoenix, Arizona, who generously consented to having some of his reminiscences and observations included in this book. The effect of these influences has been to change a simple pictorial biography into what I believe is the most comprehensive account available of the life and art of one of the greatest singers of all time.

Acknowledgements

My research over the years has taken me to San Francisco, Washington, DC, Chicago, Newark, New York, Phoenix, Oslo, London and Paris. In all those cities I received assistance from numerous people. To all who, along the way, offered me encouragement, advice and counsel, I express my sincere gratitude.

I would like to acknowledge here the help I have received from M. K. Swingle and Karl Feichtmeir, Manuscript Librarian, of the Library of the California Historical Society in San Francisco; the late Russell Hartley, Director, Judith Solomon, Assistant Director, and Douglas Duke of the Archives for the Performing Arts in San Francisco; Mr and Mrs Milton H. Esberg Jr of San Francisco; Bernice M. Nece of San Pablo, California; Claudia Cassidy in Chicago; William J. Dane, Supervising Librarian of the Art and Music Department, Newark Public Library; the late Mary Ellis Peltz, Archivist, Heloise L. Pressey, Assistant Archivist, Michael Rubinovitz, and Robert A. Tuggle (now Archivist) of the Metropolitan Opera Archives in New York; Frank C. Campbell, Chief, Music Division, New York Public Library, and Barbara Sutherland, Warren Michon and Neil Ratliff of the Library and Museum of the Performing Arts at Lincoln Center in New York; Mary Corliss of the Museum of Modern Art in New York; E. Payson Clark Jr, the late Nancy Hamilton and Edward L. Orff Jr, of New York; Øystein Gaukstad and Edwina Gundersen of the Norsk Musikksamling, Oslo; Torstein Gunnarson of Norsk Rikskringkasting, Oslo; Aslaug Rein, Karen Marie Flagstad, and the late Berit Stabben of Oslo; the late John Culshaw; the late Boris Skidelsky of the Archive Office, Royal Opera House, Covent Garden; Margaret Nicholson of the office of the Friends of Covent Garden, London; Rolf Liebermann, former General Manager of the Théâtre National de l'Opéra, Paris; and Martine Kahane, Director of the Musée de l'Opéra, Paris.

Acknowledgements

My special thanks go to Dilys Hartog and Sue Phillpott. It was Dilys Hartog's enthusiasm for the book that led to its acceptance by the publisher; she has nurtured it every step of the way. Sue Phillpott was my very capable and diligent editor; her practised eye and hand have been a boon to me.

Grateful acknowledgement is also made to the following individuals and organizations: Louis Biancolli, for quotation from *The Flagstad Manuscript*, published by G. P. Putnam's Sons, 1952; Sigurd H. Dusenberry and Mrs Milton H. Esberg Jr, for quotations from letters to Caroline Esberg from Kirsten Flagstad; Houghton Mifflin Co. and Erich Leinsdorf, for quotation from *Cadenza: A Musical Career*, by Erich Leinsdorf, published in 1976; Macmillan Publishing Co. and William Barry Furlong, for quotation from *Season with Solti*, by William Barry Furlong, published in 1974; *Musical America*, for quotation from a review by Oscar Thompson in the issue of 10 February 1935; *New York Post*, for quotation from an article by Oscar Thompson in *The New York Evening Post* of 8 October 1932; *The New York Times*, for quotations from seven reviews, copyright 1935/37/52; the New York Times Syndication Sales Corporation, for quotations from six reviews in the New York *Herald Tribune*, copyright 1935/36/37/40; *San Francisco Chronicle*, for quotation from a review by Alfred Frankenstein in the issue of 1 October 1949.

Permission to reprint extracts has been requested from the following: Alan Blyth, for quotation from his interview with Hans Hotter, which appeared in the July 1976 issue of *Opera* magazine; the *Chicago Tribune*, for quotations from columns by Claudia Cassidy, copyright 1945 and 1947; *HiFi/Stereo Review*, for quotation from an article by David Hall in the issue of November 1960; P. L. Travers, for quotation from her article entitled 'Flagstad' in the 8 April 1948 issue of the *New English Weekly*.

My heartfelt thanks go to many friends, including Astrid Haugeto of Staten Island, New York, who attended the Kirsten Flagstad Memorial Festival in Oslo in 1975 from which she sent me a quantity of informative material, and who also gave me many historical items from her personal collection; Marie E. Schumer of Bloomfield, New Jersey, widow of Harry G. Schumer, Librarian of the Metropolitan Opera from 1946 to 1968, who introduced me to many knowledgeable people, and who was a constant source of enthusiastic support; Lawrence Hess of Middlebury, Vermont,

Acknowledgements

who was present at Kirsten Flagstad's Metropolitan Opera debut in 1935; Caryl G. Beckwith of Stowe, Vermont, a close personal friend of Kirsten Flagstad's, who shared many of her reminiscences with me and who lent me a quantity of valuable material; Lorraine and David Rappeport of Bloomfield, who read the first draft of this book and offered me advice and encouragement; my colleague Dee Kneale, who read the entire final typescript and made many helpful suggestions; my brother, Richard Vogt; and, especially, Greta K. Krantz, my secretary and confidante, who typed the entire manuscript, and who put up with my many idiosyncrasies over the years – which was infinitely more difficult.

I deeply regret that my friends Beckie Blair of Bloomfield and Anne Dejulis of Belleville, New Jersey, did not live to see this book in print. Mrs Blair's generous gift of newspaper clippings on Kirsten Flagstad from the 1930s was put to good use, and Miss Dejulis' extensive collection of Flagstad memorabilia, a gift to me from her, was of exceptional research value.

Howard Vogt
Bloomfield, New Jersey
1987

1

Norway's Daughter

Shortly before 5 p.m. on Sunday 2 May 1982 I boarded a Scandinavian Airlines flight at Kennedy Airport and settled into my seat for the overnight journey to Oslo.

Early May is spring in New York but late winter in Oslo. I stepped off the plane into brisk air of twenty-five degrees Fahrenheit. A strike had brought public transport to a standstill, and there was no way to get into the city except by taxi. The drivers were vying with one another for passengers and charging three hundred kroner (about £35) for the trip.

During the ride through the Monday-morning rush-hour traffic to the Bristol Hotel, images of the as yet unseen statue of Kirsten Flagstad began to form in my mind. Arthur Dusenberry, her son-in-law, had phoned weeks earlier to ask whether I could attend the unveiling; Torstein Gunnarson, chairman of the Kirsten Flagstad International Society, had sent him a snapshot of the plaster cast which showed a life-size standing figure. He hadn't been able to make out any details. The sculptor was Joseph Grimeland, who had made the charming *Fløytespilleren* (the Flute Player), which stood in the garden of Flagstad's home, Amalienborg, in Kristiansand during her lifetime. She had bequeathed it to the hospital in which she died, and it stands today where she could have seen it from her hospital window. I wondered whether Grimeland had captured the noble bearing and the serene expression of Flagstad as skilfully as he had depicted the pastoral simplicity and childlike wonder of the three figures in his Flute Player.

The driver's voice broke my reverie. We had arrived at the Bristol.

Arthur and his son, Sigurd, Kirsten's grandson, were also staying at the Bristol, the traditional family meeting-place. Karen

1

Marie, Kirsten's sister, and other members of the family had met them at the airport the previous day. When I called their room a bit later on the Monday morning to say hello, Arthur told me to go on up: 'Mr Gunnarson is here. We're going over the plans for Wednesday.'

I shook hands with Gunnarson, whom I had met in 1976. As programme director of the Norwegian Broadcasting Company, as well as chairman of the Kirsten Flagstad International Society, he had been perhaps the prime mover in raising the funds that had enabled the society to commission the statue. Sigurd had gone off with Sjur Hall, his Grandfather Hall's son from his third marriage and half-brother of Sigurd's late mother, Else Hall Dusenberry. Arthur smiled as he commented on the intricacies of the family relationships. I excused myself and went to my room to try to get some rest, but I was too keyed up to sleep; and besides, jet lag had set in.

Later in the day, on my way down from my room, I saw a woman of medium height with grey hair and glasses, standing at the door to Arthur's room. On impulse I said, 'Are you Caryl Beckwith?' (Arthur had said that he expected her to be in Oslo for the unveiling.) 'Yes, I am,' she replied. I had finally met the woman who had been one of Kirsten Flagstad's closest friends. Over the next few days we were often together in the same group, and by the time I left for London that Friday we had decided that we liked each other.

That same day I telephoned Aslaug Rein, the Norwegian journalist and editor, and the person to whom, as a compatriot and devotee of the arts, Kirsten Flagstad, in December 1961, had entrusted the writing of her biography in Norwegian – 'in case my Norwegian public might want to know about my life's work', as she put it. We arranged to meet at about five o'clock in the cosy library lounge just off the main lobby of the hotel. We had not seen one another since October 1976, although we had talked by telephone and corresponded frequently in the intervening years. When she arrived, we greeted each other like good friends who lunch together once a week; five and a half years became only a moment in time. Like many Nordic women, Aslaug is fairly tall and somewhat angular in build. Her face, which in repose can strike one as solemn, even stern, becomes animated and very expressive when she is talking.

While we were chatting over coffee, Arthur spied us from the lobby and came over to our table. With him was a young man of medium build, with dark brown hair and a beard, whose prominent cheekbones, deep-set eyes and broad forehead reminded me at once of Kirsten Flagstad. 'Howard, I'd like you to meet my son, Sigurd,' said Arthur, as I rose to shake hands with Sigurd Hall Dusenberry, Kirsten Flagstad's grandson. 'We're on our way to Karen Marie's for dinner,' Arthur added.

I introduced them to Aslaug, and we talked for a few minutes about the plans for Wednesday. I sensed a certain shyness in Sigurd. We were together almost every day in the next week and a half, in Oslo and in London, and as we became acquainted, I surmised that there was an inherent reserve in him. It is an attractive quality, inherited from his grandmother, perhaps.

I invited Aslaug to have dinner with me in the Bristol Grill. Our conversation centred on Karen Marie and Berit Stabben, Flagstad's former housekeeper. Karen Marie had not been well, Aslaug said; her heart was giving her trouble. She would be seventy-eight in November. Berit, said Aslaug, appeared to be as strong and fit as ever. She would be at the unveiling ceremony on Wednesday and at the reception to follow at the Grand Hotel.

I got up before seven on the Wednesday morning, opened the swivel window wide, and poked my head out to see what kind of weather we could expect. It was still cloudy, and there was the feel of rain in the air.

The ceremony was scheduled to begin at eleven o'clock at the chosen site, the lawn in front of the Norges Musikkhøgskole, the Norwegian School of Music, across the street from the Royal Palace Park. I dressed and went downstairs for breakfast: one of those sumptuous Norwegian breakfasts of fish, cheese, meat, soft-boiled eggs, crisp rolls and butter, coffee, and, of course, orange juice, now a staple of Scandinavian breakfast hospitality.

Aslaug and Caryl joined Arthur, Sigurd and me at the hotel just after ten, and within fifteen minutes we were on our way, braving the chilly, blustery air to walk the half-mile or so to the school. We were still a good block away when Aslaug exclaimed, 'There it is!' She pointed to a shape covered with a pale-blue cloth, ahead of us on the right. When we arrived, there were already fifty or more people on the school lawn greeting each other or talking in small

3

groups, and passers-by, including some backpacked teenagers, were beginning to gather on the pavement. Arthur spotted Karen Marie and Berit Stabben near the chairs reserved for family and friends. Berit, dressed in her colourful national costume, greeted me with her shy smile and forthright handshake.

One section of the lawn had been reserved for the school's brass band, which was to play during the ceremony and would bring it to a close with the first performance of a composition by Knut Nystedt entitled 'Maskerade'. Music stands and chairs had been set up on a temporary plywood platform that extended across the front of the lawn to include the statue area. There were microphones on the platform, and recording equipment on the school porch. Members of the faculty and their friends had found choice viewing locations on the second- and third-floor balconies above the main entrance. Norwegian flags, their white-bordered blue crosses on red fields brightening the grey day, flew from poles on both sides of the porch and from the balconies.

Just after eleven, the steady hum of conversation subsided when Torstein Gunnarson stepped to a microphone, acknowledged the city and national officials and distinguished guests present, and made a short speech, presenting the statue to the school on behalf of the Kirsten Flagstad International Society. He then introduced Øivin Fjeldstad, the veteran Norwegian conductor, a ruggedly handsome elderly man with white hair. Fjeldstad and Flagstad had been music colleagues and friends, and had made several recordings together, including the acclaimed 'Sibelius Songs' and 'Songs from Norway' with the London Symphony Orchestra. It was to honour this professional association and friendship that Fjeldstad had been asked to unveil the statue. When he loosened the blue cloth, it fell to the pedestal, revealing the larger-than-life-size figure of Norway's daughter newly cast in bronze; it gleamed like burnished gold when a fleeting ray of sunlight broke the clouds and fell on it. The crowd applauded, as if the singer had just walked out and taken her place on the concert platform. Then the orchestral introduction of Grieg's 'Ved Ronderne' ('At Rondane') filled the air, and a hush fell over the audience as the recorded voice of Kirsten Flagstad sang, 'No ser eg atter slike fjell og dalar . . .'. Uncannily, the voice seemed to emanate from the statue. A soft, light rain began to fall.

Late that night I walked the few blocks to the National Theatre. I stood between the statues of Bjørnstjerne Bjørnson and Henrik Ibsen and looked at the theatre, its façade now faintly illuminated by the street lights. 'Here is where the voice that has been called "the voice of the century" was first heard on a stage,' I thought. 'Here is where it all began, almost seventy years ago.'

2

'A Certain Flagstad'

On Friday 12 July 1895 in Hamar, Norway, a daughter was born to Michael and Marie Nielsen Flagstad. The child was baptized in Hamar Cathedral and given the names Kirsten Malfrid. Almost forty-five years later, on Monday 8 July 1940, Kirsten Flagstad walked out onto the stage of Lewisohn Stadium in New York and was greeted by the tumultuous applause of twenty thousand people, including a fifteen-year-old boy from East Orange, New Jersey. She was the greatest Wagnerian soprano of her time – perhaps of all time.

I first heard and saw Kirsten Flagstad on the stage on 27 March 1937, in a matinée performance of Wagner's *Lohengrin* at the Metropolitan Opera House. I was twelve years old at the time and had attended my first opera performance, Verdi's *Aïda*, the previous month. We lived then in Caldwell, New Jersey.

The last time I heard Flagstad in person was on 20 March 1955. She had come to New York from Norway to sing two all-Wagner concerts in Carnegie Hall with, and for the benefit of, the financially ailing Symphony of the Air, the former NBC Symphony Orchestra. I was living then in Newark, New Jersey, and working at the Newark Public Library.

Between those two dates, I attended as many Flagstad performances as I could. Her voice and presence had a profound aesthetic and spiritual influence on my life.

My love for music must have been inborn, because my parents told me that I used to 'play the piano' on the seat of a chair before I was three, propping a book, any book, up against the back of the chair to play from. There was music in my family, mostly on my father's side. He himself had a strong baritone voice of good quality and sang for many years in a men's glee club. His sister Loretta, my

Aunt Rettie, was very musical. She could play anything on the piano by ear that she had heard only once; I can remember her dancing around her living-room with a long-handled mop, humming contentedly to the strains of music on the radio. I've always thought it was a creative way to dust. Another thing I remember very clearly is the annual ritual after Thanksgiving dinner, when Rettie and her mother, my grandmother 'Nana', used to sit down at the piano and play four-hands together, always ending up with something called 'The Seventh Regiment', a march they didn't know how to finish. They'd play on and on, laughing until the tears rolled down their cheeks, and ours. Rettie's daughter Ruth, a Juilliard graduate, became an accomplished pianist and organist. She always encouraged me in my musical interests and often played for me when I first began to study singing seriously. I took piano lessons from her when I was eleven, but she gave up on me because I wouldn't practise.

I sang in church in the choir, first as a boy alto, and then, when my voice broke, as a baritone. I sang in all the high school music productions, including *The Chimes of Normandy* and *The Bohemian Girl*. By that time, opera was the big thing in my life, and Kirsten Flagstad was my ideal.

My father took me to that performance of *Lohengrin* in 1937, and we stood at the railing behind the orchestra circle seats throughout the performance, after queuing for a couple of hours to get in. We always stood in those days, because we couldn't afford anything else. I think the price was $1.50. All I really remember about that performance is Flagstad's appearance on the balcony in Act Two, all in white, and her singing of 'Euch Lüften'. Years later I read that Henry Johansen, who was to be her second husband, had fallen in love with her at that very moment on a June night in Oslo in 1929. I can understand why. The earnest simplicity of her singing was spellbinding. All of Elsa's femininity, her basic honesty and her vulnerability were conveyed by that lovely voice. I didn't try to analyse what made it lovely; I was too young for that. But I knew that I was listening to something special.

That November, Kirsten Flagstad and Lauritz Melchior opened the season with *Tristan und Isolde*, and I remember buying the morning papers on my way to school the next day so that I could read about it. After that, Flagstad's first recording of the 'Liebestod' became a part of my life. I bought it sometime in 1938 at Chalmers

Music Store in Main Street in East Orange, where we had moved from Caldwell. I took the record over to Rettie's house to play it, because we didn't have a gramophone at home at the time. I put it on, and I remember Rettie walking into the room. There were tears in her eyes. 'Who is that, Howard?' she asked. 'Kirsten Flagstad,' I answered. She replied, 'That's the most beautiful voice I've ever heard.'

I attended my first performance of *Tristan und Isolde*, with Flagstad as Isolde, on Saturday 8 April 1939. The Christmas before, my parents had given me a radiogram, and I played the Flagstad 'Liebestod' constantly. My father fell under its spell, too, but I couldn't persuade him to go to the performance with me. The 'Liebestod' was one thing, but standing through almost four hours of *Tristan* was something else. So I went to New York alone for the second time in my life. My parents, with some misgivings, had let me go to the city by myself in March to attend a matinée performance of *Rigoletto*. I had celebrated my fourteenth birthday the previous October.

As I look back now, I see that my musical leanings were always thoroughly Romantic. My first significant contact with great music came through Walter Damrosch's 'Music Appreciation' radio concerts, which were a part of my schooling in the fifth and sixth years in 1934 and 1935 at Central School, Glen Ridge, New Jersey, where we lived at the time. It was then that I heard my first Wagner, the 'Ride of the Valkyries', and the prelude to Act Three of *Lohengrin*, which Dr Damrosch described so vividly to me that my imagination was fired with Wagner for ever after.

Verdi was my other special composer, not least because we were both born on 10 October, and I felt sure we were related in some mystical way. Dr Damrosch introduced me to him, too. At that time I was fascinated by Ancient Egypt, and as part of a school project I had made, on a cafeteria tray, a diorama of the Nile, represented by coloured paper under a piece of glass, and the pyramids, fashioned out of clay, surrounded by sand and hand-made palm trees. Then I discovered *Aïda*, and delved into the story and the music with gusto. I learned to play the Triumphal March and the final duet on the piano, and I remember being struck by the sudden key shift in the march. It wasn't until years later that I realized what a stroke of musical genius that transition from A-flat to B major was. It seems inevitable now that *Aïda* was the first opera I saw on the stage.

I went through a Tchaikovsky period in the late 1930s. The Fourth Symphony impressed me tremendously; I heard it first at a summer stadium concert in Newark and then listened avidly to my cousin Ruth's 'World's Greatest Music' series recording of it. Soon I succumbed to the Fifth and Sixth Symphonies as well. The Mozart G Minor Symphony became one of my favourites after Ruth introduced me to it; I was especially fascinated by the last movement, with its quick, dark, intense upward-leaping theme. Mendelssohn's *Italian Symphony* and *Midsummer Night's Dream* music were also great favourites; I remember being completely entranced by the Max Reinhardt film of Shakespeare's play when my Aunt Dorothy, one of my mother's four sisters, took me to see it sometime in the mid-1930s. She also took me to see the film of Paderewski playing Beethoven's Moonlight Sonata. That made a profound impression on me, too, and for weeks afterwards I struggled with the first movement on Rettie's piano, finally managing to play it all the way through from memory. But nothing I had experienced before that Saturday in April 1939 had prepared me for the impact of *Tristan und Isolde* on the stage.

The first notes of the Prelude awoke in me that feeling of completeness that comes over all of us at certain moments in our lives. We feel suddenly at one with everything, suffused with joy and wonder. That fleeting moment remains alive in our memories for ever, but we seem unable to recapture its essence. We do hold it, though, in our minds, because the intense illumination that accompanies it provides us with a living mental image of unusual clarity. I can still see, hear and feel that moment so clearly: where I was standing, with my arms resting on the deep-red velour-covered railing; the expectant hush in the auditorium; the back of conductor Artur Bodanzky's head, and the prompter's box silhouetted against the footlight glow on the rich antique gold brocade of the curtain; the drawn-out sigh in the music.

Then I became oblivious of everything but the drama unfolding before me. The curtain was a part of the drama, as the composer had intended. It parted, then rose slowly as the cellos and basses played the last six measures of the Prelude. Immediately, I could feel the tension in the figure on the couch. There was absolutely no movement, but as the Sailor sang, the tension in that figure

9

mounted until the inevitable outburst at the end. I realized then that here lay the greatness of Kirsten Flagstad's art. It was stripped of all but the essential. With Flagstad on the stage, you were witnessing a *re-presentation*, not merely a performance. She possessed what the critic Max de Schauensee so perceptively called 'an inner radiance', which was transmitted to the audience by her person, by her voice and by her rare ability to act without extraneous movement. Her incandescent portrayal of the Irish princess throughout the rest of the opera served to confirm what I had intuitively realized. There was never a striving for vocal or visual effect; every step, gesture and facial expression, every nuance of colour in the voice, sprang from the drama.

A few instances spring vividly to mind: the eerie spell cast by the mysterious interweaving of voice and words with flutes and clarinets at 'mit Heilsalben und Balsamsaft' in Isolde's Narrative; the voice, seemingly disembodied, rising in a seamless legato with tone matched to word, and accompanied by a spontaneous slow upward movement of the head, as if drawn up by the ascending vocal line and the import of the words, at 'er sah mir in die Augen', some forty measures later; the moment when pent-up emotion exploded in tone and gesture on the words 'Rache! Tod! Tod uns Beiden!' in Isolde's Curse; the entire first scene of the second act, before Tristan's entrance, when the pulse of ardent anticipation in the music could be heard in the voice from Isolde's first phrase, vibrant under the steady stream of tone, which swelled with the passionate intensity in the music, until it flooded the auditorium with Isolde's cry, 'Frau Minne will: es werde Nacht, dass hell sie dorten leuchte, wo sie dein Licht verscheuchte.' Finally, the 'Liebestod', which became in reality what it intrinsically is, the inevitable culmination of the drama, rather than just the last aria in the opera.

I have on occasion heard it said that Flagstad was no actress. To me the comment indicated a lack of knowledge, not to mention perception and understanding, of what true acting is. To this person, acting meant physical movement, an outward exercise – not an inward experience made manifest in manifold ways.

The voice itself was, and remains, unique. 'You could never mistake that voice for someone else's,' remarked a friend of mine, recently, who was present at Flagstad's Metropolitan Opera debut, as Sieglinde in *Die Walküre*, on Saturday 2 February 1935. About the atmosphere in the auditorium that afternoon, he said:

> After the first act, you knew that something unusual was happening. You could feel it in the air. When the curtain fell on Act Two, I realized I was hearing a unique voice remarkable for its freshness and soaring quality, and for its ability to communicate feeling directly to you. At the end of the performance, there was pandemonium, and I was a happy participant in it. Today, fifty years later, I still think Kirsten Flagstad was the greatest singer I've ever heard.

In a review of that debut in the 10 February 1935 issue of *Musical America*, the critic Oscar Thompson, who had heard her sing Isolde in Oslo in 1932, wrote:

> Of moderate height and normal build, with a medallion-like countenance – the nose straight from the forehead, beloved of the ancient Greeks – the singer gave an immediate impression of womanliness and freedom from pose. She was graceful and plastic, but reserved in gesture. A slight inclination of the head, a partial turn of the body, a clenching of the hands, were made to express more than the pictorial attitudinizing of those spectacular actresses who have sought to stylize their Wagner. Every motion was beautifully timed; moreover, it was rooted in the orchestra as well as the text and the psychology behind the text. The pathetic Sieglinde of the second and third acts evoked pity. The first act Sieglinde was a figure of compassion for the exhausted stranger who had stumbled into the abode of his enemy.
>
> The voice was one of ample power – it seemed larger, in fact, in the vast reaches of the Metropolitan than in the relatively small spaces of the National Theatre in Oslo. Of recognizably Scandinavian quality, it recalled for one listener the summer landscape of that vast mountainous plateau between Oslo and Bergen: a voice of crystal clarity at the top; of warm glow, as of the play of sunlight on snow, in the middle; and of dark, opaque, blue-gray shadows below. Variable as was the tonal color, this was not at the expense of a unified scale.

A memorable anecdote about this historic afternoon is related by Louis Biancolli in *The Flagstad Manuscript: An Autobiography Narrated to Louis Biancolli*, published in 1952:

The performance, of course, was broadcast. During the first intermission, the General Manager, Giulio Gatti-Casazza, was seated at a desk in his office when the telephone rang. It was Frances Alda, once a leading soprano of the company and formerly his wife, calling from her home in Great Neck, Long Island, where she had the radio turned on.

'Who was that singing Sieglinde?'

'*Perchè*?' asked the laconic Gatti-Casazza.

'*Perchè ha una bellissima voce e canta molto bene.*'

'*Una certa Flagstad . . .*'

For me, the most remarkable thing about Kirsten Flagstad's voice, next to its unique timbre, was its apparently limitless resource. It was like clear water flowing from a spring that Nature had decreed would never run dry. It was flawlessly produced – the ultimate criterion of the technique of singing. You never felt yourself tightening up when Flagstad was singing, wondering if she would make it through the next phrase; you knew there was no need to worry. Even when she appeared at the Met for the last time, in 1952, as Alcestis, and it took the voice longer to warm up, there was only a hint of effort at the end of a long, demanding phrase. She was then almost fifty-seven, and had been singing professionally for over thirty-eight years.

In quality, the Flagstad voice was *hochdramatisch*, the true Wagnerian dramatic soprano. It was unparalleled in beauty of tone, pure and full-bodied throughout its two-octave range, and it was notable for both its size and its flexibility. It overrode every orchestral fortissimo with consummate clarity and ease, and in certain passages, such as Brünnhilde's ecstatic anticipation of Siegfried's return in Act One, Scene Three of *Götterdämmerung*, and the conclusion of the 'Immolation Scene' in Act Three, it was astonishing in its power, with no loss whatsoever in its luminosity.

It is indisputably true that Flagstad's voice was destined for Wagner. But, nonetheless, it was also the ideal voice for such classical roles as Fidelio, Alcestis and Dido; and, remarkably enough, it was equally effective in the song literature, although Flagstad's formidable prowess on the operatic stage tended to obscure her considerable ability as a song recitalist.

All of this did not come about by chance. The reader will learn in detail in succeeding chapters how the groundwork for this phenomenal career was laid, and how the vicissitudes of human existence contributed to its development. A person's life affects his work in many ways: it is like a kaleidoscope, where numerous interacting fragments form a pattern. Flagstad was particularly fortunate in her family background, but not primarily because of its musical orientation: it was the foundation of discipline established by her parents that counted most. This, combined with the stolidity and stubbornness inherent in the Norwegian character, gave her the base on which to build. As well as the extraordinary sense of discipline, she showed total objectivity about her voice and art, and a remarkable self-control in dealing with the changing circumstances of her personal life and the demands and challenges of her forty-year career. There can be no doubt that, as far as her vocal instrument was concerned, she was uniquely endowed, but this did not really come to light until after many years of painstaking study and practical experience. No one but the most discerning musician would have predicted an international career for her when she first appeared on the stage in 1913. Like a great runner, she trained herself for the long race by building her voice slowly, step by step, and letting nature take its course. No great career in any field is made in any other way.

Another significant factor in her development was her innate modesty: she was not unduly impressed with herself. She was a retiring person who enjoyed her own company and that of her family and close friends. Her directness and integrity carried across the footlights and were important aspects of her appeal. She took pleasure in compliments and praise when they were deserved, but she was not given to airs and graces. When she talked about her voice or her singing, or any other aspect of her art, she always referred to them as if they existed outside of herself. Talking about a certain performance, she might say, 'Yes, the voice was good tonight'; or, 'The voice wasn't really in top form tonight, was it?' There was no ego connected with it. She had her share of foibles, idiosyncrasies and eccentricities, but they very seldom coloured her work, and never interfered with it. She could intuitively assume the temperament of the character she was portraying because she never let her own personality get in the way. At the same time, she could draw on her own considerable inner resources to mould a role without using them for personal rather than artistic ends – a rare quality in the world of opera.

13

In 1939, the year I turned fifteen, I wrote to Kirsten Flagstad and asked her if she would send me an autographed photograph of herself as Isolde. I was planning to stage *Tristan* in a puppet theatre and I wanted the picture for costume details. She sent it to me, signed 'Sincerely, Kirsten Flagstad'. I was overwhelmed. That photograph became my most prized possession, but the puppet production never materialized. I was at that age when dreams are plentiful.

The Metropolitan Opera had a World's Fair season in May 1939, and it was on Friday the 12th that I heard my first *Götterdämmerung*. The apt word for Flagstad's Brünnhilde is 'monumental': it was monumental in both conception and execution, and it remains today, in my opinion, the definitive representation of the role. What made her portrayal so awesome was that the vocal splendour was wedded to uncanny dramatic insight. Her intuitive understanding of the character and the text was so profound that her voice, in its constantly shifting tone colour, became a mirror reflecting the unfolding of a tragic destiny. She realized completely the composer's vision.

Psychologically, Brünnhilde's journey from the prologue to the 'Immolation' is immense. An heroic woman, loving and beloved, is inexorably drawn down into the abyss of human greed, malice and intrigue where, out of bewilderment, indignation and despair, she unwittingly joins forces with evil, only to realize her error and, progressing from knowledge through wisdom to understanding, atone for it and ascend to supernal heights: 'Alles, Alles, Alles weiss ich, Alles ward mir nun frei!' We are caught up in a spiritual odyssey of cosmic significance.

How did Kirsten Flagstad manage to convey this on the stage so eloquently and completely that thousands of people left the theatre in a state of exaltation akin to catharsis? The answer is – through the power of her own humanity. Her fundamental integrity precluded all artifice and superficiality on the stage, as it did in her everyday life. She herself was certainly not aware of the enormous impact she had on her audience. She was in some mysterious way the human vessel through which truth was revealed; anyone who perceived her with his mind and being, as well as his ears and eyes, can attest to that.

This same soundness carried her through the crises of her

personal life, especially the major one of the first post-war years when she was falsely, and sometimes maliciously, accused of Nazi sympathies by segments of the press, and when she was deserted by many whom she had thought of as friends, and forced to endure insults and slander. What she went through would have broken most people, but once again she wisely drew on her inner resources to quietly and confidently battle her way through to vindication and victory. It was a personal triumph of the same epic dimensions as any she had achieved on the stage.

One of my most poignant memories of Flagstad on the stage concerns the day I finally prevailed upon my still somewhat reluctant father to attend a *Tristan* performance with me. We stood behind the orchestra circle seats, just as before. I so much wanted him to enjoy it. I could feel him becoming more and more engrossed in the drama as the performance went on, but I knew what he was really waiting for. When several people failed to come back to their seats for the third act, I persuaded him to tip the usher and go and sit down. He was forty-five then, which was old, I thought – far too old to be standing through *Tristan*. Every once in a while I would tear my eyes from the stage just long enough to glance at the back of his head.

At Isolde's offstage entrance, 'Tristan! Geliebter!', a barely perceptible stir went through the house, as it always did at that moment when Flagstad's disembodied voice filled the auditorium. Then she ran on, her gold-banded mauve headdress fluttering with the movement, and we all mentally took her arm as she descended those treacherous steps and rushed to Tristan's side. The daylight on the stage was waning. With a heart-rending whispered 'Isolde!', Tristan died. And then the threnody began, lifting us to another sphere until we were suddenly jarred back to reality by the Shepherd's 'Kurwenal! Hör! Ein zweites Schiff!'. But the spell was not broken; it only faded momentarily. Then that voice, already in another world, softly intoned the transfiguring words, 'Mild und leise wie er lächelt . . .'. Isolde rose slowly, almost imperceptibly. An autumn twilight suffused the scene. Her voice rose and fell with the surge and ebb of the music, immersing itself in the sea of sound. Her arms slowly rose and her body swayed slightly to the mounting intensity of the music, until with the flood of sound at 'Welt-Atems wehendem All', she stood suddenly still with arms outstretched as if to embrace the universe. Then, as the twilight deepened, she

15

reached her goal, 'höchste Lust!', with the final pure pianissimo F-sharp floating on the ebbing sound. She sank down in Brangäne's arms to Tristan's side as the half-light faded and, with the mournful voice of the oboe suspended in the air, the final chord sounded and the curtain fell. There was absolute silence for a moment; then came the soft exhalation of pent-up breath as the trance was broken, and the mounting storm of applause.

As the house lights came up, my father left his seat and walked up the aisle. There were tears in his eyes: 'Beautiful, beautiful,' he said huskily, and my eyes, too, filled with tears because he was so moved. I never felt closer to him than at that moment.

I saved up the money I earned doing odd jobs around the house for my mother to attend Flagstad's Lewisohn Stadium concert on 8 July 1940. Edwin McArthur was to conduct the Philharmonic Symphony Orchestra in an all-Wagner programme. It cost $1.50 for a ticket in the reserved section, and I had a good seat close to the stage. I had never seen so many people in one place before in my life. There was the same air of keyed-up expectation in that huge crowd as there always was in the Opera House audience when Flagstad was to sing.

When she walked out to sing 'Elsa's Dream', I suddenly realized that I was seeing her out of theatrical costume for the first time. She wore a pale-blue gown which set off her golden-brown hair, a two-strand pearl necklace and pendant pearl earrings. There was a prolonged ovation, which she acknowledged with a warm smile and gracious nods of the head. Then she stood stock-still, her chin slightly lifted, her hands lightly clasped at her waist, and in a split second the unique spell took hold. Kirsten Flagstad had become Elsa of Brabant: without costume, without scenery, without the panoply of stage effects.

Flagstad was a great artist, and everyone present in Lewisohn Stadium that night was aware of it. Her greatness was grounded in her natural simplicity. Greatness is a spiritual quality, attained unknowingly in the quest for perfection. It proceeds from a rare combination of attributes: uncommon native ability, discovered and consistently developed through study; knowledge and appreciation of oneself; self-discipline; reflectiveness; intuitive perception; single-mindedness; perseverance; humility; openness; and the element of mystery, which evokes wonder in the beholder and enlarges his vision of life.

Before she sang a note, she had established personal contact with her audience. Her unassuming manner told them instantly that she was a human being like themselves and that she was happy to be there. When she sang, her voice, pure and effulgent, seemed to well up out of the earth beneath her feet. Her singing was spontaneous and free, with its roots deep in the Nordic past. It was like sunlight glinting on the snow-capped mountains and crystal fjords of her homeland.

She moved on from the quiet rapture of Elsa's vision, to capture the exultant mood of Elisabeth entering the Hall of Song in Act Two of *Tannhäuser*. As the orchestra played the opening bars, you could feel her tense, like an athlete about to run a race, and you realized that she produced her firm, buoyant tone by using her whole body as a resonator. The sense of complete vocal security that she always conveyed to her listeners came from her body's total involvement, of which her superb breath control was only a part.

Years later, when I was studying for a time in Chicago, my teacher, Maria Hussa–Greve, who was an opera singer, would say to me when I was trying to sustain a high-lying phrase, 'Think *down*, Howard; *down* into the body!'; and she would punctuate the words with a downward movement of the arm, followed by a turning upward with the hand cupped. And when I was visiting Kerstin Thorborg at her home in Sweden, she would say to me when we were out walking in the country, 'Listen to the cows, Howard. Do you hear how that sound they make, that "moo", comes from deep down in them? That's the way the voice is produced.' She demonstrated her 'moo' for me with the same arm movement, and made me follow suit, until suddenly we both burst out laughing as we imagined what a casual passer-by would think of us. After that, whenever she wrote to me, she would say, 'Remember the cows!'

Both singers were saying the same thing: the body must be in the tone. The sound may issue from the vocal chords, but it originates in the belly and is sustained by the whole body. This is why a singer's physical health and mental equilibrium are so important in performance. They are inseparable from his instrument.

To return to the Lewisohn Stadium concert: Flagstad's singing of one particular phrase in 'Dich, teure Halle' stands out in my memory because it demonstrated her mastery of the legato line. All the syllables of 'Aus mir entfloh der Frieden', except the first and last, are set to the same note, the higher E on the staff. Flagstad joined note to note by intoning each syllable, including the first and last, as if it were no more than a subtle variation in light on a taut golden thread, at the same time giving full weight to the meaning of the words. Fortunately for aspiring singers, this vocal magic can be heard in a recording of the 4 January 1941 performance of *Tannhäuser* broadcast from the stage of the Metropolitan.

Each succeeding selection that Flagstad sang that night was more demanding, vocally and interpretatively. 'Dich, teure Halle' was followed by the 'Liebestod', and the concert closed with the 'Immolation Scene', which brought the multitude cheering to its feet. Her entire performance was an object lesson in the art of singing.

Heredity and environment, and that mysterious force called Fate, play major roles in the shaping of every person's life. It is to consider the significance of these elements in her life that we now go back to the beginnings of the Kirsten Flagstad story.

3

The Early Years

Aslaug Rein's biography of Flagstad had been published in Norwegian in Oslo in 1967. A Norwegian born and bred, she probably knows more about Flagstad's life in Norway than anyone else alive, except for Karen Marie. But I wanted to tell the story in a different way; to tell the younger generation of singers and other musicians about her from my own perspective as a singer. I wanted to reach those who never heard her in person, and those to whom Kirsten Flagstad is only a name. And I wanted to rekindle memories in those people who heard her and saw her and responded to her unique presence.

This chapter, and chapters 4 to 9, contain parts of Aslaug Rein's biography, in my translation, and the information I derived from ten years of research, as well as my own reminiscences and observations.

The family has its roots in the broad valleys of the Hedmark region, north-east of Oslo. The farm name appears in the registers of 1723, when eastern Flagstad was deeded to Anders Olsen Frogner. Anders sold the farm to his brother Ole, who adopted the farm name Flagstad as the family name, according to the ancient Norwegian custom – farm names were regarded as higher in social rank than other names. Eastern Flagstad was handed down from father to eldest son until 1835, when it was sold out of the family.

Kirsten Flagstad's great-grandfather, Mikkel Olsen Flagstad, was born in 1798 at eastern Flagstad. When the farm was sold, he moved some distance away to Hamar where he had obtained employment as a gunsmith with the Oppland County Mounted Cavalry Corps. In 1840 Mikkel Flagstad married Olea Olsdatter Valsig, and the couple moved into a house called 'Strandstuen' (Lakeside Cottage), which was one of the five houses situated within the city limits when Hamar was incorporated on 21 March 1849. The house originally stood close to Lake Mjøsa, but it stands now on the plot of land to which it was moved in 1855, at 11 Kirkegaten, just a stone's throw from Hamar Church, and it was there that Kirsten Flagstad was born. On Friday 12 July 1985, the ninetieth anniversary of her birth, Strandstuen was established as the Flagstad Museum by the people of Hamar.

Kirsten Flagstad's great-grandfather was very musical, but the family papers do not reveal whether he played any instrument. His brother Anders, however, was sufficiently well known locally as a musician to be recorded as such. Mikkel Olsen Flagstad's two sons followed in their father's footsteps as gunsmiths in Hamar. The eldest, Kirsten's grandfather, Ole Mikkelsen Flagstad (1836–1901) was widely known not only as an excellent gunsmith but also as a sportsman and a musician. He succeeded his father as a gunsmith with the Corps, and also played horn in the Corps orchestra, while in his spare time he liked to play the violin. Ole Flagstad was a great outdoorsman, a fine skier and skater. He invented and constructed a new type of speed ice skate which he patented and which became known world-wide. He worked for some years as a gunsmith at the fort of Kongsberg. There he married Anne Kirstine Vad, and their only child, Michael, was born in Kongsberg on 4 February 1869. Later on the family moved back to Hamar, where the child grew up.

At an early age, Michael showed a decided talent for music, and his father became his first violin teacher. He was an intelligent child, a reader, and his father therefore sent him to the secondary school. After that, he had to make his own way. He tried his hand at several kinds of work, but he was unhappy in all of them. He really wanted to be a musician. Accordingly, he went to Kristiania (sometimes spelled Christiania), present-day Oslo, to take violin lessons and to study music theory. He could not afford to extend his studies, however, and could only hope to continue his education by being ambitious enough to seek work as an orchestral musician. In 1890 he was taken on as a violinist in the orchestra of the Christiania Theatre.

One day, when Michael had been playing in the orchestra for about a year, the conductor arrived accompanied by a young woman, who was noticeable for her unusually small size and her curly red hair. 'This,' the conductor announced, 'is Miss Marie Nielsen from Johnsrud at Eidsvoll. She is employed here at the theatre as a chorus coach, but will also play the piano in the orchestra when necessary.'

Marie Nielsen Johnsrud was descended from a musical family that had left its mark on Eidsvoll for generations. Her father, farmer Lars Nielsen Johnsrud (1826–1908), showed great musical talent even as a boy. He had learned to play the fiddle all by himself but was eager to get formal training, so he went to Paul Hansen Frank, a local farmer, who played the violin, was in charge of musical events at Eidsvoll, and had created a rich musical atmosphere in his own home. It did not take him long to realize that Lars Nielsen was an unusually talented pupil, and he gave him basic instruction in the violin. But Lars had higher ambitions, and went to Kristiania where he studied with the best music teachers of the day, Fredrik Ursin and Gudbrand Bøhn. Although, some time later, he had to return to Johnsrud to take charge of the farm, he did not give up his music. He played with Paul Frank and participated enthusiastically in the music life of Eidsvoll. When eventually, in 1853, he married Frank's daughter, Karen, the music centre was transferred from Frankens to Johnsrud, and a harmonium and a piano were acquired. Karen Paulsdatter was as musically gifted as her husband. It is said that when she sang the hymns in church, the other members of the congregation stopped singing in order to listen to her.

Lars Nielsen not only played the violin but was familiar with wind instruments as well, and he formed the first horn sextet in Eidsvoll. Afterwards, when the sextet was augmented with stringed instruments, Lars took over as first violinist. The group was very much in demand in the neighbourhood, to play dance music at weddings. Lars played the organ in church, too. Both he and Karen were God-fearing people who attended church regularly.

In the winter of 1859, three little girls could be seen skipping happily around the house at Johnsrud. The eldest was five years old, and the younger two, who were twins, were about three. When Lars tuned his violin, the three children would gather round him and sit listening to his playing, while his wife, occupied elsewhere, would hum the music to herself. That November, it was rumoured that the dreaded disease 'Trondheim tonsillitis' was taking a deadly toll in the districts near Eidsvoll. Small children were hit the hardest, and many had died. The disease reached

21

Eidsvoll in December and spread from farm to farm. Just before Christmas it reached Johnsrud; within a week all three children had died.

Shortly afterwards a deputation from the region came to visit Lars. 'There, you see, Lars,' said the oldest one, 'how God is punishing you for playing dance music at weddings. Now he has taken all three children from you and Karen. Put away the fiddle, and you will see that the children God may give you in the future will be spared.'

Lars could not understand how music could be sinful and how God could have punished him for playing the violin at weddings. Why, did he not also play the organ in church? He finally went to the local dean and told him about the deputation. He had to know whether the pastor was of the same opinion as the people who had been to see him. The dean shook his head and said gently, 'No, Lars, no, that is not the way God punishes. Take up your fiddle and play again! I know you are a good Christian, and playing dance music at weddings will not make you any the less so.'

A few years later little feet could again be heard at Johnsrud. Karen and Lars had five more children, of whom three lived to maturity: Hans and Christian, and Marie, who was born on 15 November 1871.

Lars Nielsen had perfect pitch, a gift all the children inherited. Even before they started school, they learned to play the violin, the harmonium and the piano. Besides farming and teaching his own children, Lars found time to take violin pupils, who came from Eidsvoll and nearby regions and were housed at Johnsrud or on the neighbouring farms. Lars struggled to teach the work-roughened hands of his pupils to dance over the strings, and he would never give up until he had succeeded in making them play the music as he felt it should sound.

Hans, the eldest son, played both fiddle and harmonium. When the old organ in Eidsvoll Church broke down, Lars often loaded the harmonium on to wagon or sled and set off with young Hans who, under the supervision of his father, accompanied the hymns. Hans loved the organ, but he did not take to the fiddle in the same way – perhaps because he remembered how tired his father used to be when he came home after playing late at weddings. Lars' younger son, Christian, went as a young man to Kristiania where he played in the military band. He was also a violinist and conductor of the Central Theatre orchestra there. Marie, the youngest of the children, was as talented musically as her brothers. She could read sheet music before she knew her ABC. Marja, as she was called at home, played the harmonium and the piano equally well, and her father was strict about her practising. She was also brought up by her mother to be handy with a needle.

One day when Lars walked into the upstairs living-room, he found his daughter bent over a lace cushion; to find her working on lace instead of practising so angered him that he took the cushion and flung it into a corner. The lace was one wild tangle and it took Marie several days to straighten it out. She thought her father had been very unfair, as she was diligent at practising the piano. When Marie was enthusiastic or angry, her blue eyes sparkled and her red hair seemed to stand like a halo around her head. This fiery head was the despair of her father. 'You had better learn a profession so you can provide for yourself, Marja,' he said seriously, 'for with that red hair of yours, you will have little chance of getting married.'

As soon as she had mastered the harmonium she was permitted to practise on the organ in the church at Langset, a nearby village. At the age of nine, she played so well that she could substitute for her father at a service, and she was soon engaged as the permanent second organist. The only problem was that she was so small. When she sat at the organ, her feet could not reach the pedals, so she brought along a friend who played the pedals for her. If, as sometimes happened, her friend could not be there, Marie had to stand almost upright to play. Her playing must have satisfied everyone, for after three years as second organist she was engaged, at the age of twelve, as the permanent organist, at an annual salary. So it was that Marie Nielsen, early in life, started earning her own money.

In order to be at Langset Church on Sunday mornings in time for service, Marie had to leave Johnsrud on the Saturday afternoon. In summer she either walked the thirteen kilometres or rode on horseback; in winter she was permitted to use one of the farm horses, and quite alone she went by sled to Vik farm, where she spent the night. On one of these trips both of her cheeks were frozen so badly that she suffered from the effects for the rest of her life. Anders Moestue, a friend and music colleague of Lars Nielsen, lived at Vik farm. Moestue looked forward eagerly to Saturdays and the arrival of Marie, so that she could accompany him. He was an able violinist, and considered these Saturday evenings the most enjoyable in the week. He admired the child's playing and her ability to read music rapidly and accurately.

In those days one could not appear in church with curls, and certainly not with red ones. That was considered sinful. So every Saturday before she left, her mother flattened down her hair with water and plaited it so tightly that not a hair could escape. Marie was given strict orders to sleep with her plaits this way and to straighten out any stray hair before she went to church.

Marie kept her position as organist of Langset Church until she was confirmed at the age of fifteen. Her father then considered it time for her to go to Kristiania for further music studies at the Conservatory. When she left, Lars observed her sadly: she was still very small, and her hair was no less red. He admonished her to study hard so that she could become self-supporting as a performer or a music teacher. Martin Ursin became Marie's piano teacher. She worked hard and was soon qualified to do some teaching herself.

When the Christiania Theatre advertised in the summer of 1891 for a chorus coach and pianist, Marie applied for the position and got it. Here it was that she met the young violinist, Michael Flagstad. They fell in love; their engagement was announced, and on 4 October 1892, before Marie was twenty-one, they were married. And so Lars Nielsen's worry that his daughter would not find a husband had been needless. As Marie's dowry he gave the young couple money, with the stipulation that it be spent only to buy a building lot so that they would have a home on their own soil. Marie and Michael continued to work at the theatre through the spring season. Then they went to Hamar, to Michael's childhood home, and there, at Strandstuen, on 5 July 1893, Marie bore her first child, a boy. He was baptized Olav.

When the Christiania Theatre opened in the autumn, the little family returned to the capital. This time, however, Michael was the only one to take his place in the orchestra. For Marie there was enough to do at home, tending the household and the baby. But they soon realized that they could not live on Michael's salary as a musician. Besides, times were uncertain for musicians. The only solution was for Michael to give up his work with the orchestra, return with his family to Hamar where they could live with Michael's parents, and take up some other kind of work. To supplement the income, Marie would give piano lessons.

Michael found work at a condensed milk factory. From the very first moment he was unhappy, but he stayed for the sake of the family. Nor did Marie get as many pupils as she had hoped. And both of them were homesick for the musical environment of Kristiania. In the autumn of 1894 they were stricken by the death of their son Olav at the age of fourteen months. Shortly afterwards, however, Marie could tell her husband that she was pregnant again.

They now heard from friends in Kristiania that conditions for orchestral musicians were much improved, but Michael dared not resettle there without regular work in addition to that of musician. He decided to return alone to learn shorthand, in the hope of getting work at the Storting, the Norwegian parliament, as a stenographer. The Storting at this time met only for a spring session, which meant that Michael could play regularly in the theatre orchestra during the autumn and, by securing a substitute when necessary at the Storting, could continue during the spring season, too. In Kristiania it would also be easier for Marie to get pupils.

Michael passed his examination and obtained the position he wanted. He was also promised work as a violinist at the Christiania Theatre. With this happy news he returned to Hamar, where he joined Marie to await the birth of their second child. On Friday 12 July 1895, Marie gave birth to a daughter, and the baby was baptized Kirsten Malfrid in Hamar Cathedral. The name 'Kirsten' was derived from 'Kirstine', her paternal grandmother's middle name.

When Kirsten Malfrid was a few months old, the Flagstad family moved into a small flat at 6 Niels Juel Street in Kristiania, close to the Western railway line. Thanks to the two positions Michael now held, the couple's financial situation was excellent, and Marie gradually obtained many pupils. These were rewarding years for the young musicians. Michael became a member of the Quartet Association and the Orchestra Association, where he made contact with musicians who became his and Marie's friends.

Kirsten was a quiet child. When she was old enough, she played by herself for hours. She heard music at home daily, but beyond humming to herself, as most children do when occupied, she showed no signs of any precocious musical talent.

On Monday 23 May 1898, two months before her third birthday, a brother was born. He was baptized Ole after his paternal grandfather. Kirsten was excited about the little boy, who to her seemed like a live doll, but was disappointed because he was too small to play with. When he was big enough to crawl around, though, he became Kirsten's favourite playmate.

One beautiful spring day, Kirsten, then almost five, was permitted to take her dolls outside the house to play while Fru Flagstad was teaching. She had strict orders to play on the pavement only, so that her mother could keep an eye on her from the balcony. But the railway line fascinated her. For once she forgot her mother's admonition. She walked down to the tracks, placed her dolls on the rails, and played quietly for a long time. Suddenly the tracks began to sing. At that moment, Fru Flagstad looked out and saw her. Terrified, she ran out into the street just as the train whooshed by. She stood there nearly paralysed with fright for her child. Then she saw Kirsten walking calmly towards her with her dolls in her arms. 'How could you sit down on the tracks!' Fru Flagstad shouted. 'You know how dangerous it is. The train might have come at any time.' She shook Kirsten till the dolls fell to the ground. 'But Mamma,' Kirsten answered, unperturbed, 'I moved away before the train came.'

With two children in the family, the flat in Niels Juel Street became too small. The Flagstads also wanted to get away from the dangerous vicinity of the railway line. So they rented a larger flat in the heart of the city, and moved there in the autumn of 1900. But they were used to living in more countrified surroundings, and disliked their new location. The dream of having their own home outside town assumed an ever rosier hue, and Marie's dowry was available with which to buy a plot of land.

Ingvald Davidsen and Emil Johannesen, two of Michael's friends and colleagues in the Orchestra Association, were also interested in acquiring their own homes, but feared the cost. Michael suggested that the three of them should try to find a plot large enough for three houses, to be built from the same blueprints, thereby reducing the cost considerably. The idea caught fire, and in the autumn of 1901 the three musicians acquired the deeds to a plot in Ivar Aasen Road, a short walk from the station in the suburb of Vinderen, on the new Holmenkollen electric trolley line. The plot was divided, and they drew lots to decide how to share out the property. Davidsen drew the northernmost section and

Johannesen the middle one. The one located farthest south, bordering on open land, became Marie and Michael's. During the late winter and spring the three houses were built. From the very beginning, with true folk humour, the neighbours dubbed the houses 'The Three Musicians'.

Kirsten celebrated her seventh birthday in the new home at Vinderen. A flagpole had been erected in the garden, and the flag was hoisted in honour of the birthday child. During the years the family lived there the flag was raised on all festive occasions, including those celebrated by the neighbours. On this birthday Kirsten could entertain her guests by playing the piano. In the preceding two or three years she had revealed such unusual musical talent that Fru Flagstad had sent her to her own music teacher of earlier days, Martin Ursin, so that from the beginning she would receive the best possible piano instruction. When she moved with the family to Vinderen she already had a small repertoire, and was to continue her studies with Ursin.

Kirsten started school in the autumn of 1902. She was a good student, both in school and in her music lessons. She enjoyed doing her schoolwork, but she hated practising the piano, as Ursin was strict and demanding, and Fru Flagstad supervised her. In fact, she sat right next to the piano and worked on her embroidery while Kirsten played. Later in life Kirsten was extremely grateful to her mother for being so strict about her practising. 'It's been such a help to me in studying my parts that I've been a good piano player. I've been able to read the piano scores of the different operas, even the most difficult Wagner operas, with ease,' she said.

Music was an integral part of daily life at Vinderen. Marie Flagstad, or Maja as all her friends called her – she had been called 'Marja' at home as a child – was eventually to become known as 'Norway's Opera Mamma', because she had worked with so many young singers. In 1902 she and Michael signed contracts with the Central Theatre, he as violinist and conductor, she as coach and accompanist. The vocal soloists came to Vinderen to be coached by Fru Flagstad, and she still taught her many piano students at home.

On top of the high Schmidt piano in the living-room at Vinderen lay Michael's violin, and on the music stand next to the piano lay piles of sheet music for piano, violin and voice. After the daily lessons were finished, Kirsten would enjoy sitting and leafing through the piles. She preferred the vocal music, and one day she

27

played through a Schubert album for contralto. It became her habit, as she played, to sing the voice part. After going through the entire album a couple of times she knew several songs by heart, and gradually she acquired quite a repertoire. Michael Flagstad loved to listen to his daughter as she sat there singing for her own enjoyment. When he lay down to rest after dinner, he often asked her to sing for him. Years later, when Kirsten had decided to become a singer, he could not understand why she was training as a soprano when she had always sung contralto.

All the residents of 'The Three Musicians' held music evenings, but most of the time they met at the Flagstads'. If they happened to have a free night simultaneously, the musicians would arrive, bringing their instruments. For a while Maja's brother Christian and his wife, and their daughter, Asta, lived with the Ingvald Davidsens. When Christian could join them, the musicians were happy because they could then play Beethoven quartets – always Beethoven, everyone's favourite composer.

Kirsten was still too small to take an active part in these performances, but she was permitted to place the stands and arrange the music on them. Then she would curl up in a chair in a corner of the room, where, quiet as a mouse, she would listen to both the music and the good-natured banter and mutual criticism of the players' various technical weaknesses. Michael Flagstad's love of the violin was deep, but both he and his friends were aware of the technical faults that he never succeeded in overcoming. While they were playing, Michael was completely absorbed in the music, and his friends overlooked his imperfect playing of passages that challenged his technique. They felt that his feeling and expression compensated for such trifles.

Kirsten called her father and his friends 'the Sunday Quartet'. Every Sunday morning they gathered round the music stands to play chamber music. If occasionally a piano part was included, Maja was called in from the kitchen, where, as if by magic, she had prepared the most delicious dishes. 'Mother was a true culinary artist as well as a musician,' said Kirsten later. 'It was miraculous what she could prepare out of almost nothing. Mother's good food contributed, I'm sure, to the fact that Father's music friends loved to come to our house, because after the music there was always a treat from Mother's kitchen.' If Fru Flagstad was needed at the piano, Kirsten had to take her place in the kitchen. She was used to helping her mother in all domestic duties that were not part of the maid's regular work, and she did what she was asked to do without protest, even if she did not enjoy it all.

When Kirsten reached the point in her music studies where her proficiency was acknowledged by 'the Sunday Quartet', she was the one who was asked to play the piano part when they wanted to play a quintet. It always made her happy when her father asked her to join them; she loved him and admired him boundlessly:

Father was a remarkable man. All his life he studied something or other, and he knew everything. He learned four languages by himself. French was his passion, as it was also Martin Ursin's, my piano teacher. When I practised scales and exercises for Ursin, he used to rattle off French irregular verbs to the same beat. He and Father carried on long philological discussions in French. From early childhood I can remember how Father sat at night reading. Mother used to be quite desperate; Father had to work mornings at the Storting and nights at the theatre. But no one could dissuade him from staying up late to study.

Undoubtedly this rich musical environment in which Kirsten grew up stimulated her and tended to liberate her musicality. She found that later, when she began her training as a singer, she had unconsciously acquired such a knowledge of music during her early years that she was far more advanced in musical comprehension than her fellow students.

Lars Flagstad, who was always called Lasse, was born in the house at Vinderen on 5 June 1903. He was named after his maternal grandfather. From the very first moment, Kirsten was given the responsibility for her little brother's care; one of her regular duties was to take him out in his carriage. She tended him carefully and joyfully, for she loved babies even at that age, and her mother always felt safe for Lasse when Kirsten had charge of him. She was infinitely patient with Lasse, but with Ole it was a different matter. There were times when Kirsten, as the elder, would consider it her right to admonish Ole, who was three years younger. He would take his revenge by teasing her till she exploded with rage. Usually she was calm and thoughtful, but when she was teased she was like a fury. She would grab the first weapon she could lay her hands on and go at him. Once she grabbed the bread knife from the kitchen

29

table. Holding the knife high, she chased him all through the house until the parents each got hold of a child and shook the rage out of them. Soon after, Kirsten and Ole would again be the best of friends.

Kirsten's home at Vinderen was like a miniature farm, with the Christmas pig in the pigsty, hens in the henhouse, and turkeys in the yard. In the garden grew potatoes and other vegetables. Michael Flagstad had purchased the empty plot next to their own property, and there he grew vegetables on a large scale. He experimented with new types of seeds and unusual kinds of edible plants. There were so many mouths to feed that it was important to stretch the household money by growing as much food as possible. One relative or more always lived with the Flagstads. When Michael's father died, his mother and his uncle Martin moved in with them. Martin Flagstad became 'Uncle Martin' to the whole neighbourhood. He tended the animals, weeded the garden, comforted the children when they were hurt, and washed their abrasions and cuts. It was to Uncle Martin that the children went with their disappointments and sorrows, as they also did when they were lonely during the many absences of their parents.

When the fields began to turn green in springtime, Kirsten was sent out to cut the new caraway shoots. She did not have to be asked twice: she loved to roam in the fields around her home on the sunny spring days. The caraway plants grew plentifully along the paths. All her life long she was to remember the song of the lark and the scent of the wild flowers: 'Possibly these wonderful memories have something to do with why I'm so terribly fond of soup made out of caraway shoots,' she once said.

It was a wonderful place that the Flagstad children and their friends had for a playground: wide fields with a view far south to the fjord, and the sombre woods in the north. There were plenty of children to play with. Ingvald Davidsen had four daughters, and with them lived Asta Nielsen, Kirsten's cousin of the same age. At the Vinderen manor there was the composer Halvdan Cleve, who also had four little girls who were Kirsten's playmates. When she was ten years old, Dr Jon Alfred Mjøen and his family moved into the house below the Flagstads', and the house was dubbed 'the house of oddities'. The Mjøen children eventually numbered six, so that for every Flagstad child there was a Mjøen of corresponding age. During the summer the whole crowd went picnicking. They built cabins, fished with worms in the Gaustad brook, and learned to swim in the water hole formed by the dam above the Mjøens' house. In the dark 'little forest', a woody knoll behind 'The Three Musicians', they played hide-and-seek, and there the little girls had their secret hideaways.

In late autumn, when ice covered the Gaustad brook, it was exciting, although strictly forbidden, to test the ice to see when it would be thick enough to skate on. One Christmas, Ole and Lasse aroused great envy when they arrived with new skates. Uncle Martin, who was something of a jack-of-all-trades, had made them in the workshop he had in the basement of the Flagstad house. Kirsten did not care much for skating, though. She longed for good skiing conditions, and went on long trips alone or with her friends. She also practised with the boys of her age on the ski jump behind the house. The Vinderen children held a big ski jump contest every winter, and one year Kirsten hauled off the first prize, a big bag of oranges. The healthy life she lived at Vinderen certainly contributed to the exceptional physique and stamina she had in later years. After all, a Wagner role requires tremendous physical exertion. In later years people often asked how she managed to maintain such an arduous singing and travel schedule. She often sang the most demanding Wagnerian roles with only a day's rest in between performances. There was a week in the late 1930s when she sang three Wagnerian roles on three consecutive days at the Metropolitan. Up until the time she became seriously ill, she had phenomenal physical stamina. In addition to that, she had tremendous willpower and, as already mentioned, an almost incredible capacity for self-discipline. She never travelled with an entourage of any kind; secretaries and maids were no part of her lifestyle. The only person who travelled with her on tour was her accompanist. There were also friends who were happy to relieve her of everyday tasks when she was staying for an extended period in one place.

As coach at the Central Theatre it was Maja Flagstad's duty to participate in the long operetta tours the theatre undertook from time to time. During her mother's absences, Kirsten was in charge at home. She records:

Even today I remember how proud I was when for the first time Mother gave me the responsibility for the household and the younger children. It must have been in the spring of 1905, because my sister Karen Marie was only six months old. She was born on 24 November 1904, the fourth and last of the flock. She received the names of our maternal grandmother and our mother.

We usually had a maid at Vinderen, but the responsibility was mine. I was only a ten-year-old, but I felt so grown-up when I went to Father every morning to ask him what he would like for dinner. Before I went to school I would give the maid orders for household purchases. As soon as I returned I had to take care of Lasse and Karen Marie. I felt as if I were their real mother and took great pains to give them as proper care as when Mother was at home. Mother must have been satisfied, because later I was always given the same responsibility when she had to leave on tours.

With four children and one or more relatives always living with the family, space in the Flagstad house was getting scarce. For a while Kirsten and Ole had to share a 'grown-up' bed in the nursery, and this led to lively feuds between them. They had figured out which side was 'closest to the Central Theatre where Mother and Father worked at night', and took turns sleeping on that side. But occasionally they got confused, and then a fierce fight developed to secure the 'best' place.

During all holidays the Flagstad children were sent to the country, either to Michael Flagstad's parents at Hamar, while Grandpa Flagstad lived, or to Maja Flagstad's brother Hans Nielsen at Johnsrud. In contrast to the lack of room at Vinderen, there was ample space at Johnsrud. Together with Hans Nielsen's own six children, Kirsten and her brothers and sister were installed in the huge attic room in the *stabbur*, a storehouse on pillars. Kirsten's cousin Asta also spent her holidays at Johnsrud, and likewise shared the attic room. There the youngsters could make all the noise they wanted without disturbing others.

They were awakened every morning at seven, and those who were big enough to work were ordered out into the fields to help. Hans Nielsen was strict, and had made it a principle that all his children should learn to play an instrument as well as help out with the farm chores. He made no exceptions with the city children when it came to helping on the farm, either. All the children enjoyed the haymaking. But when orders came to weed the turnip fields, faces grew very long indeed, although the pay was the same as for the hired help, 5 øre a row. Kirsten's cousin, Astrid Nielsen Opsahl, recalled:

> Kirsten hated weeding in the broiling sun. It was never her habit to play truant or avoid any duty, but when we were told to weed in the turnip fields she tried a trick that usually worked. She asked Father if she could play and sing instead. Father loved to listen to Kirsten, so if there were plenty of weeders anyway she was excused. While the rest of us weeded our way through the long rows, with the sun beating down on our backs, Kirsten sat by the open window playing and singing. We were a little envious of her for getting away with this, but we also loved to hear her, so we usually forgave her the 'trick'.

When Astrid, who was the same age as Kirsten, had finished her allotted rows, she would run upstairs to join Kirsten, and then the two girls would sing duets. Both knew a great many songs from operettas and popular music. Kirsten played and sang first voice; Astrid 'embroidered' with second. If they did not know the words to the music, they made them up as they went along.

Hans Nielsen appreciated the beauty of the two clear voices, and occasionally let the girls appear as soloists in church, or at a congregational assembly with one of the many choirs he conducted. Astrid Opsahl again:

> Kirsten and I must have been about nine years old when we were first permitted to sing with one of Father's choirs. We were so proud and so affected by the solemnity of the occasion that at one of the rehearsals we got completely confused. 'Come now, little ones,' Father said severely in his Eidsvoll dialect, 'no more nonsense. You must keep together better and sing more in time.'
>
> I remember Kirsten as a cheerful and obedient little girl, but she had a strong will of her own, and she was very stubborn when she had made up her mind about something. One Easter she and her brothers and sister were holidaying as usual at Johnsrud. Kirsten wanted to leave for Kristiania before the holidays were over to hear the operetta *Madame Sherry*, which

had had its first performance at the Central Theatre the day after Easter Sunday. Both Aunt Marie and Uncle Michael were playing in the orchestra. She packed up her belongings, and at the dinner table she announced that she would be leaving on the afternoon train. 'No,' said my Mother, 'stay here until you can all leave together, and this afternoon we will perform *Madame Rootbeer.*' Mother knew that Kirsten enjoyed dressing up and acting. But no, to town she must go. 'How do you intend to get to the station?' my Mother asked her; 'Bøn station is more than three miles away.' 'I walked when I came and I can walk when I leave,' Kirsten answered so emphatically that Mother realized there was no holding her back. Easter was late that year and it was warm and spring-like when Kirsten left, spick and span in a white cotton dress and with a light coat over her arm.

From the station in the city she had gone straight to the theatre. Aunt Marie said she had been quite uneasy when she saw Kirsten arrive, black with soot from the train, and with her dress all creased. But they had let her remain for the performance, watching and listening breathlessly from the orchestra pit.

In 1907 the Central Theatre toured with *The Merry Widow.* Wherever the operetta was performed, an epidemic of *Widow* fever broke out. During the summer holidays Maja Flagstad, who accompanied the children to Johnsrud, helped Kirsten and Astrid learn several of the duets. Kirsten, who was twelve, had grown rapidly, and was tall for her age. Astrid, who was smaller, sang the part of the widow, and Kirsten the part of Count Danilo. All through the summer and autumn the two cousins entertained with selections from the operetta. During the Christmas holidays they visited Vik farm, where the lovable Misses Moestue, Anders' sisters, lent them old ball gowns in which they dressed up and went from farm to farm singing duets from the *Widow.* Kirsten remembered later:

We were a great success wherever we went, and we enjoyed our success, Astrid and I. Our hosts in Eidsvoll said we were the most enjoyable of all the 'Christmas fairies' who had visited them. I was never timid about performing, although I was really a shy child. In our family, and also at Johnsrud, singing and playing were so much a part of the normal routine ⋅ that it seemed natural to entertain with what we had to offer.

Kirsten attended Slemdal elementary school until she was nine years old. Then she went to Ragna Nielsen's school, which at that time was located in Nordahl Brun Street. Ragna Nielsen was a militant suffragette, but she did not want her students to become involved in her own political battles. To preserve her anonymity, the students were given strict orders to say that they attended Mrs Nielsen's school, not Ragna Nielsen's.

Kirsten always knew her lessons, and she always received the best mark for tidiness. If ever she or her brothers and sister had difficulty with their homework, they went to their father for help, which they always received. Michael Flagstad could usually answer offhand. If he was uncertain, or if he wished to give a more precise answer, he would fetch his reference books and dictionaries. Karen Marie recalled:

That was the worst thing I could imagine, when Father did this. I wanted to be finished with the lessons quickly so I could go out and play with my friends; that was the reason I asked for help. But the result was that I had to wait while Father read page after page. I was restless with impatience, but it was impossible to sneak out until he had given the answer. Every time this happened I decided never to ask him again, even if there was something I didn't understand – but of course I forgot and did it again. Father loved to help us with our schoolwork, and he was always so kind and patient.

Fru Flagstad noticed that Kirsten enjoyed playing from new sheet music, so it seemed quite natural to her to present Kirsten, on her tenth birthday, with the vocal score of Wagner's *Lohengrin*. She received the gift gratefully and with joy, and immediately began studying the role of Elsa. Soon she knew not only Elsa's part but all the other roles in the opera. It did not bother her that the score was in German, as she knew enough of the language from her Schubert songs to enable her to sing the roles with reasonably good characterization. When her parents discovered with what enthusiasm and seriousness she studied the roles, they continued to give her opera scores. Shortly after her birthday she was given Verdi's *Aïda*. She was greatly taken with Verdi's music, and Aïda became her favourite role. Fru Claire Mjøen, who was called 'Mammi' not only by her own six children, but by all the children in the neighbourhood, said:

Many a summer night I heard Kirsten at the piano singing and playing. The girl's clear voice filled the air with delightful music, but no one at that time had any idea what heights this voice would reach, or the fame this modest blonde girl would attain. I greatly admired Maja Flagstad, who could manage to get hold of her children for practising and music lessons. None of us other mothers could manage it! It was just as difficult to get the children away from their play as it would be to turn the Gaustad brook from its right course. But when Fru Flagstad called out over the fields in her deep, powerful voice: 'Kirsten, come in to practise', or, 'Ole, get ready for your cello lesson', Kirsten and Ole would drop what they were doing and rush inside.

Kirsten made her first pocket money by playing at dances. As vice-chairman of the Kristiania Music Association, Michael Flagstad constantly received requests to provide musicians for various events. One afternoon he was called by someone who wanted a pianist for a dance that very night. He thought for a moment; then he turned to Kirsten and explained to her what the call was about. 'You can take this job, Kirsten,' he said. Kirsten got quite upset and said she could not possibly play dance music. 'Of course you can. Show that you are a true Flagstad! You read music just as easily as you read words.' 'My daughter will accept,' he said over the telephone. So the decision was made. But her father made the condition that Kirsten must be escorted home – she was only fifteen years old.

Kirsten was given the address and took the trolley to town. On her arrival she was handed a pile of dance music and played almost continuously until two o'clock in the morning. Her playing was so satisfactory that she constantly received requests to play at other dances in town, and as long as her lessons did not suffer, her parents permitted her to accept. When her friends heard she was doing this kind of work, they said they thought it beneath her dignity. This hurt Kirsten, and she asked her father his opinion. 'I think you are a good sport to help us out in a pinch,' said Flagstad, 'and you can tell your friends so from me.' It was enough for

Kirsten to know that her father admired her and was pleased with her. Her friends soon changed their views and thought she was clever to take the jobs. 'Kirsten was our ideal, and the centre of our group of friends,' said her cousin, Asta.

Song must always have been very dear to Kirsten's heart, for she never failed to listen to Fru Flagstad's students. 'Can't you wait till I come home from school to have your singing students?' she begged of her mother before leaving. And after school she would sneak into the next room to listen. Maja knew she was there, and occasionally she would call out to her, 'Kirsten, come and sing second voice with my pupil. It's easier for him to sing correctly when he hears how the duet should sound.' Kirsten was pleased that her mother needed her help. As a rule she knew the opera excerpt in question, but if not, she sang flawlessly from the score.

> I was only eleven when mother asked me to sing a duet with one of her students for the first time. Strangely enough, it was a duet from a Wagner opera, *Der fliegende Holländer*. I had to sing most of the role of Senta, one I didn't know at that time, to assist him. I can't recall that I received any praise from Mother on that occasion. For us it was natural to have a sheet of music handed to us and to play or sing without making a mistake.

In the autumn of 1911, Kirsten was confirmed. She received a new dress with a long skirt, and was given permission to put up her long wavy hair. From the day of her confirmation she was treated as an adult. Her parents had invited relatives and friends to dinner at Vinderen. Speeches were made in her honour, and many complimentary things were said about her helpfulness, her caring for the younger children, her industry at school and her zeal at the piano. In her speech her mother said:

> It's so nice that Kirsten now likes to practise and that she enjoys singing, even if it's only for her own entertainment and ours. For one thing I know – none of my children will become professional musicians or ever appear on a stage. Kirsten and I have already discussed her future, and as far as she is concerned, I can say with certainty that she will never become a musician.

During coffee, when Kirsten was asked to entertain the guests, she immediately went to the piano. She sang and played 'Elsa's Dream' from *Lohengrin*, and received much praise for her performance. One guest only, Maja's friend Ellen Schytte Jacobsen, a singing teacher, remained silent. Some days later when she met Maja she said urgently, 'If you let Kirsten continue to sing like that, she will eventually ruin what little voice she has. Let her come to me so I can teach her some technique. It won't hurt her to know what she's doing when she sings to herself, as I understand she likes to do.'

So Kirsten was sent to 'Aunt Ellen', who soon discovered what a brilliant pupil she was. After the worst faults of her singing – faults acquired during her self-training – were corrected, there emerged a clear, pure, unfailingly musical voice. Kirsten, for her part, discovered that she liked learning to sing. She easily acquired the technical foundation that her fellow students found so difficult, and had no problems in that area. She was also found to have perfect pitch. One day, after she had been studying for three months, Aunt Ellen said to her, 'Well, Kirsten, in about three years you can make your debut as a singer.' Kirsten merely laughed, and so did her parents when she told them what her teacher had said. No one took the comment seriously, Kirsten least of all. She was not planning to be a musician, but a doctor. That was her mother's dream, and hers, too. In order to begin her studies as quickly as possible, she had skipped one year at school. She was the youngest in her class, and strained to the utmost to keep up with her more mature classmates. But she was plagued by severe headaches and such violent nosebleeds that her doctor strictly forbade her to open a book during the rest of the school year. She needed a complete rest for several months. 'If the headaches cease, she can begin school again next autumn,' he said.

The severe headaches returned, however, and Kirsten was compelled to leave school for good. It was a hard blow for both her mother and herself that she had to forgo her medical studies. But Maja had to admit that music was Kirsten's field. She entered the Conservatory to study to become a piano teacher, at the same time continuing her vocal studies.

Kirsten and her friends at Vinderen were now young ladies. At an end were the childish games and sports contests. They took walks – or promenaded quietly and sedately as, at that time, young ladies were expected to do. With Sonja Mjøen, Asta Nielsen and Aadel Nørregaard she played at 'theatre' in the 'little forest', dressed in flowing garb. The young girls were at their most romantic age. Dances were arranged at the Mjøens', the Flagstads' and the Nørregaards'. After each ball Kirsten received notes and letters from admiring young gentlemen: she was very popular. She said later:

> But my youth was not spent only in dancing. At home we had our assigned duties, and I had my generous share of them. I was accustomed to work and gave little thought to the fact that my friends had more time to themselves than I had. When I had finished my tasks, I ran to join them. We exchanged small talk and confidences. In spite of our being considered adults, we were childish of mind, and so very naïve and innocent!

When Kirsten had been at the Conservatory for about six months, she was selected from among the students to assist the actress Dagmar Fischer on her recital tour in the east of Norway. The tour included Eidsvoll, where they drew a full house. Kirsten's relatives at Johnsrud, and all her friends roundabout, attended in a body. They thought it was wonderful to hear the girl who only a few years before had been running about, her plaits flying, in that very place. The Eidsvoll paper ran a detailed review, mentioning that 'Miss Fischer was given valuable assistance by a young Kristiania lady, Miss Kirsten Flagstad, who not only played piano solos, but also accompanied Miss Fischer, for instance during her declamation of the famous poem "Bergljot" by Bjørnson.' Unfortunately the tour was not financially successful, but it gave Kirsten greater self-confidence in appearing before an audience.

Her mother thought that Kirsten wasted too much time on her vocal lessons, as she was not, after all, to become a singer. Maja was of the opinion that one should not learn only for amusement – any learning should be put to use. She asked Ellen Schytte Jacobsen straight from the shoulder if Kirsten had a future as a singer. The answer was that Kirsten was unusually gifted, and that time would tell. As she had said two years before, in her opinion Kirsten could make her debut in about a year. In the end, she was permitted to continue her vocal lessons.

In January 1912 Bokken Lasson, a well known Kristiania singer of popular music, had opened her cabaret, the Chat Noir. Maja was employed as coach and pianist. The cabaret became a regular attraction in Kristiania, although this type of entertainment was new there. French popular *chansons* and café skits had never previously been presented in the capital.

The first season at the Chat Noir was to end on 17 May, Constitution Day, and Bokken Lasson thought it would be appropriate to introduce a national touch. She asked Maja if she did not have a daughter who sang, who could perhaps come and sing together with herself and another voice student. They were to present a series of Norwegian songs. As Maja herself would be there, she consented to Kirsten's participation in the performance. Maja was at the piano, giving her daughter her cues. This was Kirsten's first public performance as a singer. Her debut occurred without any fanfare. There was nothing about her voice or her person at that time to suggest future world fame.

Maja then felt it was time for Kirsten to earn some money, so she allowed her to join the actor Per Qvaernstrøm and his ensemble who, in the summer of 1912, were to run a summer theatre in Dyrmyrskogen, the woods near Kongsberg. Dyrmyrskogen was a popular excursion spot with the inhabitants of Kongsberg and adjacent districts. Since 1908, during the summer months, the stage there had been the location of a summer theatre, which attracted many visitors and gave the actors from Kristiania an opportunity to earn extra money. Many years later Kirsten Flagstad wrote to the author M. B. Landstad about her part in Qvaernstrøm's theatre in Dyrmyrskogen:

As far as I remember, I was engaged as pianist at the theatre in the summer of 1912. We began with a revue of yours, and I was in charge of the music, which consisted of only a melody, and the coaching of the actors. I had to add a bass line, of course, and 'embroider upon' the music, and even put together an overture. I played entr'acte music for *Anderson, Petterson and Lundström*. During the intermissions, I played Beethoven sonatas and Grieg, and when the fairies appeared, I even played excerpts from *Lohengrin*.

My stage debut was in *The Stork*, as the cook. I appeared only in the last act, so I was free to play the piano during the intermissions. Before my cue, Mrs Worm-Müller painted red roses on my cheeks and tightened my hair into a knot on top of my head; then up on the stage I went.

Per Qvaernstrøm played the fiddle, and I often accompanied his old-time dances in a small open pavilion; and once Gunlaug Lund and I danced a Spanish dance there. I recall with pleasure my dear colleagues, Schønemann, Mrs Worm-Müller, Strømmen and Qvaernstrøm. All of them dead by now. I was paid almost as much as Qvaernstrøm – 100 kroner a month. You have no idea how important I felt.

Kirsten's choice of music for the intermissions probably did not harmonize well with the taste of the boisterous audience that had come to be amused by the frolics of *Anderson, Petterson and Lundström*. There was loud talk while she played Beethoven's Pathétique Sonata. One night an elderly gentleman came over to her, poked her in the back with his cane, and asked whose daughter she was. When she told him, he turned on his heel and walked away, exclaiming, 'I might have known, since you play that kind of music here.' Kirsten had the feeling, nonetheless, that he intended his remark as a compliment on her choice.

4

The Young Musician

Kirsten made steady progress in her music studies. Leaving Aunt Ellen after her lessons, she would walk home through the side streets so as not to run into acquaintances. She was trying to retain the lesson in her mind, and as soon as she arrived home she would start practising what she had learned in order to make it sound the way she knew it should. In the meantime, her parents had left the Central Theatre. Michael was now conductor at the Norske Teatret, and Maja was much sought after in the capital as a coach wherever opera, operetta or choral concerts were being prepared.

In the autumn of 1913, d'Albert's opera *Tiefland* (*Lavlandet*, in Norwegian) was to be presented at the National Theatre, with Johan Halvorsen as conductor. One of Maja's pupils was scheduled to have an audition for the role of Marta, and Maja was to be her accompanist. But the young singer did not get the role, and after the audition, Halvorsen said to her: 'Unfortunately you are not right for the role of Nuri either. The role is not filled, but Nuri should be about fourteen years old, so it is difficult to find the right person.' On her way home, Maja stopped at one of the music shops, where she bought the vocal score of *Tiefland*. As soon as she arrived home she told Kirsten to learn the role of Nuri as quickly as she could. Two days later she knew the role by heart, but in German.

Maja took her daughter to the National Theatre and asked Halvorsen to listen to her. Kirsten was the thirteenth candidate to be auditioned for the part of Nuri. Halvorsen knew that the daughter of such recognized musicians as Michael and Maja Flagstad would at least be well trained.

Kirsten had sung only a few measures when Halvorsen began to listen intently. Here was someone who could sing! As soon as the audition was over, Kirsten was given the part. Her mother naturally went with her when the contract was to be prepared and signed. Kirsten was engaged for twenty performances at a salary of 50 kroner a performance, a total of 1000 kroner. Now she would be rich! She was to appear on a stage with mature singers, and even be paid!

Kirsten immediately began to learn Nuri in Norwegian, and came well prepared to the first orchestral rehearsal. Everyone was kind to the young singer, so she was not in the least nervous when Halvorsen rapped on the conductor's stand to signal the beginning of the rehearsal. When it was over, Halvorsen again rapped on the stand, then said to the orchestra: 'Gentlemen! We have reason to feel proud. Miss Flagstad is indeed the daughter of true musicians. She was the only one of the soloists who went through the rehearsal without making a mistake.'

The Danish tenor Vilhelm Herold was to sing the principal role, in addition to coaching the singers. Herold soon discovered that Kirsten felt comfortable on the stage, and did not instruct her too much as she rehearsed her small role: 'Herold patted me on the head and said to me: "Do as you please, child." He let me walk around and even knit. I was really surprised at myself. I was nervous neither at rehearsals nor at the first performance; I was merely happy to be with the cast. I wonder if the opera singer in me was born that night, although many years were to go by before I would realize it.'

Kirsten's parents wanted to give a small party for her after the first performance of *Tiefland*, on Friday 12 December 1913. In expectation of her salary she had been permitted to buy material for a dress, and throughout the day of the performance the young soprano sat at the sewing-machine making it.

Kirsten received a generous share of the applause after this successful performance. With flowers in her arms she curtsied to the royal box where King Haakon sat with his entourage. She was congratulated by the conductor and her colleagues, and Herold expressed his pride in her. In the restaurant, friends of her parents came to congratulate her. It was a momentous and memorable day for the eighteen-year-old Kirsten. The next day she read the review of the critic and composer Hjalmar Borgstrøm in the *Aftenposten*. He commented: 'Miss Kirsten Flagstad made her debut in the role of Nuri. A very melodious voice and a modest manner show great promise for the future of the young singer.' Kirsten was delighted.

If so severe a critic as Borgstrøm predicted a future for her as a singer, she must possess the necessary talent, she thought. Performing artists knew Borgstrøm's qualifications as both musician and critic.

One night during the run of the opera at the National Theatre, Vilhelm Herold was the guest of the Students' Association, where he was honoured as the celebrated artist he was. 'You must come to see and hear *Tiefland*,' he said to those seated with him, 'not only for my sake, but for the sake of little Kirsten Flagstad who has made her debut as Nuri. She is truly a "conductor's child", and, mark me, one day you will hear about her.'

Kirsten spent some of the money she first earned as an opera singer on new curtains for the living-room at Vinderen. Compared with the cheques she was to receive later in life, the sum was very modest. 'I still believe that that cheque was the one that gave me the greatest pleasure,' she said. 'Never have I felt as rich as when I held the cheque from the National Theatre in my hand. During my girlhood days I was accustomed to having only small amounts of money in my possession. To me, 1000 kroner seemed an incredible amount.'

After her successful debut, it was decided that she should concentrate on her vocal studies and work towards the career her teacher had set as a goal. Even if, as Maja's friend, Ellen Schytte Jacobsen did not charge a penny for Kirsten's lessons, a long study period would cost money, more than Kirsten possessed or than her parents could afford to spend on her education. She was advised to apply for a scholarship. Johan Halvorsen, without being requested, wrote a recommendation for her to enclose with the application. With his sure instinct, Halvorsen realized Kirsten's potentialities: 'Miss Kirsten Flagstad is without doubt, as far as both voice and talent are concerned, one of the chosen few. She is a true musician, and possesses a beautiful and resonant soprano voice. Her intonation is perfect and her sense of rhythm unfailing. I refer you to her debut in d'Albert's *Tiefland* in the difficult role of Nuri. It was a debut that justifies the greatest expectations for her future. She should have the scholarship.' Kirsten was kept waiting, however. She continued to study and to perform her daily duties at home. She also accepted invitations to sing, because she realized that she needed more experience in appearing before the public.

While she was singing at the National Theatre, her parents

received a request to provide music on Christmas Day for the inmates of the local prison. The Flagstads often received such requests, and they never refused; they decided that this time Kirsten should come along also. She commented later:

> I was greatly shaken when I sang for the inmates for the first time. They could see me and I could see them, but they could not see each other. The many pairs of eyes staring at me coldly, with indifference, even animosity, made me shiver. When Mother played the introductory chord of my first Christmas song, I closed my eyes in terror. When I had finished singing, I discovered, to my surprise, that they were looking at me with both interest and emotion.
>
> As we were about to leave, I was asked if I would consider returning on Easter Sunday to sing again. Although I dreaded facing the prisoners again, I said I would. At Easter it was much better arranged: I was placed so that the prisoners could see me without my seeing them.
>
> After the concert I was told of an incident that moved me profoundly. The warden said that one of the prisoners, who had been an inmate for several years, was to be released just before Easter. When he came to say goodbye, he asked if I was going to sing again on Easter Sunday. The warden told him I was. The prisoner then begged to remain until after Easter Sunday so that he could hear me again. 'Keep this in your heart, young lady,' the warden said. 'You will never receive a greater compliment.'

Ellen Schytte Jacobsen decided that it would be good for Kirsten to change teachers for a while, and the choice fell on the bass Albert Westwang, who had studied in Germany and enjoyed a brilliant career there. He had captivated the Kristiania music world with his big, rich voice. Westwang concentrated on improving Kirsten's breathing technique, which he said would assure her of the necessary support in long dramatic passages. He let her study 'Elisabeth's Prayer' from Wagner's *Tannhäuser*. Over and over she had to sing the long phrases, and Westwang insisted that at the end of each phrase she should still have breath left. 'I don't think he was ever satisfied,' said Kirsten. 'Considering my later career as a singer of Wagner, one would think that Westwang possessed a sixth sense. The foundation he laid for my breathing technique has been invaluable to me. It was strange that he had such foresight, because at that time there was nothing to indicate that I, with my small, light voice, would ever sing Wagner.' It is interesting to note that from early adolescence Kirsten Flagstad had a deep speaking voice, in marked contrast to her then light soprano and slender figure.

For her advanced studies Kirsten had hoped to go to Berlin, which, at that time, was the Mecca for all singers. But the outbreak of war in 1914 disrupted her plans, and she had to continue with her two teachers in Kristiania.

During this tragic winter there was need of lighter entertainment in the theatres. The National Theatre decided to present Planquette's operetta, *The Bells of Corneville* (*The Chimes of Normandy*). Conductor Johan Halvorsen offered Kirsten a principal role, that of the young girl Germaine. From the musical point of view she mastered the role, but, because her stage experience was limited, her acting was rather stiff and awkward. Halvorsen, who understood that Kirsten had difficulty with the spoken parts, had composed a little waltz which made it possible for her to sing the lines. She received much praise for her singing, but the critics were more reserved when it came to her characterization of the role of Germaine. However, Kirsten's natural charm had already made her a favourite with the audiences.

In the summer of 1915 she was engaged at the outdoor theatre in the suburb of Bygdø, appearing in the *Mountain Story* of Henrik Bjerregaard and Waldemar Thrane. Her singing and acting delighted the audience, and her performance of Aagot's 'Mountain Song' was the highpoint of the production. 'How rich and beautiful it sounded from the lips of the promising young singer,' wrote one of the critics.

That autumn a music history conference took place at the National Theatre. For the first and only time, two future Metropolitan Opera stars sang together in a Norwegian opera. The lyric soprano Kaja Eide (Eidé Norena) was engaged to sing the principal role in the two one-act operas of Gerhard Schjelderup, *Holy Night* and *Spring Night*. Kirsten was offered a small role and was thrilled to be singing on the same stage as the already famous Kaja Eide. Twenty years later, when Kirsten made her sensational debut at the Metropolitan, Eidé Norena, who had adopted that name at the beginning of her international career, was sitting in the audience and witnessed the success her Norwegian colleague enjoyed. She sent a cable to Norway, the text of which was published in a Norwegian newspaper, on the front page in bold type, the day after the debut: 'KIRSTEN FLAGSTAD'S DEBUT A BRILLIANT SUCCESS. EIDE NORENA.'

While Kirsten was studying with Albert Westwang, she un-expectedly received a private loan of 3000 kroner. She decided to go abroad for further study, and, as it was impossible to go to Germany because of the war, she chose the flourishing musical atmosphere of Stockholm.

She was now twenty-one years old, tall and slender, and very feminine. Among her admirers there were two young men, both several years older than she. Both were persistent in their court-ship. Kirsten was attracted to one of them, the son of a landowner in north-western Norway. When he proposed, she accepted, not realizing that what she felt for him was friendship, not love. It had always been her desire to marry early and have many children. More than anything else she wanted her own home: in the house at Vinderen there was nowhere she could call her own. When she was too grown up to share the nursery, there was no other place for her than downstairs in the living-room, in the corner behind the piano. That was Kirsten's 'bedroom'. In the daytime, the couch she slept on was her father's favourite place for his afternoon nap. She was not one to complain, but one day on a trip to town with her sister Karen Marie, who was nine years younger, she confided that she was unhappy at home. 'I do think that now, as a young woman, I should have my own room,' she had said with a sigh. 'But I know it's impossible because there are so many of us in the house.'

This may have been the reason for her acceptance of the proposal. Her fiancé immediately set about building a house in the region where he lived. Kirsten had strong emotions, but it was indecorous in those days for young girls to show their feelings, and she was too shy to show them. Also, in addition to being modest and reserved by nature, she had been brought up very strictly. The friends of her youth who knew her well agreed that she was almost prudish. She was always the perfect lady, never tolerating any-thing risqué. The landowner's young son, too, evidently felt that Kirsten was unduly correct. After some time he broke off the engagement. A broken engagement was a disgrace: Kirsten went about frozen and without a smile.

It was therefore a relief for her, as well as for her family, when she received the loan that enabled her to leave for Stockholm; with strict economy, she could stay for at least a year. Before she left, she withdrew her application for a scholarship. She did not consider it right to accept money from a public institution when she had acquired a private loan.

Michael and Maja Flagstad accompanied their daughter to Stockholm to introduce her into musical circles and to help her find a vocal teacher. It was fortunate indeed that the choice should fall on Dr Gillis Bratt, the well known throat specialist and vocal instructor. As far as Kirsten was concerned, it could not have been a better choice. It was Dr Bratt who 'released' her voice, and laid the foundation for her future career as the world's greatest Wagnerian soprano.

After the audition, Dr Bratt asked Kirsten if she had ever sung in public. When she said yes, he said that no one could have heard her because her voice was so small and weak. Kirsten flushed. She replied that she had received excellent reviews for her singing. Nevertheless, Dr Bratt persisted, she still had a child's voice, but he believed that it could be made stronger and fuller. Her vocal chords 'leaked' breath, but by intensive work, and because she was so musical, she would be able to overcome this defect.

This was a difficult time of extremely concentrated study for Kirsten. She had lessons twice a week with Dr Bratt, and he was very strict. Often he drove her so hard and was so dissatisfied with her work that she would start to cry. Then his mood would change immediately. He would offer her sweets from a dish that he always had in his studio, and console her, saying that in spite of everything she was making great progress. Indeed, after three months' study her voice had grown to twice its former size.

It was now clear that she wished above all to become an opera singer. Therefore it was necessary for her to learn to act on a stage, and, accordingly, she took lessons in *plastique* (the technique of making very slow movements, like a statue in motion) with a prominent dance instructor, Anna Bele, who directed the Jaques-Dalcroze School in Stockholm. Kirsten recalled:

> When I was first in Stockholm my time was spent running from one teacher to another. I had rented a room with a piano, in the home of a pleasant family. Breakfast was included, and that was fortunate because I had no time to think about food.

Between lessons I would eat hurriedly in some café where the food was reasonable. As a voice student, I had been given a pass to all opera performances, and I spent most of my evenings there. But I was happy in spite of the hard work, and I had no time to be homesick. I did miss my sister and brothers, though, whom I was used to taking care of; so when I felt lonely I would console myself by seeking out a little boy in the family.

The 3000 kroner sufficed for one year's study with Dr Bratt. I felt I was on the right road, but realized it was only Dr Bratt who could help me further in my training. It was discouraging to have to return home after only one year, without knowing whether I would have the opportunity to continue my studies in Stockholm.

Once again she was lucky. A businessman from Bergen, who had followed her development and kept track of her progress in Stockholm, gave her a cheque for 10,000 kroner – a very large sum at that time – so that she might continue her studies with Dr Bratt. His only condition was that his anonymity be preserved outside the intimate circle of the Flagstad family. Kirsten was brimming over with gratitude. She promised to spend the money wisely, to stretch it as far as possible, and to work diligently so that her benefactor would not be disappointed. Rarely have the promises of a young music student been kept so faithfully, and rarely has a donor received so much in return. Through his help, what was to become 'the voice of the century' was established.

While Kirsten was in Stockholm in the autumn of 1917, she renewed an acquaintance that was to develop into a lifelong friendship. The young Norwegian actress Grace Grung had a one-year leave of absence from the National Stage of Bergen to study speech with Dr Bratt. On one of the first nights she spent in Stockholm, she went to the Royal Opera. During an intermission she met the Flagstads, mother and daughter:

Maja stopped to say hello. Both she and Kirsten had been guests in my home during one of the many operetta tours Maja Flagstad conducted. Kirsten, who at that time was about fourteen or fifteen years old, had come with her. One evening Maja had asked Kirsten to sing a little for us, but she had

49

refused rather sharply. 'What an ungracious chit of a girl she is,' I had said to myself.

Now, when Maja heard that I also was studying in Stockholm, she said earnestly that Kirsten and I must see each other often. I looked searchingly at Kirsten, who stood a little in the background, and she seemed to me as standoffish as ever. In spite of Maja's eagerness, we did not arrange to meet. But we must have been destined to become friends – friends for life.

When Grace Grung enrolled as a pupil at the Jaques-Dalcroze School to take lessons in *plastique*, the teacher, Anna Bele, placed her in the same class as Kirsten, the only other Norwegian. After lessons they started leaving together and gradually discovered that they enjoyed each other's company. They went to the opera together, as well as to concerts and the theatre. Six months later, there was a vacancy where Kirsten lived, and Grace moved in. Their friendship became increasingly close. Kirsten said later:

> Grace was such a good influence on me. She was several years older and much more mature. Our rooms were adjoining, with a connecting door. We had agreed that while we worked we should keep the door closed. However, I often asked her to listen to me, or she would come in and ask me about a Swedish word or expression she didn't understand, and finally the door remained open most of the time.

Gillis Bratt often mentioned Kirsten to Grace Grung. 'Kirsten is very gifted,' he said. 'She has it in her to become a great singer. She works energetically and single-mindedly.' He made no secret of the fact that his goal was to prepare Kirsten for a debut at the Royal Swedish Opera. But he did not want her to audition for the Opera management until she was so well prepared that there could be no doubt about a debut. He thought that the spring of 1919, after two and a half years of training, would be the right time.

After Kirsten had studied for a year and a half, Bratt felt that she should give a concert in her home town. It would be good for her to face an audience, and it would be interesting to see what the critics in Kristiania would say about her voice at this stage in its development. Together they worked on a programme alternating German and Norwegian Lieder with Italian and German opera arias. The baritone Carl Richter, of the Royal Swedish Opera, was to assist her. Besides two individual sections each, Richter and she would sing duets from two Mozart operas. They had secured the services of the Italian-born pianist and conductor Piero Coppola as accompanist.

The concert took place in the University Auditorium on 21 March 1918. A near-full house greeted Kirsten Flagstad when she walked on stage to open with 'Ritorna vincitor' from Verdi's *Aïda*. The atmosphere was tense and expectant: the audience anticipated something special from a Flagstad. They were not disappointed. The enthusiasm mounted with each song, and the warm applause and the many repeats that were demanded clearly showed that Kirsten had fulfilled all hopes. After she and Richter had had to repeat the opera selections, the listeners remained seated to hear encores.

It was a tired but happy Kirsten who, with her arms full of flowers, was called back time after time to receive the tribute of the audience. The critics, also, expressed their approval. 'The young lady's singing was convincing proof of sound schooling,' wrote Hjalmar Borgstrøm. '. . . The voice is on the way to becoming quite big. If its further development brings with it greater authority, one can anticipate that the talented young singer will gradually attain considerable artistic stature.' Kirsten herself believed that her studies in Stockholm had been of decisive importance:

I did not leave my two first teachers, Ellen Schytte Jacobsen and Albert Westwang, because I was dissatisfied with their teaching. It was they who thought it would be wise for me to change teachers. All three teachers developed the musical gifts with which I had been so fortunately endowed; I never needed to change my 'method'. But it was Dr Bratt who discovered that my voice was too weak because my vocal cords 'leaked'. When this fault was corrected, the voice grew considerably. At the beginning of my studies with him, he asked me if I intended to teach. I answered with a decided 'no', for I already knew then that I did not want to be a teacher. Instruction would go faster if I did not need an explanation of everything I did, he said. I believe he realized at an early stage that I could become a good singer; but did he foresee that I would go as far as I actually did? I myself am surprised, but eternally grateful, that my voice was of this quality.

51

When Kirsten came home in December 1918 to celebrate Christmas with her family at Vinderen, she was eager to find out how the newly organized Opéra Comique had fared. Both her mother and her brother Ole were involved in it. Her mother could report that the Opéra was a success. People needed to enjoy themselves after the long, weary war years, and night after night they filled the theatre. The opening had come at an opportune time, and Benno Singer, the impresario, who was the producer, was both able and enterprising, Maja told Kirsten.

Benno Singer, Hungarian by birth, had arrived in Norway in the summer of 1914, the year of the Exposition, and had made a fortune from his many entertainment establishments in the Tivoli Park. He had remained in Norway during the war, and his fortune had increased. He was, however, no mere businessman. His love of opera ran deep, and he wanted to use his capital to give Kristiania a permanent opera and operetta stage. He had a large office building erected, which was also to house his opera, in Parliament Street.

The grand opening of the Opéra Comique took place on Saturday 30 November 1918, with a prologue and speeches. A festive audience had filled the theatre to see and hear the opening opera, Camille Saint-Saëns' *Samson et Dalila*. The critic Reidar Mjøen had prepared a commemorative booklet in which he set forth the history of opera in Norway. The last words, proud and triumphant, read: 'Now that the beautiful art of opera has at last come into its own in our country, it is not least because we no longer have the problem of finding singers. Indeed, we have an abundance of good singers. With the Opéra Comique, and its successor-to-be, the Norwegian Opera, the contest between opera and drama will be a thing of the past.'

Singer had asked Michael Flagstad, with whom he had worked before, to translate the libretto of *Samson et Dalila* into Norwegian. In 1915, together with Thorleif Clausen, Michael had written the revue *Futt*, which had enjoyed great success at the Théâtre Moderne. Michael had a talent for correlating text and music: his song, 'Du skulle ha sett min Klara, så rød som ei rose var'a' ('You should have seen my Klara, as red as a rose was she') had become what we would now call a 'hit'.

In the autumn of 1918, the whole house at Vinderen was practically a branch of the Opéra Comique. Michael sat at the dining-room table working on his translation; Maja coached opera arias with the soloists in the living-room; and Ole practised in the basement. Occasionally Michael wanted his family's opinion of the text he was working on. One night he read his translation of one of Dalila's arias to them: 'With silken chains I will hold him, and lead him, meek as a child . . .' Fourteen-year-old Karen Marie thought it sounded so romantic! When Michael had returned to the dining-room to continue his work, Maja let fall her sewing into her lap, and, nodding towards the dining-room, she said with infinite tenderness: 'Those silken chains, children, are the ones with which I hold Michael. It is silken chains that bind him and me together.'

'Mother was so sweet when she said that,' said Karen Marie. 'Lasse and I both realized what depth of feeling was expressed in those words and in the way in which she said them. We have often relived the mood of that night when Mother let us catch a glimpse of what she and Father meant to each other.'

Kirsten, who rejoiced with the family that *Samson et Dalila* had been such a complete success, reminisced later about family holiday customs:

> Christmas at Vinderen meant something very special to me. Father and Mother both cherished the old traditions, and I have tried to carry over our Christmas customs from Vinderen to my own home.
>
> During Christmas, Father and Mother enjoyed more leisure than at any other time of the year. They gathered friends and relatives into their home for sumptuous parties. Besides having such a good head, Father was also good with his hands, and he took great pleasure in making small figures which, at Christmas, he placed on top of the stove. The draught made the figures move, and I remember especially an old man who sawed wood and a woman who churned butter. Mother decorated the house and prepared quantities of good food. Abundance ruled at Christmas. But music, song and interesting conversation were just as important a part of our celebration as the enjoyment of Mother's opulent table.

Ole Flagstad had a schoolfriend named Ivar Andrésen, who, through the years, had been a frequent visitor at Vinderen. He felt happy in the musical environment, for his secret dream was to become a singer. Ivar's father, a well-to-do businessman, wanted him to take over his business. This particular Christmas Maja and

Ole decided to fight a battle for Ivar. In their opinion, he should have the opportunity to go to Stockholm and study with Dr Bratt. In secret, Kirsten and Ivar studied a scene from Puccini's *Tosca*, and then, one evening in the holidays, Ivar's parents were invited to dinner at the Flagstads', Over coffee, with everyone in a mellow mood after the good food, Maja suggested that they should have a little music. Chairs were removed, Ole brought out his cello, and Maja seated herself at the piano.

With a huge kitchen knife as a prop, Kirsten stood up as the threatening Tosca, while young Ivar tried to assume a dignified air as the evil Scarpia. They sang and acted the dramatic scene with great bravura, and Herr and Fru Andrésen were overcome when they heard the beautiful voice of their son. It did not take Maja long to convince the couple that Ivar had to be a singer. That Christmas season at Vinderen the foundation of Ivar Andrésen's international career as a great bass singer was laid. Karen Marie said later:

> I'm sure Mother and Ole did not know themselves how many musically talented young people they gave a start to. In the light of Maja's view that a talent should have the right to develop, it is strange that she so strongly opposed musical careers for her own children. But to her credit it must be said that when all four of us nevertheless chose careers in music, she supported us wholeheartedly. I believe she really was pleased, for I have never seen anyone as proud as Mother when one of us met with success.

Michael Flagstad no longer had much time for playing his violin. His work in the Storting took up so much time that he had had to give up his position as conductor. He had become editor of the *Storting News*, and also continued as a stenographer. Many a member of the Storting whose speech was not as smooth as it could have been would ask him to polish it a little before it went into print.

This Christmas, he would occasionally ask Kirsten and Ole to play a Beethoven trio with him. The same overwhelming pleasure seized Michael whenever he held the violin in his hands. 'Please, Kirsten, sing an A so that I can tune my fiddle,' he would say. He was proud of her perfect pitch. When he grew tired with playing, he would rest on the couch behind the piano, always with one of his beloved pipes within reach. Those pipes would lie about all over the house – until Kirsten saw her chance to tidy up. That, however, would draw thunder from the usually peaceful Flagstad: 'Where is my pipe?' 'Where it should be, on the pipe table,' Kirsten would answer.

All my life I have regretted my severity with Father. He spilled ash everywhere, which always annoyed me. But I cannot forgive myself for constantly rebuking him and scolding him for his untidiness. Father was an outstanding man, and he loved me. I should have known better than to set myself up as his judge. My abnormal sense of tidiness has bothered many others, too, I'm afraid, not only Father. In later years I have tried to be less meticulous. Others also have a right to be as they are.

Between Christmas and New Year of 1919, one of Kirsten's schoolmates, Ole Hall, rang her up, inviting her to the National Theatre. They agreed to meet at the entrance. When she arrived she was met not by Ole, but by his older brother Sigurd. He confessed that he had asked Ole to telephone for him because he was not sure that Kirsten would accept an invitation from him. Kirsten, who was a stickler for form, said she certainly would not have, but deep inside she felt flattered that Sigurd Hall wanted to take her out. He was several years older than she, and employed in his father's business. A. O. Hall's wholesale ironware firm was a well established one, with retail contacts throughout the country. Sigurd was the firm's sales representative.

It was a pleasant evening. Sigurd was charming and entertaining, and when they parted, he asked permission to see her again. The very next day he called and invited her out to dinner, and without hesitation Kirsten accepted. She fell under the spell of his charm, and of his sophisticated manner. They were constantly together during the holidays.

Sigurd Hall was a widower. He had lost his wife during the Spanish flu epidemic. Kirsten was profoundly moved when he told her about his deep grief when his wife died. Shortly after their first date, she invited him home to meet her parents. Maja's mother instinct warned her that this man might be dangerous for Kirsten, and she was very cool towards him. If they fell in love with each other, Kirsten's plans for further education in Stockholm might be ruined.

Towards the end of the holidays, Kirsten told her family that Sigurd had proposed and that she had accepted. She would not return to Stockholm to study with Dr Bratt, she said. She and Sigurd would be married in the spring of 1919, and until then she would join the Opéra Comique. 'When we get married,' she said, 'I won't sing a note except for my own pleasure.' A stormy scene ensued between mother and daughter. Maja was furious. But she knew it was to no avail: Kirsten was as stubborn as a mule when her mind was made up. In the end, Maja gave her blessing; Michael had already given his. 'The girl's happiness is the most important thing to me,' was his comment.

Kirsten *was* happy. Those who met her with Sigurd were moved when they saw the love between them. Maja capitulated completely, and became the one most eager to help Kirsten with her trousseau.

At the Opéra, Kirsten was received with enthusiasm by Benno Singer, by her colleagues and by the public. On 16 January she appeared on the stage as Martha in the Norwegian première of the opera *Der Evangelimann* by Wilhelm Kienzl. 'At last the Opéra Comique has succeeded in acquiring the *ingénue* so sorely needed,' wrote one critic after the first performance. 'One could hardly imagine a more charming *ingénue* than Miss Flagstad. Her appearance, her voice and her acting are delightful.'

Singer had promised Kirsten that she would sing Nedda in Leoncavallo's *Pagliacci*. But he had also said that she would have to take the roles he gave her, including minor roles in operetta. When he discovered how popular she was with the public, he gave her one principal role after another. In the course of four months she studied six major roles, all completely new to her. It was an abuse of her talent that could not help but affect her performances. Kirsten had undeniable talent, and a rare gift for learning a part quickly and correctly. But as an actress she was completely without experience, and her characterization of the various roles was inevitably undistinguished. But the Opéra Comique was to give her a solid foundation for her later career in opera.

As Nedda in *Pagliacci* she reached the peak of performance. Instinctively she felt that opera would have to be her main field if she was to continue to sing in public.

Kirsten and Sigurd were married on Wednesday 14 May 1919. The young bride had to appear at the theatre the same evening, as her contract with the Opéra did not run out until the end of the spring season. There was no time for a honeymoon until June, when the Opéra gave guest performances in Copenhagen with part of its ensemble. Kirsten was to appear in several of the operas to be presented there. Among other roles, she was to sing the part of the young Ganymed in *The Beautiful Galatea* of Franz von Suppé. She disliked this boy's role because she had to appear in a short tunic; she did not feel right on the stage so 'undressed', as she put it.

After the first performance in Copenhagen, she received an offer that might have changed her whole career. A Danish director who had seen her in the role of Ganymed telephoned her and offered her the starring role, with star pay, in his new musical. He promised her good songs and beautiful costumes. 'It was not difficult for me to decline,' she said. 'What surprises me, though, is that I refused on the grounds that I was an opera singer. It really was quite strange, as I had decided not to consider any engagements after I married Sigurd.' Whenever Kirsten had a free night, she and Sigurd went dancing. He was a wonderful dancer, and the young couple, so obviously in love, attracted many eyes. In nature, Kirsten and Sigurd were quite different, though. He was gregarious, and liked to be surrounded by happy people. His charm and his good humour made him the centre of a lively group of friends. Kirsten was primarily a homebody; she would have preferred to be alone with her husband, or with a few good friends who accepted her quiet, introspective personality.

Kirsten was better known to the Danish public than she realized. She was a great hit at the Danish Casino, which was crowded as long as the guest performances by the Opéra Comique lasted. Kirsten had told Benno Singer that she did not want to renew her contract. She would be completely happy taking care of her husband in their small flat in Willow Street. But when autumn arrived and Sigurd was away on business, she felt lonely. Singer offered her tempting roles, and she signed a contract for that season.

The new opera roles that Singer had promised in order to induce her to sign up with him were slow in materializing. Nedda in *Pagliacci* satisfied her artistically, and she received praise from the reviewers. But most of the time she had to appear in one lightweight, insignificant operetta after another. The Opéra had to produce light works in order to bring in the extra money needed to produce opera.

Kirsten was not satisfied with her performances that autumn. Her voice had lost its lustre, her acting was uninspired. She began to have difficulty with her long breath, and she had to strain to encompass the long passages with which she had formerly had no trouble. It made her uneasy, until she finally realized the cause. She was pregnant. Now she had a valid reason not to sign another contract. She sang until Christmas, and then prepared for her new role, the most delightful she could have hoped for.

Maja Flagstad, who was extremely proficient in all kinds of needlework, had passed on the art to her two daughters. While waiting for the baby, Kirsten busied herself happily with knitting and sewing. Every stitch in every garment was executed with minute care. If she made the slightest mistake, she undid it. Many years later, in a hotel room in New York, she sat with a friend while embroidering a piece with fine cross-stitches. At regular intervals she turned the embroidery over to see if the stitches went the same way. 'Why do you do that, Kirsten?' her friend asked. 'Nobody will look at the wrong side.' Kirsten stared at her. 'I will. Mother taught me as a child the way it was to look: as neat on the wrong side as on the right.'

On Monday 17 May 1920, Norway's Constitution Day, Kirsten gave birth to a baby girl. She and Sigurd were the proudest and happiest of parents:

I was completely absorbed in the child. I had no thought outside of her and Sigurd. Nothing in the world existed for me outside our little home; I was fully satisfied to live only for the two of them. But I will admit that the child came first. Sigurd was just as crazy about the baby as I was, so he did not feel neglected. He was exceptionally expert in taking care of her, and this in a day when it was not usual for fathers to tend babies with the zeal Sigurd showed. Our little girl was baptized Else–Marie, but soon we were calling her only Else.

For many months I did not sing a note, except when I sat at Else's crib and sang her to sleep. I thought I was finished with my singing career for ever. It seemed so distant and unreal that if anyone had told me then that I would sing again in public, I would only have laughed.

Maja Flagstad, who had raised four children and had always taken on strenuous work besides, felt that Kirsten became too absorbed in Else. When Benno Singer wanted her to return to the Opéra Comique in the autumn of 1920, and Kirsten said she was not interested, Maja tried to persuade her, but was brushed off. Maja would not give up, however. She nagged so long at Kirsten to resume her singing that she became furious: 'I do not want to go back to the Opéra Comique, and I am not in the least interested in continuing any singing career. *You* are ambitious, but I am not!'

Singer decided that *Gypsy Love* by Franz Lehár would be an appropriate opener for the Christmas season, and that the leading role would be perfect for Kirsten Flagstad Hall. But he knew it was futile to try to persuade her. Maja, who was the theatre coach, trooped up to Kirsten's apartment with the score. Kirsten, as usual, was busy tending Else. As soon as Maja was inside the door, she said: 'Now you must make up your mind, Kirsten. I have brought the vocal score of *Gypsy Love*. The main role would fit you like a glove.' Before Kirsten could protest, Maja sat down at the piano and began to play. Lehár's insinuating music filled the room. Almost against her will, Kirsten went over to the piano, humming. Soon she was singing with full voice. Maja stopped abruptly, turned around, and stared at Kirsten, who looked completely bewildered. Her voice had doubled in size. Without a word, but with a triumphant smile, Maja played on. And, with obvious pleasure, Kirsten sang through the part. When Maja left, she had Kirsten's permission to tell Singer that if he wished to offer Kirsten the role, she would accept.

No sooner had Maja left than she regretted her decision. She had forgotten about the child. Who would take care of six-month-old Else while she was at the theatre? 'I will, Kirsten,' said Sigurd, when she told him what she had let herself in for. 'Our excellent maid will take care of her in the mornings while you are at rehearsal, and on the nights you have to sing, I will be glad to take care of Else.'

Kirsten's colleagues welcomed her back heartily. They all liked her, although none of them felt they really got to know her. At the first rehearsal, singers and musicians alike were as amazed at the development of her voice as her mother had been. Also, she moved about the stage with more assurance. Marriage and motherhood seemed to have liberated her.

Gypsy Love opened on 26 December 1920. The performance was a triumph, and Kirsten Flagstad was hailed by an enthusiastic audience and a single-minded press. Benno Singer encountered no problem when he asked her to sign a contract with the Opéra for the spring season of 1921: she had to admit that she was happy to be back on the stage. She appeared in all the operetta and opera productions, singing new roles, both big and small. When someone fell ill and a substitute was needed in a hurry, she often had to learn a new role in a day. She said later:

> I had been taught at home never to refuse if help was needed. To switch from one role to another – often from day to day – gave me training in those years that has been invaluable in my career as a singer. In one season no less than four operas were presented at the Opéra Comique: Mozart's *Die Zauberflöte*; *La Fanciulla del West*, by Puccini, its first performance in Norway; and, finally, *Un Ballo in Maschera* and *Otello*, by Verdi. I had the leading role in all of them.

When Leo Slezak came from Vienna to give a guest performance in *Otello*, Kirsten and her colleagues became acquainted with international opera standards for the first time. Slezak arrived with the nimbus surrounding his colossal person that three years at the Metropolitan had given him. As early as 1910, he had made his debut there as Otello and had created a furore. But he did not like it in America, and after three years he broke off his meteoric career at the Metropolitan and returned to his beloved Vienna.

In New York he had played opposite the great star, Frances Alda. She had been the Desdemona in his farewell performance at the Metropolitan on 31 January 1913. Twenty-five years later, almost to the day, Kirsten Flagstad was to invite Frances Alda to accompany her to an *Otello* at the Metropolitan. Edwin McArthur, Kirsten's accompanist, was seated between the two singers. Just before the curtain rose, Frances leaned towards Kirsten and whispered: 'I have sung Desdemona to the great Slezak.' 'So have I,' Kirsten whispered back. 'Frances Alda looked like a living question mark,' laughed Kirsten as she told the story. 'I don't think she believed me; she evidently imagined that I had been too young to play opposite Slezak. I didn't care to elaborate on the story; it was a good one as it was!'

Benno Singer had employed his countryman, the Hungarian Alexander Varnay, as stage director of this 1921 production of *Otello*. Varnay was known and admired all over Europe for his brilliant tenor voice and his ability as an actor. As artistic manager and régisseur, he was a find. It was primarily Varnay's talents that enabled the Opéra Comique to produce a series of performances of high artistic standard, with an ensemble of excellent composition and training. He instructed authoritatively but gently, and was accordingly greatly beloved by the cast. Kirsten had become one of his favourites because she learned her roles so quickly and perfectly, and because she was so receptive to direction. 'Die Kirsten kann alles,' Varnay enthused at rehearsals. His daughter Astrid, then two years old, became a noted soprano, whom Kirsten knew and admired.

Kirsten had scarcely eight days in which to learn the role of Desdemona. She felt the time was desperately short, since she sang every night, but Varnay merely laughed and said he had no fear that she would not know her role by the time Slezak arrived. 'I was very nervous about meeting Slezak,' she recalled. 'He was considered the ideal Otello, but I had heard that offstage also he had the temperament of the role. My fear was completely unfounded. The huge man bubbled over with fun; he was, in fact, a dream. He was always up to mischief, but he charmed us all. And the public as well as the critics were enthusiastic about his performance.'

Slezak had not expected to find a Desdemona of Kirsten Flagstad's quality in the out-of-the-way town of Kristiania. One night, when they had played exceptionally well together, he burst into her dressing-room without knocking, embraced her and cried out enthusiastically, 'When I leave, Kirsten, I want to take you along! We shall travel all over the world together with *Otello*!' Kirsten merely laughed. She knew he said the same thing to all his leading ladies. He always fell in love with them a little – a little too much, she thought. One night she left the stage in tears, declaring that she would never again play with 'that impudent man'. Great persuasion was exercised by Varnay and Maja to make her promise to continue. Only when Slezak knelt before her, begging forgiveness, did she relent.

In spite of playing to capacity houses, this production was so expensive that it swallowed up most of the theatre's capital. A few light operas were presented in the hope of saving the situation, but when this failed, Singer realized that the Opéra Comique had to stop producing opera at the end of the spring season. He had overextended himself in the attempt to give Kristiania a permanent opera. New capital was raised, and Singer engaged a new director who, from the autumn of 1921, was to run the Opéra as a revue theatre. To impress the change upon the public, it was renamed the Casino.

The new management wished to acquire Kirsten's services. She had been connected with the old theatre and had proved to be a very strong attraction. She was offered excellent terms as a revue star, but again she turned down the offer on the grounds that she was an opera singer. She felt that she could now use the designation with greater justification: she had, after all, received high praise from the reviewers for her operatic performances.

She returned to her domestic duties. To her surprise, she discovered that they did not fill her with the joy she had anticipated. It was no longer enough for her to be only wife and mother. Her talent demanded expression. She was now an accepted singer, constantly in demand; nobody – except her own conscience – expected her to give up her career. She was a trifle wounded in her pride as a mother when she discovered that Else fared very well without having her around all the time. In addition, Sigurd enjoyed having her perform in public and be praised, and he encouraged her to accept the offers she received. Maja suggested that Kirsten should prepare a concert programme – 'just in case', as she said. To her satisfaction, she found that this time not much persuasion was needed to get her to agree.

In October 1921, Kirsten was asked to be the soloist with the Philharmonic Society Orchestra. Shortly afterwards a similar offer arrived from the Harmonien in Bergen. Because she had followed her mother's advice, she was able to submit a concert programme, which was accepted.

She sang at these concerts as a mature and assured artist. Her voice was again full and rich, and her delivery had an authority that formerly the critics claimed she had lacked. Kirsten Flagstad was now a singer to be reckoned with, and she could not conceal from herself that she enjoyed performing. Maja knew how to make the most of her daughter's love of singing. She suggested that she should learn Rossini's *Stabat Mater*, which was in the process of being studied by a group of singers in Kristiania who were without employment that autumn. Maja was not happy with life unless she was overburdened with work. She rushed from rehearsals to performances, from coaching sessions to teaching her own pupils at Vinderen. In between, she managed her household. If any gap between her engagements became too long, she grew dissatisfied and would create work for herself, as was the case with this performance of *Stabat Mater*.

During rehearsals she would harass her soloists. Seasoned singers like Hildur Øverland, Simon Edwardsen, Eric Janson and Kirsten herself again found themselves 'at school', for Maja let nothing pass but the best. Painstaking and meticulous, she sat at the organ conducting everything. After the first performance in Hamar Church on Christmas Day, 1921, Maja and her soloists travelled around in the east of the country, presenting *Stabat Mater* in a number of churches. The tour brought the five artists praise and recognition, but the financial outcome, unfortunately, was nowhere near commensurate with the artistic triumph.

Sigurd had promised to take care of Else while Kirsten was on concert tours.

He had a fantastic way with children and was an exceptional father. While I was away, he also took charge of the household. He was familiar with cooking and other domestic duties, and never hesitated to tackle any job. During the time we were without a maid, it was Sigurd who prepared the meals. Else loved her father, and the two had such fun together that I don't think she missed me much when I was away.

Sigurd had another excellent quality that meant a great deal in our marriage: he was never jealous of my work. He was never grumpy when he came home and did not find everything shipshape. When we got married, I had thought he was very spoiled. His mother was a charming person of whom I became very fond, but she had allowed him to eat only what he liked and to skip what he thought he didn't like. Fru Hall was endowed with an even disposition, which Sigurd had inherited. I myself was not so well balanced in this respect.

For the first time, in the spring of 1922, Kirsten sang the soprano part in Beethoven's Ninth Symphony, performed by the Philharmonic in Kristiania. 'How many times I sang the same soprano part later, I can't remember,' she said. 'I only know that I had an almost unearthly sensation every time I participated in this sublime work of Beethoven's.' The concert tours brought her new experiences, artistic and human. Among other things, she learned to appreciate the advantages of a steady engagement at a theatre.

Halfdan Nobel Roede, businessman, patron of the arts and benefactor, had opened a small, intimate theatre, the Mayol, in the building belonging to the Students' Association in University Street, Kristiania. Cultivated and charming, Nobel Roede was well known in the town, and moved with equal grace in business and artistic circles. The Mayol had opened on New Year's Day, 1921, with Rudolf Rasmussen as its first director. His idea was to run it as a literary avant-garde theatre. One of the greatest artistic triumphs during Rasmussen's tenure was the guest performance by the celebrated European actor, Alexander Moissi.

The public was enthusiastic about the productions at the Mayol, but the theatre was a financial failure. After one year, Rasmussen had to close. The Danish musician and theatre director, Carl Johan Biering–Petersen, who had first come to Kristiania from Copenhagen with his ensemble in the summer of 1919 to present operettas at the Opéra Comique, had rented the Mayol as a summer theatre during the days of Rasmussen's directorship. As it was now unoccupied, Biering–Petersen came to Kristiania to discuss with Norwegian artists the possibility of running the Mayol on a year-round basis. Nobel Roede's only stipulation when leasing the theatre was that at least half the artists engaged be Norwegian.

OW GUIDE
OOF SYSTEMS
POLICE NETWORK
WITH COMMS PHOBIA

5

The Emerging Opera Singer

Kirsten Flagstad was almost twenty-seven when Biering–Petersen proposed to engage her as prima donna of his newly established company at the Mayol in the spring of 1922. She accepted his offer, and embarked on a series of appearances in revues, operettas and light operas which was to last for over five years, continuing, after the demise of the Mayol in the autumn of 1924, on the stage of the Casino, the former Opéra Comique, where Benno Singer was producer and Thorleif Clausen artistic director. Biering–Petersen left Norway and returned to Denmark when the Mayol failed, but one of his young Danish singers, Ellen Cruckow, remained behind: she had married Ole Flagstad in 1922.

Although the musical material with which Kirsten had to work ran the gamut from frivolous and superficial to lightweight, these musicals, as we would call them today, kept her singing and acting in front of the public – which proved to be valuable experience while her voice continued to develop and she became more sure of herself on the stage. The steady diet of operettas was broken for the first time on 22 November 1924, when she appeared at the Casino as Micaëla in Bizet's *Carmen*, with Erica Darbo in the title role. Of Kirsten's performance the critic Hjalmar Borgstrøm wrote: 'With full justice she was singled out for special applause. Her Micaëla was perfectly delightful, both in singing and expression.' She sang in forty-six additional performances.

Her next operatic role was that of Ragnhild in *The Sailor's Bride* by her countryman, Sigwardt Aspestrand, which opened at the Casino on 12 December 1925, twelve years to the day after her debut as Nuri at the National Theatre. The Casino was now managed by Thorleif Clausen, who had succeeded Benno Singer when that enterprising gentleman – who, as Kirsten observed, 'deserved our gratitude for his efforts to establish a permanent opera stage in Kristiania' – disposed of his various Norwegian interests after suffering severe financial losses, and subsequently left the country.

A turning-point in Kirsten's career came in December 1926 when Gounod's *Faust* was produced at the Casino, thanks to the healthy coffers generated by the public's enthusiasm for two of Emmerich Kálmán's showy operettas, *The Queen of the Carnival* and *The Circus Princess*. *The Queen* garnered 141 performances, and *The Princess* seventy-nine. Kirsten sang the title role in both.

The role of Marguerite was a challenge for which Kirsten Flagstad, at thirty-one, was fully prepared. The cast of this *Faust* included Theodor Andresen in the title role, and the eminent Swedish bass, Åke Wallgren, as Méphistophélès. The first performance took place on 7 December 1926, and the next day a reviewer interpreted the feelings of those present:

> It was with tense anticipation that theatre-goers took their seats in the Casino last night. How would the theatre manage to carry out such a risky experiment as a production of *Faust*? But when the Swedish guest, Åke Wallgren, filled the theatre with his powerful voice, all nervousness disappeared. Quite on a par with the Swedish guest was Kirsten Flagstad Hall, who undoubtedly has never sung more beautifully nor acted more convincingly than yesterday. The pure, uncomplicated personality of Gretchen [Marguerite] is so much more a part of her real self than those circus princesses and carnival queens that it has been her fate to blow life into. She appeared charmingly young and warm in the garden scene, and in the prison scene there was a tragic nobility about her acting that stirred one's emotions and made one regret more than ever that we have no opera stage where her talent could be used to better advantage.

There were forty more performances.

Shortly afterwards Kirsten received a letter from John Forsell, head of the Royal Swedish Opera, asking her to come to Stockholm to discuss a possible engagement. She went for an interview, but when she revealed to Forsell that she had studied singing with Dr Gillis Bratt, whose teaching method was anathema to him, he told her she would have to change her way of singing if she wanted to audition for his company. She promptly refused, and that was ostensibly the end of her association with John Forsell and the Royal Swedish Opera. But as fate would have it, Kirsten Flagstad did sing on that stage, and at Forsell's invitation, after her success in America in the mid-1930s. She appeared as Elisabeth in *Tannhäuser*, and, fortunately for the world, she had *not* changed her vocal method.

During this period Kirsten and her husband, Sigurd, began to drift apart. Their marriage was no longer happy: the fundamental problem, which neither of them recognized in the beginning because each had genuine feeling for the other, was that their temperaments were incompatible. Kirsten was by nature a serious person; she was extremely conscientious about fulfilling both her commitments at the theatre and her responsibilities at home, especially the care of their young daughter, Else. As a result she was often tired from overwork, and then she could become dull and irritable. Sigurd was a responsible husband and father, but his approach to life was easygoing, even when his ironware business was flagging and the couple was hard put to make ends meet, despite two incomes. Kirsten became annoyed at what, in her opinion, was Sigurd's cavalier attitude towards difficult situations, while Sigurd complained about what he perceived as Kirsten's excessively serious outlook on life.

In addition to the strain in the relationship between her and Sigurd, Kirsten was preoccupied with the financial plight of her parents. In the spring of 1924 Michael and Maja were forced to sell their house at Vinderen. They moved, with Lasse and Karen Marie, into a flat in University Street in Kristiania, not far from where Kirsten, Sigurd and Else lived. Maja took the event in her stride. Michael, on the other hand, was deeply affected by the move: he missed the garden, his vegetable plot, the animals and the workshop in the basement. As for the young people, Karen Marie summed up the feelings of her brother and herself: 'It was like being pulled up by the roots when we had to move out of the house at Vinderen. We felt we couldn't bear it, to leave the house, our friends, the free life in the woods and meadows. Even today I can feel the pain I suffered when I had to leave it all. Later we succeeded in buying back the house. For many years it was Ole and Ellen's home.'

A lighthearted episode in 1926 helped to lift Kirsten's spirits. The impresario Anton Heiberg asked her to join his summer theatre at

Bygdø during her holiday from the Casino. She accepted, mainly because she needed the income. Else was sent to stay with Sigurd's parents at their country home. Kirsten recalled that summer with amusement:

> It was a strenuous but happy time. Mother directed the orchestra, and my sister Karen Marie made her debut in *The Cousin from Batavia* by Künnecke, which Heiberg had selected as the summer operetta. 'When Heiberg moves to Bygdø, good weather leaves,' people said. The adage unfortunately came true that summer of 1926. We certainly experienced open-air theatre, with no roof over us or the public. Karen Marie and I sang a duet with the text, 'What gorgeous weather, how nice to be together, in the lovely light of the sun.' The rain came down in sheets while we sang, and we were soaked to the skin. The noise of the rain as it pounded on the stage floor was so loud that we could hardly hear our own voices. But the audiences stuck it out, evidently enjoying the comedy. After the duet Karen Marie was supposed to jump and land on a table. She usually landed in a pool of water, splashing it in all directions, to the riotous delight of the public. But it was a joyous summer, in spite of all the rain.

In March 1927 the Oslo Philharmonic Society Orchestra (the name of the capital had been changed back to Oslo, its original name, in January 1925) commemorated the one hundredth anniversary of Beethoven's death with a concert performance of *Fidelio*. Kirsten sang the title role, that of the disguised heroine Leonore. The warm reception her performance elicited from the critics led her to decide that the spring season of 1927 would be her last at the Casino. It was her good fortune that she could make her last appearances in an opera, Gluck's *Orfeo ed Euridice*, rather than in an operetta. She sang Euridice opposite the Orfeo of the noted German contralto, Emmi Leisner. Both singers were applauded in the press. One reviewer wrote, 'Leisner and Flagstad dominate, with glorious voices the like of which are rarely heard from the Casino stage.'

Two of Kirsten's colleagues at the Casino, the tenor Conrad Arnesen and the conductor Olav Kielland, were engaged by the Stora Teatern in Göteborg, Sweden, for the 1927–8 season. When the theatre management let it be known that a dramatic soprano was needed for the autumn of 1928, both recommended Kirsten. She was invited for an audition and was engaged on the spot.

Kirsten's first assignment at the Stora Teatern was the role of Agathe in *Der Freischütz*, by Carl Maria von Weber. The first performance, which took place on 4 October 1928, proved to be a milestone in her now blossoming career as an opera singer. The members of the capacity audience applauded the new soprano from Norway with obvious enthusiasm, and the critics agreed with their assessment. 'One only needed to hear Agathe's introductory aria to realize that here was a musical talent of the finest quality,' wrote one of them. 'And her technique equalled her natural gifts. Kirsten Flagstad will, after her triumph yesterday, become Göteborg's musical magnet. The great soprano roles of opera literature await her.' She sang Agathe in the twenty-seven ensuing performances.

Earlier in the year, Kirsten and Sigurd had agreed to a legal separation, and Sigurd had left for Canada to seek new markets for his business. When Kirsten signed the contract with the Stora Teatern, she had decided to take Else with her to Göteborg. During the summer she had appeared in operetta in Helsinki, with the Norwegian tenor Carl Struve, a member of the Royal Swedish Opera in Stockholm whom she had known since 1914 when they sang together at the National Theatre in Kristiania. Struve's comments about Kirsten in this summer of 1928, when she celebrated her thirty-third birthday, are interesting:

It was quite a different Kirsten I was to appear with now from the very young vocal student with whom I had sung at the National Theatre. Now she was assured, at least as far as her voice was concerned. She was of course at the beginning of a world career, although none of us knew it at the time. But her acting was still rather stiff. She obviously had difficulty letting herself go in the frothy episodes of which there are so many in the operettas *Her Excellency*, *The Orange Duchess* and *Countess Maritza*, in which we sang together. At the theatre she was always a good sport, helpful and agreeable. But the minute the rehearsal or performance was over, she disappeared. I can't recall that she joined us in our circle of friends at any time. She spent all her spare time with Else. We realized that she had personal problems that summer and did not nag her to join us.

The most important aspect of Kirsten's six-year tenure at the Stora Teatern was the opportunity it offered her to learn and to perform in distinctly professional operatic surroundings. She was expected to study each role thoroughly, which meant immersing herself first in the text, then in the music, and then in the drama. Out of this would come a fuller intellectual, emotional and psychological understanding of the character she was to portray, and she was given both the time and the instruction she needed to achieve this. No longer was she required to learn a role virtually overnight, with no time for reflection before she stepped out onto the stage. Inwardly, she breathed a sigh of relief when she realized that the Stora Teatern provided the artistic atmosphere for which she had longed. Here was the environment in which, like a healthy plant in fertile soil, she could thrive.

Mikal in *Saul and David*, by Denmark's foremost composer, Carl Nielsen, was Kirsten's second role in Göteborg. The opera had received its première in Copenhagen in 1903, when the composer was thirty-eight. He looked upon it as an immature work, and was reluctant to give his consent to a production at the Stora Teatern when he was first contacted by the management. However, through the persistence of Olav Kielland, by this time the principal conductor of the theatre orchestra, who had long admired the work and wished to perform it, the composer relented and gave the project his blessing. The revival was a success, and in the part of Mikal, Kirsten Flagstad made her mark as a dramatic soprano. She described the effect of the new environment on her own development:

We went to rehearsal as to a sacred ritual. Every one of us was dedicated to the idea of doing his very best. As the rehearsals progressed, I felt that I acted in a new and much freer way. It was as if something in me had loosened. The inhibitions that had hampered me whenever I had sung in Norway disappeared. I had sung many dramatic roles but had never succeeded in penetrating and transmitting the dramatic core. In other words, I had never been able to let myself go. I had always had the feeling that the audience knew me too well as a person and might ascribe to me the characteristics of the individual I was acting on the stage. It was a stupid and childish idea, of course, but it had constrained me. In

Göteborg I was a stranger, and there I could let myself go. It was a wonderful feeling to realize that I had mastered not only the singing, but also the acting.

The composer came from Copenhagen to conduct his opera several times. *Saul and David* was produced in both Stockholm and Copenhagen following its successful revival in Göteborg on 29 November 1928.

Verdi's *Aïda* was chosen to open the 1929 spring season at the Stora Teatern, with Kirsten in the title role. By this time she was a thorough professional, adept at realizing on stage the artistic aims of both stage director and conductor. Matti Rubinstein, the conductor, recalled the impression she had made on him and the other musicians:

> She was a marvel. Her first notes on the stage at the very first audition told us that here was a singing talent quite out of the ordinary. When she came to the first orchestral rehearsal, something happened that I had never previously experienced, and never experienced again. As Kirsten sang her first aria, the members of the orchestra, one by one, laid aside their instruments and just listened to the glorious tones that poured from her throat. When the last note had died away, the orchestra rose, to the last man, and applauded.
>
> It was a joy to work with Kirsten Flagstad. She was one of those rare artists who ease the burden of a conductor. I consider the fact that I witnessed the beginning of her fantastic career, and perhaps contributed ever so slightly to it, one of my fondest memories as a musician. It was, after all, in Göteborg that her extraordinary development as an opera singer really began.

Kirsten continued to think about and work on her acting technique, but she was essentially an intuitive artist who came alive only before an audience. She was forthright about her instinctive approach to acting:

> I never really put myself into a role at a rehearsal. I always sang full voice when I practised and when I sang at rehearsals, but as far as acting was concerned, I held back. Only when I stood on the stage in a performance, alone with the character, so to speak, with no interruption, could I identify with the person I

was to act. Then everything fell into place – the character, the way in which to stand and move, facial expression, gestures. I don't know if others feel the same way, but, in my case, the character is created during the performance. I remember what the stage director said to me after the first performance of *Aïda*: 'Now I see what you can really accomplish.' It has been the same way throughout my operatic career.

The first performance took place on 7 March 1929, and there were sixteen additional performances. Conrad Arnesen was her Radames, and Kerstin Thorborg, the Swedish mezzo-soprano with whom she was to sing so many times in later years at the Metropolitan Opera in New York, made guest appearances as Amneris.

Kirsten's eight-year-old daughter Else had returned to Norway with her mother for the Christmas holidays in 1928, and had remained there in the care of Ole and Ellen Flagstad, Kirsten's brother and sister-in-law, when Kirsten returned to Göteborg in the New Year. Else had not been happy in Sweden, primarily because, not knowing the language, she had difficulty with her schoolwork and found it hard to make friends. In Norway, where she was surrounded by members of the family and could chatter away with girlfriends in her own language, she was contented, even though she missed her mother. Kirsten certainly did not like being separated from Else, but she knew that Göteborg was the place for her, Kirsten, to be at this time in her life. At the Stora Teatern she could gain valuable experience as an opera singer and earn enough money to support herself and Else.

It was during this period in the late 1920s that Kirsten first became acutely aware of the predicament that was to trouble her increasingly for the rest of her singing career – namely, the tug of war between her need to fulfil herself artistically, which led eventually to her becoming a public personality, and her desire to lead a private life. She disliked elaborate social functions, and tended to avoid them as often as possible. On the other hand, she could be the life of the party if such an event happened to catch her in an exuberant, extrovert mood. Her natural reticence, always a part of her stage personality, was perceived in the early years as stiffness and awkwardness. However, by the time she appeared on the international scene in the great roles for which she was destined, her innate reserve had become incorporated into the character she was portraying and was perceived as nobility of bearing. This was an evolutionary process, guided by intuition. The struggle between her public self and her private self was never resolved: she had to live in two worlds, keeping them in balance as best she could. The tension this created in her may have made her uncomfortable, but it may also have generated that decisive edge in her performances that made them so memorable.

Puccini's *La Bohème* followed Verdi's *Aïda* at the Stora Teatern, and Kirsten was assigned the role of Mimi, a part for which she was unsuited in physique and temperament, if not in voice. She dutifully sang in six performances in April, and her singing was applauded by public and press. But there was general agreement that she had been miscast.

When it was announced that she was to sing the title role in Puccini's *Tosca* on tour with the company, some of the opera-goers of Göteborg no doubt thought that the management had miscast her a second time. They could not visualize her as the tempestuous Roman diva. But they were wrong. Tosca had long been one of Kirsten's favourite roles, and she had looked forward to the day when she could do justice to it on the stage. She had studied the score thoroughly over the years, and she now felt prepared to meet the challenge that the role represented for her, both vocally and dramatically. With a smile, she recalled the Christmas season at Vinderen in 1918 when she and Ivar Andrésen, then twenty-two, had sung and acted the highly charged Tosca–Scarpia scene from the second act to impress Ivar's parents with their son's talent. Now Ivar was singing regularly in London and Bayreuth, and she was the Stora Teatern's leading dramatic soprano. She was certain that she was ready to undertake the heavier dramatic roles, and she was determined that her Tosca would demonstrate this to the public. Her confidence in herself was firmly based on reason and insight, and it proved to be justified. 'In the violent scenes of the second act and at the murder of Scarpia, Miss Flagstad acted with such intensity that we in the theatre trembled with excitement,' wrote one reviewer. She also looked stunning on the stage, every inch the imperious, passionate figure created by Sardou and Puccini.

Kirsten sang Wagner for the first time in public when she

appeared in concert with the Göteborg Orchestra in 1929. She had chosen 'Elisabeth's Prayer' from *Tannhäuser*, and her choice of this sustained, moving invocation again confirmed her intuitive awareness of what was right for her at the time. One reviewer noted that she sang 'with deep feeling and with a beauty of tone that approached the sublime', and another expressed what must have been the hope of many music lovers when he wrote, 'May Kirsten Flagstad soon have the opportunity to sing a Wagner role on our opera stage. Her voice as well as her dramatic ability seem to point towards the great opera roles of Wagner.'

The Norwegian Opera Association had decided to present Wagner's *Lohengrin* at the National Theatre in June 1929. Kirsten received a letter from the association while she was on tour in *Tosca*, asking if she would sing Elsa in the production. Her answer was 'yes'. The time had come for her to sing an entire Wagner role on stage, and here was her opportunity.

The role of Elsa was close to Kirsten's heart. She had learned it and all the other roles in *Lohengrin* in German when, as a child of ten, she had received a copy of the vocal score as a gift from her parents. Now she set about memorizing the role in Norwegian for the coming performances in Oslo. She took the score with her on a trip to Germany and Italy with a friend in May, and studied it whenever she had the chance. In Berlin she sang an audition, secretly arranged by her friend, for Otto Klemperer of the Kroll Opera. She was offered an engagement, but she could not consider it then because she was under contract to the Stora Teatern in Göteborg.

Kirsten had been in Berlin once before, in 1913, when she had accompanied her mother to the German capital. Maja had hoped to lay the groundwork for Kirsten's further singing studies there, but the plan was thwarted by the outbreak of the First World War. Kirsten remembered this earlier visit for another reason: her mother's unique handling of the German language. Kirsten was eighteen and had recently studied German at school, but her natural shyness, coupled with her fear of making mistakes, made her tongue-tied in the presence of native Germans. Maja, on the other hand, was undaunted, even though her German was far from fluent. While Kirsten had stood speechless and blushing, casting about tensely for gender, number and case, Maja had ploughed ahead willy-nilly and made herself understood in a highly un-grammatical way. 'But Mother,' Kirsten had whispered to her, 'you're speaking all wrong!' 'Oh, who cares, dear – you can see they understand me, and that's all that counts,' Maja had replied.

After a few days in Italy, Kirsten and her companion boarded the train for home. When they arrived in Stockholm, they said their goodbyes, and Kirsten continued on to Oslo. Every once in a while her mind would wander from the music she was studying. She would suddenly find herself gazing out of the train window with images of her daughter Else tumbling through her mind. She longed to see her child again after being separated from her for several months.

Oslo's opera lovers looked forward eagerly to the short summer season now presented annually by the Norwegian Opera Associ-ation. No matter how light and balmy the June nights, the National Theatre was sold out for every performance. Karl Aagaard Østvig, the Norwegian tenor who had been hailed as 'the ideal Lohengrin of the Vienna Opera', had been engaged as director of the production of Wagner's opera to be presented by the association in June 1929. He was one of many Norwegian singers who had been compelled to pursue an operatic career elsewhere in Europe because there was no established opera stage in his homeland.

A stream of ticket-holders, buzzing with excited conversation, converged on the National Theatre on Friday 14 June 1929 for the first performance of Østvig's production of *Lohengrin*. Their interest had been aroused especially by the news that two Norwegian artists, Bjørn Talén and Kirsten Flagstad, would sing the principal roles of Lohengrin and Elsa. Shortly before curtain time, as the audience were chatting softly with each other or leafing through their programmes, a tall, distinguished-looking gentleman in his mid-forties entered the auditorium and was shown to his seat. His name was Henry Johansen. He was a prominent Norwegian businessman with extensive interests in timber and property, including several of Oslo's finest hotels. He was a sponsor of the Norwegian Opera Association's summer opera season.

As the first ethereal strains of the *Lohengrin* Prelude filled the auditorium, one can imagine that Henry Johansen settled back in his seat and closed his eyes. He felt relaxed and comfortable now after a long day of business meetings. He enjoyed music, especially opera, and he counted himself among those who wanted opera to become an important part of Oslo's, and Norway's, cultural life. He knew he had made a wise decision when he agreed to back this season financially. What he did not know was that this night would mark the beginning of a major event in his life.

The first act was well received by the capacity audience. During the intermission they spoke with enthusiasm about Østvig's direction and about the quality of the voices, especially that of Kirsten Flagstad as Elsa. Those who had heard her before were amazed at her development. Could this be the same Kirsten Flagstad who had sung in one operetta after another only a few years ago?

Henry Johansen went out into the foyer, where he encountered a group of business associates. He joined in their conversation, but his mind kept straying from the subject. He was thinking about the young woman whose performance as Elsa was making such an impression on him. He took out his pocket watch to check the time. Good! The second act would soon begin. He excused himself and returned to his seat. Quickly he read the synopsis of the act in his programme. So Miss Flagstad's next appearance would be on the balcony. He listened rather impatiently to the vehement exchange between Ortrud and Telramund, all the while keeping an eye on the balcony so as not to miss Elsa's entrance. And suddenly there she was, a lovely figure in white, with long blonde hair falling over her shoulders and down her back. What a striking picture she made, thought Johansen. He leaned forward in his seat as she began to sing her apostrophe to the evening air. And what a voice! I must meet this woman, he decided, as he settled back to enjoy the music.

Reidar Mjøen, who had succeeded Hjalmar Borgstrøm as music critic of the *Aftenposten*, wrote at the end of his review of the first performance: 'Without detracting from the accomplishments of the other principals, it must be said that Fru Flagstad Hall is the main attraction of this production.' She had more than fulfilled all expectations. Kirsten remembered the occasion well:

I was so happy about the success of the performance. All of us felt that it had gone extremely well. In an elated mood, we who had taken part went over to the Grand Hotel. We had reserved a special room where we intended to have a little celebration. When we went through the Mirror Hall, the main dining-

Strandstuen, the house in Hamar, Norway, where Kirsten Flagstad was born. Standing, from left to right: Anne Kirstine Flagstad, Kirsten's paternal grandmother; a young lady of the household; Marie Flagstad, Kirsten's mother; Ole Mikkelsen Flagstad, Kirsten's paternal grandfather; and Michael Flagstad, her father. Seated: Olea Flagstad, Kirsten's paternal great-grandmother. Photo 1894.

Michael and Marie Flagstad with one-year-old Kirsten, 1896.

The four Flagstad children in front of the old Schmidt piano in the living-room at Vinderen, spring 1905. From left to right: Ole, Lasse, and Kirsten holding six-month-old Karen Marie.

Kirsten at sixteen, in the autumn of 1911, does her homework in the living-room at Vinderen while her father looks over a Storting report.

Kirsten as Germaine in *The Bells of Corne-ville* by Robert Planquette, at the National Theatre, Kristiania, autumn 1914.

Kirsten as Delia Gill in *The Queen of the Movies* by Jean Gilbert, at the Mayol theatre, Kristiania, April 1924.

The Cousin from Batavia, by Eduard Künnecke, in rehearsal at the summer theatre in Bygdø, 1926, with Kirsten (second from left) and Karen Marie Flagstad (second from right).

Flagstad as Aïda in the Verdi opera at the Stora Teatern, Göteborg, March 1929.

Hildur Øverland as Ortrud and Flagstad as Elsa in Act II, Scene ii of *Lohengrin*, June 1929.

Act I of *Lohengrin* at the National Theatre, Oslo, June 1929, with (centre) Flagstad as Elsa and Bjørn Talén as Lohengrin.

Flagstad as Lucie and Conrad Arnesen as Vicomte Olivier de Brichanteau in Act II of *Den Stora Okända* (*Donna Juanita*) by Franz von Suppé, at the Stora Teatern, Göteborg, October 1929.

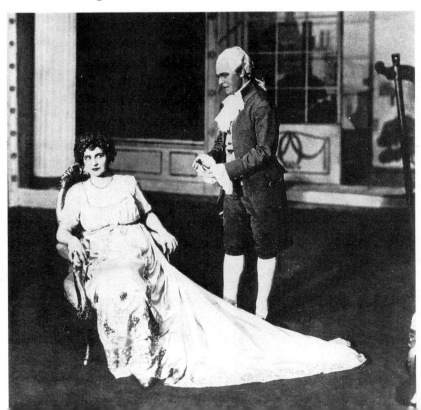

Flagstad as Floria Tosca in Act I of Puccini's *Tosca* at the National Theatre, Oslo, June 1929.

Flagstad as Anita and Conrad Arnesen as Max, in Křenek's *Jonny spielt auf* at the Stora Teatern, April 1930.

Elof Benktander as Garibaldo and Flagstad in the title role, in Act I, Scene ii of Handel's *Rodelinda* at the Stora Teatern, February 1932.

Flagstad as a coy Eva in *Die Meistersinger* at the National Theatre, Oslo, June 1933.

Two young admirers present flowers to Kirsten Flagstad on board the *Drottningholm* in Göteborg on 27 December 1934, just before the ship sailed for New York.

Flagstad as Sieglinde in *Die Walküre* at the 1934 Bayreuth Festival.

Kirsten and her daughter, Else, at a country garden party near London, May 1937.

Edwin McArthur and Kirsten Flagstad outside the McArthur family home in Denver, Colorado, October 1935.

Kirsten sings for the children of working mothers at a New York day nursery, 1936.

room, we were applauded by the people there. A little while later a colleague of mine came over to me and said there was a gentleman in the Mirror Hall who wanted to meet me. He wished to thank me for my Elsa.

It must have been the successful performance and the festive mood I was in that induced me to go with my colleague. As we entered the Mirror Hall, a handsome gentleman rose from his table and came towards us. My colleague introduced us, and Henry Johansen, for he it was, took my hand and kissed it. 'Your singing tonight has moved me deeply,' he said, as he looked into my eyes. I remember that I blushed as I murmured my thanks. It was so unusual for anyone to be so respectful. We remained standing, looking at each other without knowing what else to say. Then Henry Johansen asked if our group from the theatre would join him at his home for a little informal party. My colleagues were enthusiastic. Several of them had previously been guests in Mr Johansen's home and knew it would be delightful. So off we went in taxis to number 6 Tidemand Street.

While the host went to get refreshments, we made ourselves comfortable in the beautiful rooms. I sat down in a chair that stood invitingly in a corner of the living-room. I noticed that some of my colleagues were looking at me in slight surprise. When Henry Johansen came in and saw me in the chair, he hesitated and looked as if he was about to say something. But he proceeded, placed a tray of drinks on a table, and asked us to help ourselves to whatever we wanted. With a glass of champagne in each hand, he walked over to me and offered me one of the glasses. We drank to each other's health, and he sat down on the arm of the chair, again thanking me for my beautiful singing.

My brother Ole, who had been with us, rang me up the next day and said I must have made a deep impression on the host since he had let me stay seated in his very special chair without saying anything. Ole knew from previous occasions that Henry Johansen never let anyone sit in that chair. I brushed it off and said it had been purely by chance that he let me remain there; I dared not tell Ole that Henry had made a deep impression on me the moment we met in the Mirror Hall.

Shortly after Ole's call, Henry rang and invited me out to

dinner, and my heart pounded at the thought of meeting him again. The third time we were out together, Henry proposed to me. We were having dinner at the Bristol. Suddenly he leaned over the table, laid his hand on mine, and said simply, 'You do love me, Miss Flagstad, don't you?' I blushed and whispered, 'Yes, I do.' He said he had fallen in love with me the very moment I appeared on the balcony in Act Two of *Lohengrin* and sang 'Euch Lüften'.

Henry Johansen was a widower and had four children. His twin sons, Henry and Frederic, were twenty-three; his elder daughter, Kate, was nineteen, and travelling abroad; and his younger daughter, Annie, was ten. When Henry learned that I was not divorced, as he had thought, but separated, he looked at me solemnly and said that by no means did he want to come between me and my husband. I said that three months of the second year of separation had already passed, and that I had written to my husband, who was living in Canada, and asked him for a divorce. What I did not tell him was that I had written the very day after the party at 6 Tidemand Street. Only much later did Henry Johansen find out about that!

While Kirsten was singing Elsa at the National Theatre, requests to see and hear her in another opera poured in from all quarters. Puccini's *Tosca* could be produced at short notice, and Kirsten welcomed the opportunity to sing the role again. 'I was eager to find out if my countrymen would agree that I had overcome my inhibitions in dramatic acting,' she said. The critics had evidently been wondering about her dramatic ability, too. One of them wrote after the first performance on 22 June 1929:

> The sold-out sign was illuminated last night outside the National Theatre, and inside the atmosphere was tense. That Fru Flagstad Hall would *sing* the part well, no one was in doubt; but could she also give dramatic life to the role? Thunderous applause and many curtain calls after each act were the answer, and Fru Hall deserved the acclaim in full measure. Her Tosca is also an outstanding dramatic character-ization.

The last night she sang Tosca, a certain gentleman in an orchestra seat observed the performance with more than casual interest. He was the powerful chairman and chief financial supporter of the

Metropolitan Opera, Otto H. Kahn, who was on holiday in Scandinavia. Kahn always had both ear and eye open for talented, attractive singers who might be engaged by the Metropolitan. He had barely heard mention of the young Norwegian soprano who had made a name for herself at the Stora Teatern in Göteborg, but he was overwhelmed with her performance. She was a singer of international standard. He sent Kirsten his card, expressing his admiration for her excellent Tosca. 'I glanced at the card and put it aside,' she said. 'The name Otto Kahn meant nothing to me, and the fact that he was a director of the Metropolitan was so hazy and so far removed from my world that it really made no impression on me.'

The Oslo papers got wind of the incident. Sensing a story, they rang her up, asking, 'Is it true, Miss Flagstad, that you have received an offer from the Metropolitan?' She informed them that she had not even met Otto Kahn and therefore could not possibly have discussed any prospective engagement with him. The idea had been concocted out of thin air, and the papers had better forget all about it.

Kirsten was occupied with matters far removed from possible talent scouts, even if they appeared in the person of a director of the Metropolitan. She was in love, happily in love, for the second time in her life. What worried her was that she had received no reply to her letter to Sigurd in which she asked for a divorce. She and Henry had agreed to keep to themselves for a while that they were more than good friends. But Oslo was too small, and both of them were too well known, for the relationship to go unnoticed for long. Kirsten had confided in her family, with whom she had been living in University Street during the summer. Henry telephoned every day, and Michael Flagstad took the calls. He would then go to Kirsten and say the call was for her. 'Who is it?' she would ask, knowing only too well who it was. 'A gentleman at his best age,' her father would answer solemnly. Henry Johansen was thirteen years older than Kirsten. 'I thought Father was so sweet when he put it that way that I continued to play our little game,' she said.

Her contract with the Stora Teatern included the autumn season of 1929, and when her holiday was over, she returned to take part in rehearsals. Else continued to live with Ole and Ellen and was so happy that neither she nor her mother found parting so difficult this time. And Henry promised to visit Göteborg as often as his business would permit. They had agreed to announce their engagement in the autumn and to marry at Christmas. Sigurd's letter with the divorce papers would surely arrive before that.

And it did arrive, together with a statement that he agreed to a divorce. But the statement was not legal: he had forgotten to have it authenticated at the Norwegian Consulate in Montreal. Kirsten had to return the papers and ask him to take care of the necessary formalities. She heard nothing more from him for several months. At last a letter came, but without the divorce papers; and what Sigurd wrote gave Kirsten and Henry a shock. He had decided that he could not agree to a divorce after all; he still loved Kirsten, he wrote, and hoped they could re-establish their marriage. Much could happen during the six months that remained of their second year of legal separation. 'Let us wait to make a final decision, Kirsten, until at least the two years of legal separation have passed,' he wrote in conclusion. Kirsten recalled:

> There was nothing else to do but wait. And I must confess that I was somehow touched by the reason for Sigurd's refusal. I knew, however, that we could never resume the old relationship; we were too different. My feelings for Henry had come suddenly, but they were strong and deep. I wrote to Sigurd and told him I had met a man I wished to marry. Henry and I had announced our engagement at a party Henry gave for me and my colleagues in Göteborg, before Sigurd's letter arrived. My resignation from the theatre was to take effect at the New Year. I knew the management of the Stora Teatern would be happy to have me as long as I wished to stay, so I signed up for three months of the spring season. To my delight, I was asked to sing Eva in *Die Meistersinger* by Wagner, and Conrad Arnesen was to sing Walther. That was a bright spot after the disappointment of Sigurd's letter.

The two artists had sung in many operas together, with great success. They looked good together on the stage, and their voices blended well. During the 1929 autumn season they had sung Otello and Desdemona, and reaped thunderous applause. After the first performance, one of the reviewers wrote: 'The Stora Teatern has been called, jokingly, "the Norwegian Opera" by people in

Göteborg. The Norwegian pair, Flagstad–Arnesen, are in fact so superb that the name is fully justified.'

Conrad Arnesen's beautiful voice, his attractive appearance and his engaging personality, both on stage and off, had won him many friends and admirers. Kirsten commented:

As Otello he did not perhaps convey the primitive wildness that characterized Leo Slezak's performance, but he acted the role with authority and temperament. It was impressive that he could portray a character like that, because it was so foreign to his own nature; he was the most refined and considerate of men. Conrad and his wife were exceptionally good to me. When they noticed that I was homesick for my family, they invited me home to their own cosy flat. At a beautifully set table, with wonderful homemade food, we would talk endlessly – in Norwegian. Otherwise we spoke Swedish, of course, both on the stage and off.

While Kirsten was performing in *Otello,* a letter arrived, forwarded from Oslo. The name of the Metropolitan Opera House was engraved on the envelope, and the letter was signed by Eric Semon, the European representative of the Metropolitan. He requested that Kirsten send him extracts from reviews, translated into English, and all the stage portraits available. The material should be forwarded to New York as soon as possible. She could not understand why she should receive such a request from the Metropolitan representative. After all, she was completely unknown outside Scandinavia. She did not associate it with Otto Kahn's greeting after the *Tosca* performance at the National Theatre, but he it was who, on his return to New York, had asked his European agent to get in touch with her.

Kirsten did not answer Semon's letter. It was difficult to obtain reviews and have them translated. Three weeks later a second request arrived. So as not to seem ungracious, she collected some reviews and had them translated. With the papers she sent some picture postcards of herself in various roles – though the postcards gave a poor impression of how she really looked on the stage.

It took me two weeks to get all this done. I was annoyed to be put to so much trouble because of something so remote as an eventual audition with the Metropolitan Opera. I had enough to do in Göteborg, and, besides, I was nervous at the thought of meeting Henry's four children in the near future; his elder daughter, Kate, was to come home for Christmas from abroad, and the meeting was to take place then. But I know I could have sung at the Metropolitan five years before I did if I had only shown a little more interest. I heard nothing further after I wrote; but it's hardly strange that the august gentlemen lost interest in a singer who did so little to publicize herself. Besides, I'm convinced it was as it should be that I didn't sing at the Metropolitan until 1935. I certainly was not sufficiently mature as an artist to take on the great Wagnerian parts before then.

Henry Johansen's children were as nervous about meeting Kirsten as she was about meeting them. They knew she was a professional singer, and that implied to them everything that was the opposite of their quiet, ordinary existence. A person who sang in public must, from their point of view, be wholly unqualified to enter their family. Johansen's daughter, Kate Johansen Gjerdrum, recalled later:

> I shall never forget my first meeting with Kirsten. My brothers and sister and I had gathered in the hall, and there, bunched together, we stood and waited for her and Father. We jumped when we heard Father's key in the door. A moment later, he and Kirsten stood in the doorway. Kirsten was wearing a simple black velvet dress with a white lace collar. With a shy smile she stood and looked at us. I melted completely and went over and embraced her. That broke the ice. Kirsten won us over immediately with her natural, modest personality.
>
> I think it meant a great deal to Kirsten that I accepted her from the very beginning. Father and I had become very close after Mother died. Kirsten knew this, and in no way attempted to change or disrupt our relationship. I think she was also very wise not to try to behave like a mother to us; she became more like a friend, and that she has continued to be ever since. We became very fond of her. After that first meeting we saw her only once or twice more before she went back to Göteborg after Christmas.
>
> Once in a while Father took me along when he went to see Kirsten in Göteborg. I remember that I was very excited about

seeing her on the stage. She sang Eva in Wagner's *Meister-singer*. I was overwhelmed by how beautifully she sang and how lovely she looked on the stage. From the time I first saw her and heard her, I have been a great fan of hers.

The spring season of 1930 was to be Kirsten's last as an opera singer. She intended to retire from the stage when she became Mrs Henry Johansen.

Eva in *Die Meistersinger* was her most important assignment that spring. The role offered her little scope for dramatic acting, but the character was close to her own nature. The stage director allowed her to develop her portrayal in accord with her own honest, straightforward personality. Her voice was beginning to assume a Wagnerian fullness. After the first performance on 18 February 1930, one of the reviewers wrote: 'Kirsten Flagstad is a truly ideal Eva. It is doubtful that there is a soprano who can sing the role better, even on the greatest opera stages.'

It was a disappointment for Kirsten, as it was for her public, that she was to make her last appearance at the Stora Teatern in a role as unsuitable as that of Anita in *Jonny spielt auf*, by Křenek. The theatre manager undoubtedly wished to capitalize on the popularity she and Conrad Arnesen had enjoyed in Göteborg. Kirsten commented:

I hated the role, but I had to sing what the management decided on, of course. It never occurred to me to protest. I must confess, though, that I begged to be released from this assignment. But in vain. It was not an experience to remember with pleasure after the years at the Stora Teatern – that is, apart from the farewell performance itself. That was the only time *Jonny spielt auf* drew a full house. The opera was almost a fiasco.

The evening of Kirsten Flagstad's farewell, the theatre was filled with a richly dressed audience. When the curtain fell, she was deluged with flowers. Over and over again she was called out to acknowledge the standing ovation. Finally the curtain rose and the manager came on stage, followed by her colleagues at the opera. Before presenting Kirsten with a silver bowl engraved with the names of all her colleagues, he said:

We all regret that Miss Flagstad has decided to retire from the stage after tonight. There will be a great void at the Stora Teatern after you leave, Miss Flagstad. We wish to thank you for what you have given us as an artist during the two years you have been here. We also wish to thank you for what you have meant to all of us as a friend and colleague. If you should ever change your mind, you will always be welcome at the Stora Teatern in Göteborg.

Kirsten and Henry had decided that they wished to be married at the Norwegian Consulate in Antwerp. With his daughter Kate, they motored around Europe, while waiting for Kirsten's divorce papers to arrive from Norway. In Vienna they attended a perform-ance of Wagner's *Tristan und Isolde*, which Kirsten was hearing for the first time. The music affected her so strongly that after the first act she was emotionally exhausted and wanted to leave. 'The others wanted to hear the whole opera, so I dozed through the last two acts,' she said. 'Since I didn't know the music beforehand, that was really too much Wagner for me in one night. I remember that Henry leaned over to me and whispered, "This is something you cannot sing, young lady!" "You are certainly right about that – this is too heavy for me," I said.'

They were finally informed that the divorce papers had arrived, and they were married at the Consulate on Saturday 31 May 1930. Kirsten had become 'an ordinary Norwegian housewife'. She intended to live a quiet home life, with a little music 'just for the family'.

I have included in this book some comments and observations from Arthur V. Dusenberry, Kirsten Flagstad's son-in-law, who lives today in Phoenix, Arizona, where he and his family settled in 1953, and where he subsequently set up a small manufacturing business. His late wife, Else, was Kirsten's only child, by her first husband, Sigurd Hall, from whom she was divorced in 1930.

Arthur Dusenberry had been born and brought up on a farm near Bozeman, Montana. He met Else Hall for the first time in June 1939 at the Diamond J Ranch outside Bozeman, where he was working at the time. The Diamond J was what was known as a dude ranch – a ranch run as a holiday resort. Dude ranches were very popular in the 1930s, when the United States was just emerging from the Depression, and only the well-to-do had any money left; many

New Yorkers went out West to spend the summer months on these ranches. Katherine and Jack Hall (no relation to Sigurd), who were New York friends of Kirsten's, were regular summer visitors at the Diamond J. For various reasons Else did not want to go back home to Norway that summer with her mother, so she was sent out to the ranch with the Halls. She and Arthur were married a year later.

I first wrote to Arthur in July 1980, asking him if he would consider writing a piece for this book containing personal reminiscences of his close relationship with Kirsten Flagstad. I sent him a copy of the typescript as it was then, and we subsequently agreed that I would come to Phoenix in late September that year so that we could discuss the idea in person.

I found Arthur a warm, vital and generous person, and it was not long before we were chatting away like old friends. He agreed to jot down reminiscences as they came to him, in preparation for a preface or epilogue for this book, but we decided later that it would work out much better if I made another trip to Phoenix, this time bringing with me a cassette recorder so that we could tape our memories and thoughts in ordinary conversation. So it came about that I visited him again in late June 1981, and we recorded almost two hours of conversation about his family. He was amazed that I had never met Kirsten Flagstad. I told him that when I was a boy I had been much too shy to ever think of going backstage and introducing myself to a singer I admired. I had met Kerstin Thorborg only because a mutual friend had introduced us. I asked Arthur if he had ever met Sigurd Hall:

Yes, I knew him. He was a very lovable man, very charming – too charming in a way, I suppose. He was quite a ladies' man, you see – very popular – and that was really more than Kirsten could cope with. The Hall boys had been spoiled by their mother and more or less ground down by a tyrannical father. Grandfather Hall had built up quite a substantial ironware business in Norway, and Sigurd, who was the oldest living son, would in time have inherited the firm. But he really wasn't of a disposition to take a grip on such an enterprise, and the family business fell apart after Grandfather Hall's death. Sigurd married again, for the third time, after he and Kirsten were divorced – as you know, he was a widower when he and Kirsten were married – and I believe this last marriage proved to be a happy one. Else and I knew his wife, Vera, and their son, Sjur, too. I met all of them when we were in Norway in 1948. That trip was Else's first visit home in ten years.

Kirsten had been remarried for less than four months when she had to answer either yes or no to an invitation to sing in public. The Philharmonic Society Orchestra asked her if she would take part in an important concert in October. Her impulse was to refuse, but she decided to participate after all – just this once. She found it a colossal task to get her voice into shape again – which made her realize that it was foolish to be out of practice, even if, as she thought, she was going to sing only for her own enjoyment. In any case, her great talent had to have an outlet, and it was not long before she realized – not for the first time – that life as a devoted wife and homemaker, happy as it was, did not fulfil the artistic side of her nature. Having agreed to sing again in public, 'just this once', it was difficult for her to refuse the next time she received an offer. So when the Harmonien in Bergen contacted her, their offer was accepted. In March 1931 she presented a song recital in the University Hall, accompanied by Daniel Løvdal. She had to admit that it was a joy to sing to an audience again.

In June the Norwegian Opera Association planned to present its annual summer opera season at the National Theatre, and Kirsten was asked to sing the title role in *Aïda*. She waged a battle within herself, but the singer in her won out.

Erling Krogh, who sang Radames, recalled:

Kirsten was remarkable as Aïda. Her acting was more relaxed and natural than it had been in the past. On the stage she was calm; at least it seemed so to us who acted with her. I remember an incident that occurred at one of the performances, which shows how secure she was. My mind suddenly went blank in the last scene of the last act. I was completely lost. Kirsten realized immediately what had happened. She moved calmly towards me and sang the first bars very softly into my ear. With that my mind cleared, and I was all right again. The stage was semi-dark, so the audience, fortunately, did not notice what had happened.

After substituting at the Stora Teatern in Göteborg in the autumn of 1931 for the principal soprano – who had had to withdraw from

Weinberger's *Švanda* because of illness – Kirsten was enticed by the general manager into a commitment to sing the title role in Handel's *Rodelinda* in February 1932:

> He knew I felt it was marvellous to sing again from a stage. He said there would be plenty of time for me to study the role, as the performances were not scheduled until February. When I returned to Oslo, I had the vocal score in my luggage. It was more difficult than I had imagined to resist the artist in me, and when I found out that my husband liked to have me perform, I drifted back into my career as a singer.

After the first performance of *Rodelinda*, on 16 February 1932, the Göteborg critics agreed that her voice had again grown fuller. Some felt that it was perhaps too voluminous for a composer like Handel. 'Wagner is the right composer for the great and glorious voice of Kirsten Flagstad,' wrote one.

Her husband had come to Göteborg for the opening, and he attended the party that her colleagues at the Stora Teatern gave for her. During the evening he said to her, 'When we heard *Tristan und Isolde* in Vienna, Kirsten, I said you would never be equal to such a tremendous part, do you remember?' 'Yes indeed, and I was wholly in agreement,' she answered. 'But why do you mention that now, Henry?' 'Because after hearing you tonight, I'm convinced you can now sing the role of Isolde,' he replied.

A month later, the Norwegian Opera Association asked her to take part in the summer performances at the National Theatre – as Isolde. She refused. She would not undertake a role as gruelling as that – not yet, anyway. But when she learned that she would not sing in the opening performances, but only in the last five, she felt she could accept. The Opera Association had secured the services of the Swedish Wagnerian soprano Nanny Larsén-Todsen for the first five performances. She had sung Isolde at Bayreuth and was known as an exceptional interpreter of this difficult role. Two Norwegian artists who had also sung at Bayreuth – the tenor Gunnar Graarud and the bass Ivar Andrésen, Kirsten's longtime friend – were to appear as Tristan and King Marke. Kirsten felt that, because she would follow Larsén-Todsen, public expectations of her own portrayal would not run so high. Actually, she was eager to test herself in the part, one of Wagner's great creations for the dramatic soprano voice.

Maja Flagstad had coached most of the qualified male and female singers in Norway in the opera's roles, but she had never worked with Kirsten. Now she offered to coach her daughter in the role of Isolde. She judged that if they worked together several hours a day, Kirsten would know the role by the time rehearsals at the theatre were scheduled to begin.

> Mother came over to Tidemand Street every morning to coach me. We worked on one scene after another. For the first time I was to take part in an opera that would be sung in German. Isolde is a severe test for the voice: either it can be completely destroyed; or it can grow, as mine did. I didn't spare my voice. After a while the seams of my dresses split. The capacity of my lungs increased by several centimetres, while my weight remained the same. Mother was merciless as a coach – she wouldn't tolerate the slightest inaccuracy. In the middle of a passage she would stop, look at me sternly, and say: 'Kirsten, there is a sixteenth-note rest here. It has not been placed here as a decoration – remember that.' I have remembered that ever since.
>
> The more I became immersed and then absorbed in Wagner's music, the more enthusiastic I became about it. It was incredible that his magnificent music had meant so little to me during all the years I'd been singing. But then I hadn't been mature enough earlier, musically speaking.

There was sharp advance criticism of the Opera Association's plan to produce *Tristan und Isolde*. Many felt that it was far too difficult a work to tackle; some claimed that Norway did not have enough qualified singers, and that the ones available were not sufficiently experienced in operatic routine.

Mathieu Berckenhoff was one of the advocates of the plan to produce *Tristan*, and he was a man who usually achieved what he set out to accomplish. Years later he succeeded in organizing TONO, the Norwegian Composer Association's International Music Bureau in Oslo, of which he was for many years the dynamic head. Berckenhoff was never in doubt that both the orchestral and the vocal artists would measure up to the task, but he bowed to the pressure that Larsén-Todsen should sing Isolde on the opening night and the following four nights. Then Kirsten Flagstad would take over.

The Norwegian conductor Odd Grüner-Hegge would be at the helm. He too wondered whether Kirsten could handle the tremendous part, which in the first act alone demands almost continuous singing for an hour and a quarter. But when she reported for the first piano rehearsal with him, she not only sang the entire part flawlessly, but also had worked out a dramatic conception of the role. No one had expected Kirsten to master the dramatic aspect as had the far more experienced Larsén-Todsen, but neither did anyone anticipate that she would take hold of the role as decisively as she did the first time she sang it. Her first performance was convincing proof of her ability; it was also the introduction to an international singing career – a career the extent of which she never could have imagined.

'It fulfilled every expectation,' wrote the *Aftenposten*'s reviewer after Kirsten's first performance on Wednesday 29 June 1932. 'By virtue of her youth and brilliant vocal art, Kirsten Flagstad triumphed as Isolde. Her interpretation of the role confirmed that we have in her a Wagnerian singer for whom we may cherish the greatest expectations. If the lady *wishes*, it will not be long before she can appear both at Bayreuth and at the Metropolitan!'

After one performance, Kirsten received a visit from the Wagnerian soprano Ellen Gulbranson, who had sung at Bayreuth many times. 'It is a pity, Miss Flagstad, that you are not singing abroad,' she said. 'You should not bury your beautiful voice here at home. You should try to go to Bayreuth. There you would learn the Wagner style, because it is Wagnerian roles that your voice was meant for.' 'Thank you for your advice, but I'm sure I haven't the slightest chance of singing at the Bayreuth Festival, where they engage only the very best,' Kirsten replied. 'Besides, I am not considering any career abroad as a singer. I am happily married, and if I continue to sing, I will be fully satisfied to sing here at home.'

Mme Gulbranson shook her head at this indifference. Deciding to take matters into her own hands, she wrote to Winifred Wagner about the gifted Norwegian singer who had scored such a success as Isolde. Was there any chance that she might have an audition at Bayreuth? Winifred Wagner, impressed by a recommendation from Ellen Gulbranson, answered that Miss Flagstad would be welcome to audition in July when the singers for the following year's Festival would be selected.

Ellen Gulbranson brought Kirsten this letter in person, and urged her to act upon it. Out of respect for her senior colleague, Kirsten acquiesced. She was cordially received by Frau Wagner, who, after the death of her husband Siegfried in 1930, had assumed the management of the Festivals in Bayreuth. Frau Wagner introduced her to Dr Heinz Tietjen, the musical director of the Festival, and to Professor Carl Kittel, who was to accompany Kirsten on the piano at the audition. 'Please come to the house to see me after the audition so we can have a little chat,' said Frau Wagner as she prepared to hear the first singer.

While Kirsten sat listening in the auditorium, she noticed that most of the singers acted as they sang, with gestures and facial expressions. 'Should I risk doing that myself?' she wondered. She decided she would; it certainly would be better than just standing there and singing. When her turn came she said she would sing Isolde's Narrative from the first act. She asked Professor Kittel to omit one part that had been cut in the performances in Oslo and that she had not had time to study for the audition.

The first part went well, she felt. When Professor Kittel came to the section she had not learned thoroughly, he forgot and played on. Kirsten stopped, saying that, unfortunately, she did not know this part. 'Just continue,' called out Dr Tietjen from the auditorium. So she did – but she had become nervous. She felt that she finished the Narrative very poorly. She then asked if she could sing the 'Liebestod'. 'No, thank you, that will not be necessary,' said Dr Tietjen. 'We have heard enough. Thank you, Miss Flagstad. Who is next, please?' 'Well, so that was enough!' said Kirsten to herself. 'That means only one thing: that I am not good enough for Bayreuth. But of course, I knew that beforehand. I should never have come here.'

When she went to see Frau Wagner at her home, she was amazed to hear that the audition had been successful and that she was to be offered an engagement. They had liked both her singing and her acting very much. Winifred Wagner explained:

You have great prospects as a Wagner singer. You are the first soprano we have heard who chose to sing Isolde's Narrative. *Everyone* wants to sing the 'Liebestod', Miss Flagstad. If you are willing to sing minor roles at the Festival next year, we would be happy to have you. You must also learn some roles in case you are called on to substitute for someone. While you are singing in Bayreuth you can also study the particular style we use here. If you are interested, I will show you around the Festspielhaus now before you have to catch your train.

Kirsten noted:

> Everything I saw and heard fascinated me and increased my interest in Wagner and his operas. A whole new world was opening up for me. As we stood on the enormous stage, now in semi-darkness, I felt imbued with the distinctive atmosphere. I was deeply grateful for the opportunity to sing in Bayreuth. I wanted to preserve my impressions to use as inspiration when I began to study the roles I had been assigned. What an experience it was, that one day I spent in Wagner's own theatre! Looking back, I would say it was one of the most strenuous and eventful days of my life.

The Oslo newspapers soon got wind of the news and telephoned her at home for more information. She told them that she was to sing the Third Norn in *Götterdämmerung* and Ortlinde in *Die Walküre* – 'very small parts, but they will give me the opportunity to learn the Wagnerian style.' In order to be prepared as an understudy, she had been asked by Frau Wagner to study Eva in *Die Meistersinger*, as well as Sieglinde in *Die Walküre*.

To honour 'the new Bayreuth singer', the Norwegian Opera Association scheduled performances of *Tristan und Isolde* at the National Theatre in August 1932. This time Kirsten was to sing Isolde in all performances. Alexander Kipnis replaced Ivar Andrésen, who was ill, in the role of King Marke. Kipnis, a Russian by birth, was one of the most notable basses singing in Europe at that time. He had already performed in America as a member of the famous Chicago Opera Company, and he was to sing for several seasons at the Metropolitan in New York in the 1940s.

At the rehearsals he was overwhelmed by the magnificence of Kirsten's voice, and the feeling she expressed in her acting also made a deep impression on him. After the first performance he came to her dressing-room to compliment her on her achievement. Kirsten recalled later:

Kipnis tried to speak with me in German. The performance was sung in German, so I suppose he thought I knew the language. I knew German of course, but I didn't dare use it in conversation, so I answered only in words of one syllable. Then he switched to English, hoping that I knew this language better. I didn't, so there wasn't much of a conversation. I simply sat there, blushing and unhappy because of my lack of courage. Luckily, Kipnis didn't tell anyone abroad what an idiot the Norwegian Isolde had been. To the contrary, he recommended me to opera managers in both Europe and America. And I was soon to discover what it meant to be recommended by Kipnis. He opened up the way for me.

In August 1933 Kirsten Flagstad and Alexander Kipnis met in Bayreuth. By that time she could express herself very well in German, and they laughed heartily together over her clumsiness the previous year.

When the news spread in Scandinavia that Kirsten was going to Bayreuth, offers came pouring in. She accepted only those that gave her the chance to sing Wagner. She appeared in two concerts in February 1933, one in Oslo and one in Bergen, in commemoration of the fiftieth anniversary of Wagner's death. Then, on 7 June 1933, she sang Eva in *Die Meistersinger* at the National Theatre with her colleague and friend, Conrad Arnesen, as Walther. After the performance, one of the critics wrote:

Kirsten Flagstad's Eva cannot be praised too highly. Her clear, firm, bell-like voice can always be heard above the orchestra, no matter how heavy the orchestration. Musically as well as dramatically she fills this role of a young girl to perfection, and it is a proud moment both for her, who has so conscientiously and meticulously pursued her studies, and for Norwegian vocal art, that Bayreuth is ready to welcome her.

Kirsten said later:

A few days after the performance at the National Theatre, Mother and I travelled to Bayreuth. We had no sooner arrived than work began for me. At first I coached with Professor Kittel, and he was, if possible, even stricter than Mother had been. Every phrase, every passage, had to be learned as perfectly as possible. It was like starting at the bottom again, as if I had never sung a note of Wagner. At times I was so tired that I had to go straight to bed after rehearsal. But I liked the intense work, and enjoyed myself in the Bayreuth environment. After the coaching sessions, the stage rehearsals for *Die Walküre* began. They were really strenuous. A high mountain peak had been constructed on the stage, and we Valkyries had to run up and down it again and again, singing at the top of our lungs, until we literally had no breath left. Then we had a rest – that is, we sat down to watch others rehearse.

Every detail of a production at Bayreuth is rehearsed. At the first performance, the curtain rises on a model presentation. In spite of the hard work, it was a pleasure to be involved in something so perfect, to be part of such a perfect whole.

Frau Wagner and Dr Tietjen were pleased with her efforts, and told her to study Sieglinde and Gutrune for the 1934 Festival.

Heinz Tietjen, who was also music director of the Berlin State Opera, had offered Kirsten an engagement in Berlin after her first audition in Bayreuth. She had declined because she preferred to remain in Oslo. When they parted after the Festival in 1933, he repeated his offer, but again she declined because she did not want to leave her family. Tietjen found this incomprehensible, but said:

All the same, you are welcome to come to Berlin at the beginning of May next year. I will work on Sieglinde in *Die Walküre* with you then. You should be coached in the role before you return to Bayreuth. You still have a lot to learn before you master the Wagnerian style. Unfortunately I will not have time to coach you in Gutrune in *Götterdämmerung*, but you will receive help from Professor Kittel when you return to Bayreuth. Auf wiedersehen in Berlin, Miss Flagstad.

Kirsten accepted this offer with thanks.

After spending several days in Oslo, where numerous invitations to appear in the autumn season awaited her, she went to the Johansen summer home, Amalienborg, outside Kristiansand. Her husband had a timber business there, and the house was part of the estate. As always, Kirsten enjoyed the quiet home life. Nevertheless, something had changed – not in the environment, but in herself. She was now an opera singer on holiday. She could no longer halt the singing career she had intended to abandon when she remarried. She realized that from now on she would have to divide her time between her career and her home, and she had the feeling that she would gradually have less and less time to be a private person.

Among the offers she received was one from the Brussels Opera. The manager wrote that he knew of her reputation as a Wagnerian singer and hoped she would agree to sing Sieglinde in a performance of *Die Walküre* at the Opera at the end of May 1934. Kirsten reflected:

> I couldn't imagine how they could possibly have heard of me in Brussels, but the offer was tempting, and it would mean stage experience before I appeared in the role at Bayreuth. Now I was glad that Dr Tietjen had offered to help me with this role in particular. I would be fully prepared to sing Sieglinde in Brussels after he had coached me, even though I would be portraying this character on the stage for the first time.

Kirsten Flagstad sang in several concerts in Norway and Sweden in the autumn and winter of 1933–4, but she spent most of her time studying her two Wagner roles. As she worked, she became more and more caught up in the lovely young Sieglinde. She looked forward to singing the role, and was sure she could master it with Tietjen's help. At the beginning of May 1934 she went to Berlin to see him, but he was busy with Richard Strauss festivals and could not see her. He seemed to have completely forgotten his offer. She telephoned for an appointment, and he scheduled one, but he postponed it from one day to the next. The date of the Brussels performance was drawing near and she had not even seen Tietjen, let alone been coached by him in the role of Sieglinde. She became nervous – not from fear of not knowing the part, but from probably having to sing it on the stage without prior guidance in developing the character. Finally she had to leave Berlin without having worked with Tietjen at all.

> I calmed myself down by thinking that they wouldn't insist upon the special Wagnerian style in Brussels. When I met the manager, I asked him how he could know me as a Wagner singer. 'Alexander Kipnis recommended you,' he answered. But the next thing he said almost scared the life out of me. He

said he was happy that I was familiar with the Bayreuth style, because I was to sing with an all-German ensemble and there would not be time to have more than one general rehearsal before the performance on 24 May.

That came as a shock, but it was too late to withdraw. I was on the point of revealing that I had never sung Sieglinde before, but I caught myself in time. He would discover that himself soon enough! Whatever I say or do, there will be a scandal, I thought. So I chose to remain silent.

She felt completely helpless. From the musical point of view, she knew the part inside out, but she was wholly unfamiliar with the staging. At the rehearsal, the directions she had read in the score were as if swept from her mind. It was not long before 'Hunding' realized that something was wrong. He whispered to her: 'How often have you sung Sieglinde, Miss Flagstad? There is something here that doesn't click. Either you have sung the part too often, or not at all. Which is it?' 'I'll tell you after the performance,' she whispered back. Not for the life of her did she dare tell anyone until after the opening that it was the first time she had sung Sieglinde on the stage.

Never in my life have I dreaded a performance as much as that one. But my lucky star was with me; I can't explain it in any other way. During the performance, the stage movements came about naturally. I had command of the role. When the curtain fell on the last act, I almost cried with relief. I was completely exhausted from the nervous tension. I revealed to 'Hunding' that I had never sung the part before. He didn't believe me – thought I was bragging. I considered his reaction the greatest compliment he could have paid me because it meant that I hadn't performed like a rank beginner.

While Kirsten was in Brussels, she met Lauritz Melchior for the first time. He was to sing in *Siegfried* the day after she sang Sieglinde. Kirsten had heard Melchior as Tannhäuser at the Casino in Kristiania in the summer of 1919. She told the jovial Danish tenor that he had made an indelible impression on her; he was flattered, and the two had many pleasant chats together. Eight months later, when she met him again at the Metropolitan, he had no recollection of the earlier meeting. 'It was quite apparent that I hadn't made any special impression on him!' she said. 'But I was then only a young unknown Norwegian singer who happened to have an engagement in Brussels, so it isn't really strange that he didn't remember me.'

When Kirsten arrived in Bayreuth to take part in the really difficult rehearsals for *Die Walküre*, she met Dr Tietjen, who deplored the fact that he had not been able to see her in Berlin. It had been only a verbal promise, so she could not reproach him, but he had placed her in a desperate situation, and the fright still gripped her. It affected her acting in the performance at Bayreuth on 7 August 1934. A reviewer wrote: 'Miss Flagstad was very inhibited in the first act, but seemed more relaxed later. She sang beautifully, however, with a rich, pure, full-toned soprano that holds the greatest promise for the future.' The critics hoped to see her as a regular guest at the Festival. Her debut at the Metropolitan the next year was to decide her future, and it so happened that she was unable to accept an offer from Bayreuth again.

While in Bayreuth, Kirsten received a bona fide offer from the United States. A letter arrived from Fritz Reiner, forwarded from Oslo. He was conducting in Philadelphia, and offered her a guest performance as Isolde in October 1934. He proposed to engage her on the strength of the glowing report of her ability that the American music critic, Oscar Thompson, had written for the magazine *Musical America* and the *New York Evening Post* in 1932. Thompson had heard Kirsten when she sang Isolde at the National Theatre in Oslo in August that same year, and had written a detailed account of the performance. In the *New York Evening Post* of Saturday 8 October he wrote:

The Isolde of this particular performance was Kirsten Flagstad, an artist of vocal and dramatic gifts which might well be envied and admired in the foremost opera houses of the world. Few, indeed, have been the recent embodiments of the Irish princess that could boast of the beauty of voice and grace of delivery that characterized this one. Here was singing without forcing, singing true to pitch, singing expressive and persuasive from the first numbed utterances of Isolde to the final exaltations of the 'Liebestod'.

Mme Flagstad is no fledgling. Soon she is to celebrate twenty years of stage singing. But she had retained for Isolde the charm of youth, and if she was not in all respects a truly heroic figure, she was a winning and appealing one. It is curious that the German opera houses have overlooked an artist so admirably equipped. A native of Oslo, her successes have been chiefly there and in the Swedish opera at Gothenburg [Göteborg].

Kirsten later commented:

My American career might have been entirely different if I had been able to accept the offer from Philadelphia. But I couldn't go, because I was under contract to sing in Göteborg from September to December of that year. I telephoned the opera manager at the Stora Teatern and asked if he could shift my dates a little so that I could sing in Philadelphia in October. But it wasn't possible, so I had to write to Fritz Reiner and say I was sorry I couldn't come.

One week before her engagement in Bayreuth was to end, a telegram arrived from St Moritz: 'Are you interested in singing dramatic Wagnerian parts like Isolde and Brünnhilde at Metropolitan next season? Stop. Keep this to yourself until later. Letter follows. Stop. If interested, please answer by telegram. Eric Semon.' Kirsten was numbed. What were the implications of this telegram? She had to talk with someone. A telephone call to her husband might be considered a breach of the imposed silence, but she felt she needed his advice. She called him, and he was delighted at the news and very proud on her behalf. 'But what of you if something comes of this?' she asked. 'I'll come with you. Say that you are interested,' Henry told her. Later, Kirsten commented:

I was not at all happy when I sent the telegram to Mr Semon. My determination to give up my career after my marriage had completely collapsed. The quiet home life I had so looked forward to had lasted less than three months. Then I had slid into work again – and had liked it. After all, I was a singer! I was torn by conflicting emotions while I waited in Bayreuth for the promised letter. I didn't have time to brood, however. I had been asked to take part in a performance of Beethoven's Ninth Symphony, and was practising for this in between singing my roles at the Festspielhaus.

Richard Strauss was to conduct Beethoven's Ninth. Kirsten

looked forward to meeting the man whose beautiful songs she had sung in public on several occasions. But Strauss did not appear until he was about to conduct, and disappeared as quickly afterwards, so, to her great disappointment, there was no opportunity to meet him. (They were to meet for the first time many years later, whereupon they became good friends.) After the performance, the chorus master, Hugo Rüdel, came up to her, bowed respectfully, and said, 'I have heard, coached and conducted more performances of Beethoven's Ninth Symphony than I can count, but I was to be in my late seventies before I was privileged to hear a soprano soloist like you, Miss Flagstad.'

Then came the letter from Eric Semon, asking her to come to St Moritz to audition for the general manager and a conductor of the Metropolitan. For the audition she was to know as much as possible of the three Brünnhildes, Isolde, and Leonore in *Fidelio*. She had just six days in which to study the roles.

> First I had to get hold of the scores, and in Bayreuth I could only obtain the scores of the operas given that year. Professor Kittel helped me a little with *Götterdämmerung* in the hope that I would be able to learn the part of Brünnhilde by heart. Then I memorized what I remembered of Isolde and Leonore. But it was a hopelessly short time in which to do it. Nevertheless, I decided to go to St Moritz. I said to myself, 'Let come what comes. If they don't want me, it really doesn't make any difference to me.'

When Kirsten met Eric Semon, she reminded him of the two letters he had written to her in 1929. He had no recollection of them: he had never previously been in contact with her, he said. 'How did it happen that you contacted me now, then?' she asked. 'Alexander Kipnis suggested it,' he replied.

After the meeting with Semon, she went to her hotel to rest after the strenuous journey; she had been sitting in an overheated train compartment since five o'clock in the morning. No sooner had she reached her room than the telephone rang. It was the coach and accompanist Hermann Weigert, asking her to come to a rehearsal as quickly as she could. She protested that she could not sing a note until she had rested a little. 'You must come at once, Miss Flagstad. There is a piano in the salon of my hotel and we can work there.'

As she entered the hotel salon, she saw that it was crowded with people. They had all streamed in when he sat down at the piano, and were evidently waiting to be entertained. Kirsten got quite upset. She was always shy about practising in front of people, and now, in addition, she was dead tired. Weigert, however, seemed quite unperturbed. He asked what she was going to sing at the audition. She explained to him what difficulties she had had in acquiring the music, and said there was not much she could sing by heart apart from Sieglinde. 'No one is interested in that,' he said curtly. 'Do you know anything from the *Götterdämmerung* Brünnhilde?' 'I will try,' she said. Trembling and uncertain because of the unwelcome audience, she sang, but Weigert did not seem impressed. 'Do you know anything at all by heart?' he asked rather rudely. Kirsten recollected:

Then I got angry. 'Isolde,' I answered, and I added somewhat sarcastically that that was what I had been asked to prepare. Mr Weigert's unpleasant disposition was beginning to get on my nerves. After all, I had been *asked* to come to St Moritz. I myself had not lifted a finger to seek an audition with the manager of the Metropolitan. And then I had to stand there and let myself be treated like a schoolgirl who didn't know her lessons, in the presence of all those strange people.

I said I would like to sing 'Dich, teure Halle' from *Tann-häuser*. I was fond of it and knew it by heart. 'It's all right with me,' said Mr Weigert without enthusiasm. I could tell that he considered the whole thing hopeless. He became a little more agreeable after I had sung the aria. 'Do you know Brünnhilde's Battle Cry from *Die Walküre*?' he asked. I said yes, and he looked for the music. Now, I thought, I'll show him that I can really sing. My fatigue vanished in a split second. I let loose with the Battle Cry and he nearly tumbled off the piano stool. I sang it out so lustily that it rebounded; I didn't care if the whole hotel heard me. The sheer joy of singing quite overwhelmed me.

Mr Weigert was as if transformed. He arose, grasped my hand, and said warmly, 'You will be engaged, I am certain. Sing the Battle Cry in the same way tomorrow and you will be engaged by the Metropolitan!' I wasn't so sure about that, but I did consider it a triumph that I'd been able to convince Mr Weigert that I had something to offer.

The audition for the general manager, Giulio Gatti-Casazza, was set for eleven o'clock the next day. It was a sultry August morning, without a touch of wind. At Gatti-Casazza's hotel, Kirsten met the English soprano Elizabeth Delius, who had also been invited for an audition. Miss Delius, who was short and chubby, was dressed in an evening gown. Kirsten wore a simple dress with matching jacket. Both singers were to have a short preliminary rehearsal with Mr Weigert. The room in which the audition was to take place was furnished with groups of overstuffed chairs. A thick carpet covered the entire floor and heavy draperies were hung in front of doors and windows, deadening all resonance.

When Kirsten heard Elizabeth Delius, she said to herself, 'I don't stand a chance.' She had a magnificent voice and knew everything by heart. While Miss Delius was singing, Kirsten saw something gleaming on the carpet. She picked up the object, which turned out to be a small coin, a Swiss fifty-centime piece. 'This may be a lucky coin,' she thought, and put it in her jacket pocket. 'Maybe the audition won't be a complete fiasco.'

Immediately afterwards the gentlemen from the Metropolitan entered, and the audition could begin. Kirsten and Elizabeth Delius were to sing the same music, so that minute comparisons could be made. The conductor, Artur Bodanzky, went over to Kirsten and inquired about her repertoire. She told him how difficult it had been to obtain the various vocal scores; as a result, she said, she did not know all the parts by heart. He smiled at her and said, 'Well then, you'll have to do the best you can.' His smile gave her a little courage.

Kirsten felt inadequate compared to Elizabeth Delius. When she was asked to sing Brünnhilde's Battle Cry, she remembered Weigert's advice and sang out with all the voice she possessed. 'You were flat,' said Bodanzky, 'Sing it again.' Kirsten did so. 'Sing it once more,' cried Bodanzky. When she had sung 'Hojo-to-ho' for the third time, he smiled and said, 'Now it is fine!' Then Elizabeth Delius was asked to sing the Battle Cry. She was not asked to repeat it. 'I wonder what that means,' thought Kirsten. She could not interpret the gentlemen's reaction, but she thought Bodanzky had seemed interested when she sang the *Walküre* Battle Cry.

After the audition, the ladies were asked to wait outside while the gentlemen conferred. Half an hour later they emerged. As they passed, Gatti-Casazza came over to Kirsten, smiled, and said, 'Au revoir'. His greeting confused her, but Elizabeth Delius interpreted it to mean that they had chosen Kirsten. 'They will take you,' she said to her. Eric Semon and Hermann Weigert escorted them to the foyer and suggested they should all have lunch together. Elizabeth Delius wanted to return to her hotel first to change her clothes. As soon as she left, Semon turned to Kirsten and burst out, 'Now I can say it! You will be engaged by the Metropolitan, Madame Flagstad. The contract will reach you in less than two weeks. Before that time you must not let it be known that you have been engaged.'

Kirsten was speechless. She had not truly comprehended that the audition could result in an engagement:

If I had known then what this engagement would lead to, I really believe I would have refused it on the spot. It meant that for the next two years I would have to stand in the limelight, more or less live out of suitcases, and work, work, only work. I might well have preferred to do a little singing at home in Oslo. But naturally I was also proud that I would now sing in 'the world's greatest opera house'. Before I left St Moritz, that same day, I had a last meeting with Mr Bodanzky. He gave me a list of the parts I should study: the three Brünnhildes, Isolde, unabridged; Leonore in *Fidelio*; and the Marschallin in *Der Rosenkavalier* by Richard Strauss. His parting words to me were: 'Come to New York as soon as you know these roles. And above all, do not go and get fat! Your slender, youthful figure is not the least reason you were preferred.'

The contract arrived exactly two weeks later, as Semon had promised. It specified an engagement of nine weeks, from 28 January to 31 March 1935. She would be paid $550 a week. In addition to the roles that Bodanzky had asked her to prepare, the contract also stipulated that she should be ready to sing Elsa in *Lohengrin*, Elisabeth in *Tannhäuser* and Sieglinde in *Die Walküre*.

Kirsten telephoned her mother and asked her to come over to Tidemand Street as soon as she could. 'I have a big surprise for you,' she said.

When Mother arrived, she looked quite excited. I don't know what she expected to hear. When she saw the contract from the Metropolitan, she began to cry. 'Your Father should have lived to see this,' she whispered. Father had died in 1930 –

from a heart attack – and none of us had got over the loss. He was only sixty-one. He had worn himself out by working at two professions simultaneously year after year, and then, in addition, by studying late into the night. After Father's death, we 'children' meant everything to Mother. I believe it was one of the happiest days of her life when she learned that her daughter had been engaged by the Metropolitan.

Then word reached the newspapers, and Kirsten's name became known the world over. Telegrams, flowers and friendly greetings arrived at 6 Tidemand Street.

She asked to be released from her guest appearances in Göteborg; she needed every spare hour to study the roles she had to know when she arrived at the Metropolitan. From the Stora Teatern came the following reply: 'We know your capacity, Miss Flagstad. You can manage your performances here and learn your parts for the Metropolitan as well. As we do not want to miss the opportunity of introducing you as a future world star, we regret that we cannot release you from your contract. Welcome to Göteborg!' Kirsten noted later:

> Even though I would have preferred to be released from the performances so that I could leave sooner for the United States, I looked forward with pleasure to singing again at the Stora Teatern. The theatre, my colleagues and the town all had a special place in my heart. I shall never forget the years I sang at the Stora Teatern. Without the schooling and the experience I received there, I would not have been prepared for a career in America.

Her first role as guest artist in Göteborg was Elisabeth in *Tannhäuser*. Kirsten had never before portrayed this loving, faithful woman on the stage. She had to change her appearance very little to illuminate the role: a touch of make-up, a wig the same golden brown as her own hair, the appropriate costume, and she became Elisabeth. She also possessed many of the inner qualities of the character. After the first performance on Friday 5 October 1934, one of the reviewers wrote: 'Miss Flagstad offers great and genuine art. She has a wonderful voice, acts with true human feeling, and expresses convincingly the distinctive quality of the character. Her entrance into the Hall of Song with the jubilant aria of greeting instantly raised the performance to the highest level.'

Kirsten's many friends in Göteborg complained that they did not see much of her any more. Every day she locked herself in her hotel room and worked on memorizing roles. Then she rushed to the theatre for the evening performance, then straight back to the hotel, to fall exhausted into bed. She had stipulated a ten-day leave before the beginning of rehearsals for *Fidelio*, in which she was to make her farewell appearances before the journey to New York. During that time, at the suggestion of Artur Bodanzky, she was to go to Prague to study her Metropolitan roles with Professor Georg Szell.

Professor Szell treated me like a beginner. He bullied me and scared me nearly out of my wits with his outbursts of rage over the most minor mistakes. All I saw of Prague was the street below my hotel window. After ten days of inhuman drudgery, Professor Szell declared that I didn't need to worry about my roles; that I knew them cold. He said he would personally write to Artur Bodanzky and tell him that. For the first time, he smiled. If only once earlier he had spoken an encouraging word to me, I would have felt so much better. I was a complete stranger in Prague, and I felt terribly alone.

Professor Szell undoubtedly meant well. Later in life I met others who considered it proper to use this approach – to 'frighten' talent out of you, so to speak. I don't agree with them. I believe you can achieve the same or even better results with an encouraging, friendly word – when it is deserved, of course!

The first performance of *Fidelio* at the Stora Teatern in Göteborg, on Monday 10 December 1934, became a high point of Kirsten Flagstad's career as an opera singer in Europe. The inner character of Leonore is very close to that of Elisabeth in *Tannhäuser*. Accordingly, Kirsten had no difficulty in expressing it.

Her imminent engagement at the Metropolitan acted as a magnet on the public. Tickets were snatched up as soon as they went on sale. Friends and admirers from Oslo, Copenhagen and Stockholm arrived in the city and lined up at the box office with her Göteborg public. They all wanted to hear her one more time before she crossed the ocean.

Kirsten Flagstad seldom spoke in terms of a favourite role, but Leonore in *Fidelio* was unquestionably one role she cherished. She commented:

103

What marvellous music Beethoven has given us in his only opera. Nothing can be compared with *Fidelio* – nothing! It is pure and human throughout, and brings out the best qualities in an artist.

To bring a character to life on stage is such an extraordinary, liberating experience that it cannot be adequately described in words. When suddenly you know within yourself that you have mastered a role, that you identify completely with the character you are portraying – then the magical transformation can take place. I have experienced this myself. I might have sung a part many times; then one night, I would perceive in a flash the innermost nature of the character. What an incredible moment that was! I felt exalted and freed. Such an experience more than compensates for all the toil and the almost superhuman effort that an artist's career demands.

The farewell evening in Göteborg was both happy and sad. What did the future have in store for me? Would New York receive me as kindly as Göteborg had? And would I ever again have colleagues as friendly and helpful as those at the Stora Teatern? I knew I was saying goodbye to the Scandinavian public, but for how long?

Had she known that she would never again set foot on the Göteborg stage, the stage that had served as a proving ground for her as an artist, the sadness she felt that night would have far outweighed the joy.

Else, who was now fourteen, was not to accompany her mother to the United States; she had to remain in Norway to complete her schooling. The keen disappointment of not being able to take her with her cast a shadow over the expectation and excitement Kirsten felt about the journey and her encounter with New York. Mother and daughter had a last phone conversation before Kirsten and her husband boarded the *Drottningholm* in Göteborg on a grey, windy day in late December.

Friends came on board to see her off, and many of her admirers assembled on the pier to wish her godspeed. Kirsten stood on deck gazing back at the city, hoping to keep it in sight as long as possible. One of the Göteborg journalists asked if she was looking forward to her Metropolitan engagement. 'I look forward most to coming back home when the engagement is over,' she said, to his astonishment.

'It will surely be no later than May,' she added. The same reporter asked if it was true that she had received an offer from South America. 'Yes, I have,' she answered, 'but first I want to see how I get on in New York. Then my husband and I will return home and think things over.'

The resulting newspaper headline read: 'Kirsten is homesick before she leaves!'

6

The International Artist

After a smooth passage, the *Drottningholm* made its way slowly up the Hudson River on the afternoon of Monday 7 January 1935, her progress impeded by thick fog. The captain informed the passengers that if the fog did not lift, the ship could not enter her berth until the next day.

Kirsten was up on deck hoping to catch her first glimpse of New York. Suddenly the bank of fog rolled away, as if a curtain had risen on a stage, and she saw the Statue of Liberty, and then the Manhattan skyline, brilliantly illuminated in the dusk. Then the curtain fell, and everything was grey again. 'It was a fantastic sight,' she said. 'I'll never forget the impression it made on me. It may sound trite, but I had the feeling that the curtain had gone up on my New York debut. True enough, we didn't go ashore until the following day. My husband and I were driven to the Astor Hotel where we had a quick breakfast. Then we walked to the Metropolitan Opera House, a few blocks down Broadway.'

Kirsten was anxious to see the Opera House building; before they realized it, they were standing in front of it. Her first impression was that it looked dingy and uninviting, but it had a certain distinction, even with skyscrapers on every side. And what had it not held of music and song! She and Johansen found their way to the modest entrance to the offices of the Metropolitan on 39th Street. She was received by Gatti-Casazza, Artur Bodanzky and the assistant general manager, Edward Ziegler. The gentlemen were friendly, but not effusive. They did not yet know what a golden bird they had caught in St Moritz. Bodanzky noted with satisfaction that she was as slender and youthful as she had been at the audition.

Before she left, she was told that she would replace the German Wagnerian soprano Frida Leider, who had asked to be released from her contract because, it was said, she did not like the raw winter climate of New York. At the time Kirsten had auditioned in St Moritz, Frida Leider was still in two minds about returning to the Met. Had she known that the management was auditioning dramatic sopranos, she might have decided to go back. On 10 January Kirsten and her husband attended the performance of *Siegfried* at the Metropolitan in which Lauritz Melchior sang the title role and the Austrian soprano Anny Konetzni sang Brünnhilde. Mme Konetzni, who had made her Met debut on 26 December as Brünnhilde in *Die Walküre*, had been engaged before Kirsten as a temporary replacement for Frida Leider during the first weeks of the 1934–5 season. Her contract with the Vienna State Opera precluded her remaining in New York beyond January.

Not long after her arrival in New York, Kirsten met her husband's brother Alfred, his wife Margaret, and their nine-year-old daughter Sigrid. The two couples saw each other often.

Maja anxiously awaited news from Kirsten. She had asked her to write as soon as possible, but she knew her aversion to letter-writing. She usually expressed herself in telegram style, as in this note, written from London, when she was at the height of her career: 'Dear Mother, I am well, and have plenty to do. I know that this is what you want to know. The rest you can hear from others. Your Kirsten.' Maja was therefore very surprised when, only three weeks after Kirsten's arrival in New York, she received a long letter from her, dated 15 January 1935:

My dearest Mother!

I know you have been waiting to hear from me, but I wanted to wait till I had something definite to report. The trip was fine . . . and we enjoyed the rest . . . and the pleasant company on board. . . .

We live in the centre of the city, on Broadway. I have only a five-minute walk to the Opera, which is very practical. The weather was very warm the first few days, but now we have clear sunshine, cold, and snow that will not last. The climate is said to be dangerous for singers.

We are often invited out, but I have to ask most people to wait until later, as I have so much to do and am dead tired early in the evening, probably because of the many new impressions, the language and the work. My English surprises me – I manage nicely; and besides English I also have constantly to speak German, so my brain is somewhat overworked. I am overwhelmed with all kinds of requests for advertising and publicity, but answer none.

And then the Metropolitan – an insignificant-looking building. The auditorium, which holds 4,660 people [actually about 3,700, including standing room, in 1935], is beautiful and comfortable – but the stage and backstage! Henry and I called on the general manager, who was very pleasant. Nervous as could be, I explained the situation as well as I could, and was released from singing the Marschallin in *Rosenkavalier*. That was the first big weight off my mind. I understood that I would have to audition for the other roles before any decisions were made in regard to performances, and was asked to come for an audition the next day, when Bodanzky would hear me.

We had *Götterdämmerung*, and I was beside myself with fright. Except for practising all parts every day on board ship, I hadn't sung a note for several days; text, everything, was swept from my mind. Bodanzky said it would be better to wait and give me a respite with my part until Sunday. So I practised two hours daily, and was coached by the stage director, Wymetal [Wilhelm von Wymetal Jr], and gradually, as my nerves calmed down, my usual assurance returned. Another reason, to be sure, was that everyone was so pleasant and kind to me.

Paul Althouse, the tenor who sings Siegfried, was practically knocked over when I had sung a few tones, and some days later he told me that the whole theatre was talking about me, and everyone was listening at the doors when I sang. . . . Then I was informed that on Tuesday – that is, today – I was to have an orchestra rehearsal in costume and make-up for the first act – they wanted to see how I would manage. On Sunday Bodanzky had heard that I sang the part faultlessly, and was extremely friendly and encouraging. . . .

Last night I slept poorly, but arose at 7.45 a.m. and was only a little nervous. I had arranged for the costume, a new off-white gown, very becoming, and a new brown wig, which looked lovely – and then the fun began. Althouse was also in costume, and we had a horse that whinnied in competition with us. After I had sung the first bars, we came to a halt. I was singing into the wings, I was told. We had to start again from the beginning. Then the whole of the first section, right up to the high C, was perfect. There was a pause, and Bodanzky cried out, 'Flagstad, ausgezeichnet!' [Flagstad, superb!], whereupon the orchestra beat on their instruments and the people in the auditorium applauded. Then came the scene with Waltraute, and then Siegfried, and believe it or not, I didn't make a mistake. When we had finished, Bodanzky went out into the auditorium and let someone else conduct the end of the first section all over again, and when I sang the high C, applause broke loose from the orchestra, the auditorium and the stagehands, with cries of bravo. Bodanzky came up and was very enthusiastic, and so was Mr Ziegler. Well, all were more than enthusiastic, and the stage director said I was so capable and lovely that I did not need to do anything special – my appearance on the stage and my bearing were enough. Such a demonstration by the orchestra was unheard of here, they said.

Then I was summoned to manager Gatti-Casazza, with Bodanzky, and it was decided that I would make my debut as Sieglinde on 2 February, as Isolde on the 6th, as the *Walküre* Brünnhilde on the 15th, and as the *Siegfried* Brünnhilde on the 22nd. Bodanzky warned me against the agents who would come in droves, and he asked me to consult with him on everything. He pinches and pats my cheek and treats me like a little girl. Yes, everyone here seems to think I am ten years younger than I am, and that is wonderful.

One day I met Kaja Eide [Eidé Norena, Norwegian lyric soprano] here – she is singing Gilda on Friday [actually, the Thursday]. She inquired about you. Well, this is all the news I have. I hope to hear from you soon, and that you are well. Tell the family about this letter, but preferably no one else until after the first performance.

Heartfelt greetings from your Kirsten.

P.S. 'The Tenner', 'the Diplomat' and 'the Spindle' [names associated with the card game patience]: I won all three today. K.

To the discerning reader, this letter reveals more about Kirsten

Flagstad's character than any number of pages that someone else might write about her.

'I don't believe I can be called superstitious, but I notice small things that may mean luck,' she once said, 'as, for example, that I win games of patience [worth telling her mother about in the letter, since the games she played were so intricate that she seldom won them], and that I found the little coin before the audition in St Moritz. I have had the coin set in a bracelet which I often wear.'

There is no doubt that Kirsten's first stage rehearsal was something of a sensation. When Bodanzky heard from the auditorium how her voice carried above the strongest orchestra sound, he rushed to Gatti-Casazza, shouting, 'Gatti, Gatti, you must come and hear her!' After the rehearsal, everyone in the house sensed that here was a singer quite out of the ordinary, even by Metropolitan standards. Nevertheless, the management dared not give her any special publicity before her debut on the afternoon of Saturday 2 February 1935. They knew their exacting public only too well, not to mention the music critics of New York who more than once had lambasted singers of European fame on whom the Metropolitan had set its hopes, artistically and financially.

Therefore, Kirsten was entirely unprepared for what was to come, and worked on her part as calmly as if she was at home in Oslo. She became a little nervous when she learned that she was to have no stage rehearsal before her debut, but singers who appeared at the Metropolitan were expected to be so experienced that they could perform immediately. Bodanzky had advised her to attend as many performances at the Metropolitan as possible before she herself was to appear, to get an idea of the size of the stage, and especially of the sound of the orchestra so that she could judge how much voice was needed in order to be heard over it at all times.

When Eidé Norena sang Gilda in *Rigoletto* on 17 January, Kirsten and her husband attended. They both thought she sang magnificently. During the intermission they stood in the foyer, a little apart, observing. They knew no one, and thought no one knew them. Suddenly, however, an elegantly dressed woman detached herself from the crowd and came over to them. 'Are you not the young singer who had the audition the other day?' she asked, turning to Kirsten. 'Yes,' Kirsten answered, shyly, because of the attention they attracted. 'My name is Becky Hamilton, and my husband, Morgan, is one of the shareholders of the Opera. Your singing made a profound impression on me, and I am very excited about your debut next month. Would you and your husband do me the honour of coming to our home for dinner next week so that we can become a little better acquainted?' The dinner at the Hamiltons' was the beginning of a warm lifelong friendship between Kirsten and Becky Hamilton.

At the debut, Mrs Hamilton sat in her box and looked over the richly decorated auditorium, all in deep red and gold. She had heard Kirsten sing Gutrune in Bayreuth in 1934, and had put a mark next to Kirsten's name on her programme, which was her custom when she heard a voice that impressed her. Now she was interested in finding out how the Norwegian singer would be received by the Metropolitan public. There were quite a few empty seats. Gatti had purposely chosen a Saturday matinée for Kirsten Flagstad's debut, because the audience was generally the smallest of the week. He wanted to have a definite indication of how she would perform before he let her loose on one of the 'good' days.

The cast included Paul Althouse as Siegmund, Emanuel List as Hunding, Friedrich Schorr as Wotan, Gertrud Kappel as Brünn-hilde, and Maria Olszewska as Fricka, with Artur Bodanzky conducting. After Kirsten had sung her first phrases, an expectant hush seemed to pervade the auditorium. In spite of the coarse garment she wore as Sieglinde, she looked lovely. And her voice carried effortlessly over the orchestra. When the curtain fell on the first act, there was a moment of absolute silence throughout the auditorium. Then the applause broke loose like an avalanche. Over and over again the performers appeared in front of the curtain, but the audience wanted Kirsten to come out alone and would not give up until she did – once, twice, three times.

In a small studio in the Opera House sat the former Metropolitan star, Geraldine Farrar. The Saturday matinées were broadcast, and Miss Farrar, during the intermissions, reported to the listeners which well known people were present, how they were dressed and what impression the performance seemed to be making on them. Now, completely overwhelmed by the new singer she had just heard, she did not know how to begin. She laid aside her written script and improvised: 'Ladies and gentlemen,' she began, 'today we are witnessing one of the greatest events that can happen during an opera performance. A singer completely unknown to us has transported the audience to ecstasy with her marvellous voice and artistic personality. A new star is born!'

When the curtain fell after the third act, the audience rushed up to the stage and stood there in a phalanx, clapping, stamping and congratulating. When Kirsten came out alone in front of the curtain, people threw their programmes up in the air, and shouts of 'Bravo!' welled up in unison. With a shy smile, she curtsied in grateful acknowledgement. The Metropolitan public had taken the new singer to their hearts at the very first meeting.

Kirsten's stepdaughter, Kate Johansen, was one of the few Norwegians present at the debut:

I had gone around in Oslo becoming more and more eager to be present. Secretly I bought a ticket for a Danish ship that would reach New York a few days before Kirsten's first performance. When the ship was in mid-ocean, I wired Father and Kirsten that I was on my way. They were accustomed to surprises on my part, so I was welcomed with delight. The Saturday Kirsten was to make her debut, she wandered around the hotel rooms as calmly as if she had been at home in Tidemand Street. Father and I were the ones who were nervous: we were so accustomed to Kirsten' taking care of herself and not fussing over anything that it didn't occur to us to escort her to the Metropolitan when she left to get ready for the performance.

As we sat in the auditorium and observed the sophisticated audience, seemingly occupied only with chattering with acquaintances, I wondered with dread how Kirsten would get on. After the first act, we calmed down. Then when everyone stormed up to the stage after the performance, I got cold shivers down my back.

Kirsten had asked us to go to her dressing-room after the performance. We pushed our way through a crowd of fans waiting outside her dressing-room door, and there she stood, still in costume, and with her arms full of flowers. She laughed a bit nervously, as she usually did when she was moved. She didn't know how to react to such an overwhelming tribute as the one she was now receiving.

The Sunday papers carried enthusiastic reviews. Among them

was one by Lawrence Gilman, the respected music critic of the *New York Herald Tribune*:

It is a pleasure to salute in Mme Kirsten Flagstad . . . an artist of surprising and delightful quality. . . . Mme Flagstad is that *rara avis* in the Wagnerian woods – a singer with a voice, with looks, with youth. . . . The voice itself is both lovely and *puissant*. In its deeper register it is movingly warm and rich and expressive, and yesterday it recalled to wistful Wagnerites the irrecoverable magic of Olive [Fremstad] the immortal. The upper voice is powerful and true, and does not harden under stress.

The singing that we heard yesterday is that of a musician with taste and brains and sensibility, with poetic and dramatic insight. . . . [Kirsten Flagstad's] acting is noteworthy for its restraint and poise. . . . [She] expresses volumes with a turn of the head or a lifting of the hand. She was at times a bit inflexible yesterday; but that may possibly have been due to nervousness.

Kirsten herself recalled:

I'll never forget the day when I leaped from complete obscurity to world fame, for I actually became world-famous with my Metropolitan debut. While I stood in the wings waiting for my cue, I was of course more tense and nervous than usual. I'd been told that the acoustics of the house were difficult, so I was afraid that the voice would not carry over the orchestra pit. But the moment I stood on the stage, face to face with the audience, all nervousness disappeared. My customary calm and assurance returned. The contact with the audience gave me the stimulus I needed to give of my best. It has always been that way with me. On the stage I feel at home, be it in Oslo or Bayreuth, or at the Metropolitan. . . .

During the first intermission, my colleagues came and congratulated me. They had all been so kind and helpful. Paul Althouse said that the performance was being broadcast, and asked if I had any idea how many listeners there might be. 'Perhaps a hundred thousand,' I said, thinking I was exaggerating. 'You can figure on ten million,' he laughed. More than three times the population of Norway! That I could never have imagined.

What completely took my breath away was the tribute of the audience to me personally. I was not unfamiliar with applause, but the way the Americans showed their enthusiasm completely overwhelmed me. I felt ecstatic when it was all over, and I realized that my debut had been a success. But I was so dead tired that I only wanted to rest. My husband, Kate, and I walked back to the hotel, as fortunately no arrangements had been made to celebrate my debut.

The management of the Metropolitan no longer had any reason to smuggle their new singer onto the stage. They gave the press as much information as they could. During the four days between Kirsten's first and second performances, the Flagstad phenomenon was much discussed and written about in musical circles. Who was she? Where did she come from? What had she sung previously, and where? Everyone wanted to know as much as possible about her personal life and her earlier career. Lawrence Gilman had compared her to a former great soprano of the Metropolitan, Olive Fremstad. Would Flagstad's Isolde become as renowned as Fremstad's? People guessed, speculated and wagered.

New York heard Kirsten Flagstad's Isolde for the first time on Wednesday 6 February 1935. The 'Sold Out' sign for that performance went up the day after her debut. The other principals of the *Tristan* cast were Lauritz Melchior as Tristan, Ludwig Hofmann as King Marke, Maria Olszewska as Brangäne, and Friedrich Schorr as Kurwenal. Artur Bodanzky was again the conductor. It was not considered good form for box-holders to arrive on time, but when they learned that Kirsten Flagstad was to sing Isolde, they were there on the dot. Instead of 'the top ten' of New York society, it was now Flagstad who was the subject of discussion from box to box. The expectant atmosphere that pervaded the auditorium and the foyers had even penetrated the 'diamond horseshoe'. 'For once I was really nervous,' Kirsten noted. 'Expectations ran so high after what had been written about me since my debut that I was afraid I couldn't live up to them. Besides, Isolde is a far greater and much more difficult role than Sieglinde. While I sat waiting in my dressing-room, I felt quite shaky, but I tried to conceal it.'

Her portrayal of the Irish princess was a triumph. It was acclaimed by the audience and described in superlative terms in the press. In the *Herald Tribune* the next day, Lawrence Gilman wrote:

Last night's performance of *Tristan* at the Metropolitan was made unforgettable for its hearers by a transcendently beautiful and moving impersonation of Isolde – an embodiment so sensitively musical, so fine-grained in its imaginative and intellectual texture, so lofty in its pathos and simplicity, of so memorable a loveliness, that experienced opera-goers sought among their memories of legendary days to find its like.

They did not find it. For one of the characteristics of Mme Kirsten Flagstad's Isolde is that it is wholly individual. This remarkable Norwegian artist . . . patterns after no model or tradition in her conception of Isolde. She has her own vision of the character, one which finds its origin in the music and the poetry of Wagner's drama; and she gives it complete validity and persuasive truth. . . .

This Isolde is a young woman of royal dignity and grace, comely and girlish and grave, made desperate by the tragic passion that has enmeshed her. Afterward, she is an incarnation of poignant loveliness and ardor as the woman rapturously possessed and possessing; and finally she is the death-devoted and mystical celebrant, no longer of this earth, a creature of disembodied ecstasy.

This process of spiritual unfolding is exquisitely indicated by Mme Flagstad, with a simplicity as subtle and restrained in method as it is irresistibly moving in effect. . . . And always, throughout, Mme Flagstad is the finely musical artist who knows the significance of the words she sings, and the shape and rhythm of the musical phrases that enclose them, and the quality of the tones they need for their conveyance.

Always the voice itself is pure and noble and expressive, of a beauty that is often ravishing to the ear, and a power and clarity that are equal to every demand that is made upon it by the music.

Gilman was not alone in his assessment. Olin Downes of the *New York Times*, W. J. Henderson of the *New York Sun* and Samuel Chotzinoff of the *New York Evening Post* were among the other critics who responded to Flagstad's Isolde with words reserved for the great occasions in the musical life of the city. In his book *Written in the Sand*, the late Carl Søyland, longtime editor-in-chief of the Brooklyn-based Norwegian language newspaper, *Nordisk Tidende*, reminisced about this performance:

There were surely many opera-goers who experienced a crescendo of excitement that night. Over and above the full, rich sound of the orchestra, they listened to the new voice which soared and shone with a beauty hitherto unheard. A hurricane broke loose when the last tone died away. The audience had been at the point of explosion and had to give vent to their emotions. It was one of the unforgettable nights at the Opera.

While long queues formed at the box office as people sought to buy tickets for Flagstad's next performances, others – photographers, cosmeticians, masseurs, piano-makers – thronged to her hotel to offer her their services, exactly as Bodanzky had predicted. The hotel switchboard was jammed with calls to her suite, and the bellboys brought up box after box of flowers. Kirsten began to suspect that the American mentality was rather different from the Scandinavian, and that it might be difficult to cope with such sincere but aggressive forms of tribute if she continued to enjoy success at the Metropolitan.

Invitations of all kinds were received, and politely but firmly declined. When she realized that she was expected to be a social personality as well as an opera singer, she made it clear that she could not and would not be both. She preferred to spend her time in study and preparation of the roles she was scheduled to sing. She commented later:

> I worked and worked all the time with Mr Weigert. He was fantastically kind and patient. Words cannot describe his goodwill and helpfulness to me. Stage rehearsals with orchestra were rare, but I was given some coaching, and the staging was explained to me. My third role, the *Walküre* Brünnhilde, I had never sung before, but that also went well, I'm happy to say.
>
> After that performance on 15 February, I was all in, physically and emotionally. The intense pressure was beginning to take its toll. I was so fatigued that I became a victim of New York's perilous climate, which had played havoc with so many other singers before me. An attack of laryngitis, accompanied by a high fever, literally knocked me out. My illness forced me to withdraw from several sold-out performances, including what would have been my first *Siegfried*

Brünnhilde, on 22 February. That was the worst – to lie in bed knowing that I had to disappoint thousands of people. As soon as I had recovered enough to sing again, I appeared, this time as the *Götterdämmerung* Brünnhilde, on 28 February, my first performance of the role. But I couldn't hear a single tone, either from the orchestra or from my colleagues. The infection had also attacked my ears. I could never have carried on had I not been so fortunate as to have absolute pitch. The conductor had to give me special signs for my cues. It was a terrible time; my nerves were strained to breaking-point. For two years after that illness, my hearing was considerably impaired.

Oscar Thompson reviewed the performance of *Die Walküre* for the *New York Times*. Of the eight paragraphs in his article, six are devoted to the new soprano from Norway. After noting that Flagstad was singing the role of Brünnhilde for the first time on any stage, and singing it without the benefit of even one orchestral rehearsal, he wrote:

Some plain indications of this limited preparation aside, the Metropolitan's latest acquisition sustained the reputation she has built up, almost overnight, of being one of the most richly endowed and resourceful Wagnerian artists of the day. . . .

The voice was no less remarkable than at the singer's earlier performances. There were the same freedom and solidity in its production, the same power, the same restraint and intelligence in its use, and, when need be, the fire, that were revelations of her singing when she scored her first success. . . . Mme Flagstad's big voice is not one of those that require an orchestra under them; among her richest and most expressive phrases [in the second act] were those in which the voice stood forth alone, the tone altering its color with the words and mirroring thoughts and emotions like a mobile face.

From her first entrance in the third act, the soprano sang with a new assurance and an added splendor of voice. Brünnhilde's final appeal to Wotan was of an intensity and power, as well as a beauty of sound, to make altogether intelligible the result on Wotan's will. Other recent Brünnhildes have sounded the pathetic note quite as effectually as

117

Mme Flagstad. None has reached quite the peaks of exaltation she attained in moments of this scene.

Kirsten's colleagues in this performance were Paul Althouse as Siegmund, Maria Müller as Sieglinde, Emanuel List as Hunding, Ludwig Hofmann as Wotan, and Karin Branzell as Fricka. Artur Bodanzky conducted.

'Epic Portrayal of Brünnhilde in *Götterdämmerung* Wins Ovation for Mme Flagstad', reads the headline of Olin Downes' review in the *New York Times* of the matinée performance of the final work in Wagner's *Ring* on Thursday 28 February 1935:

. . . yesterday, as [Mme Flagstad's] Brünnhilde of *Götterdämmerung* developed, and grew to a climax of epic proportions and of the most moving tragedy, it seemed that the half of her capacities had yet to be told.

It is to be borne in mind that this was a performance undertaken after an exhausting illness, and for the first time, in that part, on any stage. The results were of a nature to be remembered by everyone present, and of a quality to remind us of the feebleness of most contemporaneous musical effort, creative or interpretative as may be. Because for once, a truly magnificent voice and a nature to feel profoundly and communicate with surpassing sincerity and vision the greatness of Wagner had materialized. The effort was to restore certain gigantic manifestations of art to their proper proportions in the observer's consciousness, and these proportions, these rich and tremendous utterances, made a good deal of our contemporaneous expressions appear fussy, petty and pretentious. . . . [Mme Flagstad's voice] is a trained instrument of almost endless resource, equal to a first act of *Götterdämmerung* with the Siegfried duet, and the tremendous drama of the second act, with the curse uttered on the spear-head, and the all-encompassing final scene. . . .

The interpretation rose, as steadily as the music-drama itself, to the moment when Brünnhilde stands revealed, the instrument for the final sacrifice, sybil and prophetess of the destruction of the gods.

No one who saw it will forget that entrance, the apostrophe to what had been and was to be; the tender homage to the fallen hero; the majesty of the gesture that commanded the preparation of the funeral pyre; the realization by her to whom at last everything was revealed of the inevitable end, and the cleansing atonement that it was her destiny to proffer.

The performance was conducted by Artur Bodanzky, and the noteworthy cast included Lauritz Melchior as Siegfried, Friedrich Schorr as Gunther, Emanuel List as Hagen, Editha Fleischer as Gutrune, and Karin Branzell as Waltraute.

When Kirsten Flagstad arrived on the scene, the Metropolitan Opera had been in the throes of a severe financial crisis. The first years of the Depression and President Roosevelt's 'New Deal' had had a disastrous effect on opera attendance. Time and again the shareholders had been called upon to contribute huge sums of money to keep the operatic ship afloat. Then, with one stroke, the picture changed. The Opera House was filled to capacity every time Flagstad sang. The seventeen sold-out performances in which she appeared that first season, in New York and on tour, following her debut, brought the Metropolitan its largest income for many years. She also took part in three Sunday evening gala concerts, and in the gala performance for Giulio Gatti-Casazza on 19 March 1935.

Following her first four roles at the Metropolitan, Kirsten sang Elisabeth in *Tannhäuser* and Elsa in *Lohengrin*. Of her portrayal of Elisabeth on 15 March Oscar Thompson wrote the next day in the *New York Times*:

> . . . it had the now familiar splendor of voice in 'Dich teure Halle' and in moments of the scene with Tannhäuser . . . [it] was of rare poignancy in its disclosure of the emotions with which Elisabeth was stirred. . . .
>
> It was not in [the] lyric passages, however . . . that Mme Flagstad contributed that which was truly memorable in this performance. The great finale of the Wartburg scene was her triumph. Though the ensemble has been better achieved in some of its particulars, the soprano's dominance of it was of thrilling pathos and power. There were moments as of a kind of transfiguration, not only in her singing but her appearance . . . Her entrance between the swords was not more compelling to the eye than the picture of mute anguish she presented, her face hidden in her sleeve, her body slumped

upon the throne, before she flung herself among the raging men.

Lauritz Melchior sang the title role, and the cast included Karin Branzell as Venus, Friedrich Schorr as Wolfram and Emanuel List as the Landgrave. Bodanzky conducted.

Olin Downes reviewed in the *New York Times* the 18 March performance of *Lohengrin* in which Kirsten sang her first Elsa at the Metropolitan (she had already sung the role in Brooklyn on 5 March):

> Mme Flagstad's Elsa is beautifully and earnestly conceived, although the role does not call out her greatest qualities as singer or interpreter. She began the recital of the dream with a singular effect of intimacy and introspection. The climax when it came rang in her tones, a triumph of faith and a kindling pronouncement that heralded inevitably the appearance of the rescuing knight. This fine scale of values obtained all through the performance and gave the more effect to dramatic outbursts when the voice was sheer white flame and the woman and artist was revealed at her full height as a great interpreter.

Bodanzky conducted the performance, with Melchior as Lohengrin, Branzell as Ortrud, Schorr as Telramund and Ludwig Hofmann as King Henry.

Kirsten was asked to prepare Kundry in *Parsifal* as soon as she could. They did not ask *if* she could learn the role, merely *how soon*. 'Ask Mr Weigert,' she answered. 'He is the only one who can tell you that.' (She had merely glanced at the part earlier, and had said to herself that she could not possibly manage to learn it.) Weigert thought that perhaps Kirsten could sing Kundry after several weeks of intensive study. She sighed resignedly, and set about learning what she considered to be the most difficult female role Wagner had created. Eleven days after her first session with Weigert, he could report to the general manager that Mme Flagstad had mastered the role, at least vocally.

The public, who had made her their absolute favourite, were equally enthusiastic no matter what she sang, but some of the reviewers, who by now knew her musical qualifications, began to look for more variation in her acting. They wrote that she seemed stiff, that she did not act enough. Kirsten reflected:

I suppose they were right when they said that. In part it was on purpose that I didn't move a great deal. I hoped in this way to give the Wagnerian characters the dignity I felt Wagner had given them in his music. In part, too, it was because of the severe pressure of work. I simply couldn't handle more than the musical requirements. When I learned a part in New York, I also studied all the other parts in the opera because I had to know the entire *mise en scène*. If, at the Metropolitan, we had had stage rehearsals before the first performance, as was the custom in Europe, I would not have had to learn more than my own part.

In the beginning I listened to the others and tried to surmise their intentions so that gradually there could be a real ensemble. When I wasn't singing, I listened to everyone intently. Only after I had sung a part several times could I hope to fully portray the character. If, in my first season at the Metropolitan, I had attempted to delve into my roles psychologically, I would surely have collapsed. I had to undertake the study of a role and its presentation on the stage as a job that had to be done, and to do that job as well as I could.

Kirsten Flagstad sang Kundry in *Parsifal* for the first time on Wednesday 17 April 1935, during the series of post-season performances at the Metropolitan. Her colleagues included Melchior in the title role, Schorr as Amfortas, List as Gurnemanz and Gustav Schützendorf as Klingsor, with Bodanzky again on the podium.

The following day, in the *New York Times*, Olin Downes wrote of

. . . the astonishing effect of Mme Flagstad's performance. Astonishing if only for the reason that Mme Flagstad took this, the most enigmatic of Wagnerian women's parts, for the first time on any stage, and presented it with a distinction, an eloquence of gesture and song, and a conviction which would have implied long acquaintance with the role. . . . In the last decade in New York no Kundry has approached in significance and glory of song the interpretation of last night.

. . . Mme Flagstad did not attempt a new and unheard-of treatment of the character, or try to conceal and palliate her inexperience by any far-fetched devices. She followed Wagner's text and Wagner's directions implicitly, carrying

121

them out in spirit and in letter. The fact that she sang the part
with the same superb wealth of resource and ease of execution
as she has sung the other big Wagnerian roles was one of the
features of the occasion. Another was that she not only sang
magnificently, but characterized by the color as well as the
quality of the tone. . . .

Then there was the plasticity of the acting and the subtlety of
the conception, at one with the composer's. . . . Here is the
apotheosis of the Venus of *Tannhäuser*, with new overtones
and sophistications. Simple as Mme Flagstad is always,
unpretending in her directness and sincerity as an actress, she
caught these overtones, and developed her second act to a
wonderful climax.

There was a second performance on 19 April. Lawrence Gilman's
article in the *Herald Tribune* the following day was devoted to
Kirsten Flagstad's portrayal of Kundry and her overall accomplish-
ment during the eleven weeks since her debut:

The Metropolitan opera season . . . came to an unofficial and
definitive close at yesterday's special Good Friday matinée,
with a performance of *Parsifal* made unforgettable by the
Kundry of Kirsten Flagstad. . . . She embodied [the role] . . .
with a perfection of imaginative rectitude, a transilluminating
beauty and intensity, that searched the heart of Wagner's
music and his drama and left them, for sensitive observers,
newly revealed and overwhelming. . . .

Thus ends a musico-dramatic saga of personal achievement
which would be difficult to match. . . . In each of [the seven]
formidable roles [she sang] she has disclosed significances that
had long been disregarded, implications that had been forgotten or undisclosed. . . . She has illuminated depths,
extracted essences, intensified meanings. She has left each
character that she embodied more veracious and moving and
significant than it had been before. She has touched nothing
that she has not exalted and enriched and deepened by her
imaginative penetration, her ennobling and exquisite art, her
consecrational devoutness as an artist.

She has restored an old tradition and created a new one. She
has reminded us that consummate musicianship and the
utmost beauty of delivered song are not alien to dramatic

truth, but its deepest source and its most perfect instrument. . . . And she taught us a new tradition and new esthetic
gospel: that acting is . . . a process of inner sculpturing upon
the outward form, a lighting and intensification from within.

Yesterday, in that third act of *Parsifal* which is so cruel a test
for any actress, she stood for long moments, motionless, in the
rough garments of Kundry the penitent, grave and sad and
inarticulate, looking backward through the ages and her many
pasts. She made no gesture, no change of pose, she scarcely
moved her head; yet in the pose itself, in the vision within the
eyes, in the contour and plane and pallor of the beautiful
profile, she gave us a poignant sense of that eternal moment in
which the spirit rests in its pilgrimage that is outside of time –
she gave us the nameless tragedy and grief and loneliness of
Kundry, the woman of uncounted incarnations, the symbol of
Nature and of life itself.

Yet her gift as an actress is not only for this intensification of
repose. At that moment when Kundry is summoned by
Klingsor from the gulf of sleep and time and endlessly
recurrent death, her tearing cry as she awakens to the
realization of her endless task had all the anguish of
rebirth. . . .

Always, since first she came among us, she has made us
marvel as we beheld 'the thing itself, as in its image it
transformed itself'.

After a whirlwind trip to Detroit for an Easter Sunday evening
radio broadcast on 21 April, Kirsten presented her first recital in
America, for a New York charity, on the 23rd. The next day she
sailed for Norway on the *Stavangerfjord*. She had in her possession
the only signed contract for the Metropolitan's 1935–6 season. She
also took with her some songs by American composers recommended by Edwin McArthur, the twenty-seven-year-old American
pianist, to consider in preparing four recital programmes for a
planned concert tour in the United States and Canada in the
autumn. McArthur, whose letter of application was the first to
reach her after her Metropolitan debut, and whom she had
auditioned on the advice of Marks Levine, her manager, was to be
her accompanist on the tour.

Her presence on board ship created a stir, and when she arrived home, she was continuously fêted and honoured. King Haakon presented her with the Medal of Honour in gold, in recognition of the renown that her achievement had brought to Norway. As soon as all the hubbub had died down, Kirsten tried to unwind and let the fatigue and tension that had built up in her over the last four months drain out of her mind and body; she was so on edge that the slightest disturbance made her cry. After a few weeks of relaxation she began to regain her equilibrium. One day she sat down at the piano and began to play through a volume of Schubert Lieder. The lovely melodies lifted her spirits, and she began to hum the vocal lines. Soon she was singing one song after another to her own accompaniment. And then suddenly she stopped. She realized at that moment that singing Wagner for three months had so increased the size of her voice that she was finding it difficult to achieve the flexibility required to interpret the intimate moods of the Lieder: 'I soon discovered that it would take more hard work than I had imagined to polish the songs I had sung all my life, to master them so that they could be presented from a concert platform.'

On Friday 12 July 1935, Kirsten Flagstad celebrated her fortieth birthday, surrounded by her family. The world of Wagner, of fame, of reporters and of aggressive admirers seemed mercifully far away.

Gatti-Casazza was succeeded upon his retirement as general manager of the Metropolitan by Herbert Witherspoon, an American, who had been an operatic basso and a member of the faculty of the Juilliard School of Music. In May 1935 Witherspoon was stricken in his office with a heart attack, and died. One of his associates, the Canadian-born tenor Edward Johnson, who had had a distinguished career on the operatic stage, was named to succeed him.

Johnson immediately began to set in motion some of his own ideas for the coming season. He decided to capitalize on Kirsten Flagstad's popularity by presenting her in a new role, one entirely different in style from the Wagnerian roles in which she had triumphed: the title role in *Norma*, Vincenzo Bellini's great opera. He hoped she would score as great a success as Norma as she had as

Isolde. In a telegram, he asked her to study the part during the summer.

Kirsten had sung leading roles in quite a few Italian operas, but she had always sung them in Norwegian or Swedish. She was not really familiar with the Italian bel canto style. Nevertheless, she began to study the Bellini role with her usual dedication and attention to detail. The music had such a limpid, flowing quality that she fell in love with it. She would be prepared to sing it in an audition for the general manager and his staff when she returned to New York in late September.

This time Else was to accompany her mother to New York. Kirsten would try to place her fifteen-year-old daughter in a school in the vicinity, so that they could see each other as often as possible. She looked forward to showing Else the great city, and to Else's seeing for herself what success her mother enjoyed at the Metropolitan. 'When I told her that a flower had been named after me, a lily of the amaryllis family, she was really impressed. The lily is here at my home, and it blooms in April. But I have so seldom been home in April that I have seen it bloom only a few times,' Kirsten recollected. A dahlia was also named after her. Under the heading 'Michell's Top-Quality Dahlias, Decorative Types', in a catalogue of about 1950 from Michell's Garden Store, Philadelphia, is the following entry: 'Kirsten Flagstad. ID [Informal Decorative]. Rich gold suffused lightly with apricot. Blooms very early and continuously throughout the season.' This poet of the catalogue was evidently clairvoyant as well.

When Kirsten and Else arrived in New York on 26 September 1935, Kirsten immediately requested a meeting with Edward Johnson. She told him she would be glad to sing through the part of Norma so that the music staff of the Italian repertoire could form an opinion on her suitability for the role. If they were pleased, she would ask them to advise her on preparing it for performance.

Her Norma was well received, but the conductor, Ettore Panizza, felt that she would benefit from going through the part with the Italian coach, Riccardo Dellera. The first thing he asked Kirsten to do was to disregard all tempi indicated in the score. 'In Italy, it is traditional for singers to put in their own glissandi, tremolandi and other embellishments,' he explained. 'And the last note of a passage must be held much longer than the composer has marked.'

If there was anything Kirsten Flagstad disliked, it was 'thinking up' something the composer had not indicated. She had never held a note so much as a half-beat longer than the composer had specified. Her intonation was perfect; she slid neither up nor down. And now she was being asked to prepare a role in a way she thought was a veritable travesty of the composer's wishes. After working with Dellera for three hours, she had lost all desire to sing Norma. She asked Edward Johnson to excuse her from singing it, and to her relief, he agreed. He never again asked her to sing a role from the Italian repertoire. She remained with Wagner and Beethoven.

I asked Arthur Dusenberry, during our conversation in 1981, about Kirsten Flagstad's relationship with the management of the Metropolitan before the war, and he told me:

Kirsten really would have enjoyed performing in works other than those by Wagner, but the management wouldn't hear of it because the public wanted to hear her in the Wagner roles and was willing to buy out the house, even at premium prices, to hear her as Isolde, Brünnhilde and the other Wagner heroines. Of course, she did sing Leonore in Beethoven's *Fidelio*, but it wasn't until 1952, after Mr Bing [Rudolf Bing, Edward Johnson's successor as general manager] had invited her back to the Metropolitan after the war, that she was able to sing one of the great classical roles, Alcestis in the Gluck opera. It was their loss that American audiences never heard and saw her in some of the roles she had sung in her earlier Scandinavian career, such as Rodelinda, Agathe in *Der Freischütz*, Aïda and Tosca. But the politics and economics of opera production in this country at that time, and the various managements' no doubt necessary obeisance to both, wouldn't permit it. It's true that Edward Johnson wanted her to sing Norma at the Metropolitan during the 1935–6 season, but Kirsten did not feel comfortable with that role. From what I've read, the situation is different today: outstanding singers are given opportunities to broaden their artistic bases.

Else was enrolled in an excellent girls' school half an hour's ride from New York. The school had its own box at the Metropolitan, so Else could be present whenever her mother sang there. But before that, she accompanied her to Worcester, Massachusetts, for a concert there on 4 October 1935, opening the three-month concert tour.

Kirsten was anxious to find out how she would be received by an American concert audience. She found it much more demanding to stand alone on a stage and hold the listeners' attention for several hours than to take part in an opera. After all that had been written about her since her success at the Metropolitan, expectations were running almost too high.

When she walked on stage at the concert hall in Worcester, she was greeted with thunderous applause from a full house. After acknowledging the welcome, she took her place by the grand piano, her right hand resting lightly on the instrument, while her left arm hung relaxed at her side. And thus she stood, almost motionless, throughout the concert. In the beginning, the American audiences were surprised by this complete serenity and control, accustomed as they were to the grand manner of many divas on the concert platform. But when Kirsten's voice filled each hall with a beauty of tone hitherto unheard, full of expression from the softest pianissimo to the most powerful forte, they succumbed completely, just as the Metropolitan audiences had.

Judging by the enthusiastic public acclaim, Kirsten's first concert tour was an unqualified triumph. The music critics, however, were not of one mind. Some praised her performances to the skies, but others found her approach too calm, too passionless to aptly express the moods of the songs, especially the German Lieder. They mainly felt that what was lacking was artistic comprehension of and insight into the texts. Kirsten did not disagree with them:

The reviewers were quite right in saying that I did not fully convey the moods of the songs. To become an accomplished Lieder singer requires nearly a lifetime of dedication. This matter of being able to interpret the 'soul' of a song – well, I don't like the expression, but I don't know any other word that conveys what I want to say – is, in my opinion, a singer's real goal. Before one steps out onto a stage or a platform, the vocal technique must be solid and completely dependable.

Meeting the American concert public was a wonderful experience. We Europeans have little cause to shrug our shoulders about American taste. We assume that superficial art dominates, but nothing could be further from the truth. I

127

think that in many ways the Americans are ahead of the Europeans when it comes to musical training. Young and old take music courses. The universities, where I often sang, have outstanding music departments. The Americans were knowledgeable about European composers, both classical and modern. At first I had only familiar songs on my programme, but then I grew bolder and replaced them with others that I particularly loved, without taking into consideration that they were less familiar. It turned out to be just the right thing to do; the Americans like to hear new works.

Edwin McArthur was a real find. He played everything, including the Norwegian songs, from memory, and was an altogether remarkable accompanist. Outside the concert hall, he was the best helper I could have found. He looked after me so well that I became quite spoiled!

On the first concert tour, McArthur introduced a little ritual to which he and Kirsten always adhered during the seventeen years they worked together. One hour before the concert, he would arrive at her hotel. While she put the finishing touches to her gown and make-up in her bedroom, he would seat himself at the piano in the living-room and play popular music of all kinds. Once in a while he would sing the text in a voice that he himself described as 'dreadful'. Kirsten found that listening to the light music put her in a good mood, and helped her to relax before the concert. When he had played five or six popular songs of the day, she would come in, saying with a smile, 'I love to hear those melodies; now I am ready to go.' From the time she was a teenager, Kirsten had enjoyed popular music, and when the day's practising was over, she used to sneak in time to play and sing the latest songs. Safely out of the range of Maja's eagle eye, she would even sing them at parties, with great success.

After the first concert, Kirsten initiated Edwin McArthur into the fine art of opening a bottle of champagne. When he had tried to open it with a corkscrew, Kirsten had laughed, taken the bottle from him, and deftly opened it. As she handed it back to him, she said, 'Edwin, to know how to open a bottle of champagne is just as important for you as to know how to play!' As a reward after a successful concert, she would treat herself to several glasses.

Before and after concerts, Kirsten wanted to be alone in her dressing-room and have no visitors. It became McArthur's job to see that she was not disturbed, and he followed her orders so explicitly that he even made enemies of old music friends. But when she said 'no one', he knew she meant it. She noted later:

> I know I was severely criticized for my need to isolate myself before and after performances, but I could not concentrate and be sociable at the same time. Those who wished to express their enthusiasm often forgot that I was under great pressure to do my best. Afterwards, when I had given all I had, I was so exhausted that I simply *had* to rest for a while so that I could pull myself together. If only the public had understood that I met them as an artist, not as a private person. Gradually they did begin to understand, but on my first concert tour my penchant for isolation was the cause of much unpleasantness. When I was on the stage or on the platform, there was complete rapport between me and my public, but otherwise I really disappointed them, I'm afraid.

The concert tour ended with a recital at Carnegie Hall in New York on 11 December 1935. For the first time she stood in front of the audience which, in years to come, she was to call 'my special one'. Carnegie Hall, with its marvellous acoustics, also became the American concert hall that she loved the most. It was soon an unbreakable rule that she end every concert season with one or more recitals there. Most of them were for charity, and her performances on that stage brought in enormous sums for a great variety of causes.

The first time she sang from this world-renowned platform, she was greeted by an overflow audience of distinguished people who gave her a standing ovation. Else, who had come from school to stay with her mother at her hotel during the Christmas holiday, had not yet fully realized that Kirsten Flagstad was a musical sensation. The reception she was accorded in Carnegie Hall almost took the girl's breath away.

Kirsten made her San Francisco Opera debut on the stage of the War Memorial Opera House on Monday 4 November 1935, as Brünnhilde in *Die Walküre* in the company's first presentation of the complete *Ring* cycle. And it was there, two days later, that she sang the *Siegfried* Brünnhilde for the first time in her career. This period in San Francisco was memorable for her personally, too, for she met the woman who was to become her closest friend in America, Caroline Lilienthal Esberg.

Kirsten's second season at the Metropolitan began auspiciously with Isolde on 30 December. The audience, and most of the critics, agreed that her voice, even after a long and strenuous concert tour, sounded as fresh, free and radiant as it had the previous season. Kirsten said later:

> I was working all the time, but such is an artist's life. You don't decide for yourself how many concerts or opera performances you will sing. It's the people who want to hear them who set the tempo. And, of course, the managers, who want to take advantage of an artist's popularity. I only had to make sure that my schedule was accurate and up-to-date. I have to smile when people say, 'How wonderful it must be to be a singer, to go travelling around and be fêted and adored.' They forget what lies behind all this – years of hard work and self-denial. It is an artist's obligation to appear before the public rested, relaxed, ready to give his best. But that doesn't come about by chance.
>
> I had to rest whenever I had the opportunity. Even on stage, during a performance, I could find time for a little rest. In Act One of *Parsifal* there are long passages in which Kundry, lying on the ground, doesn't sing. I had learned the part in record time, so I wasn't as secure as I should have been, and on stage I had to concentrate completely whenever I was singing. In between, I saw my chance to relax. Once I nearly got into trouble. I simply fell asleep on the stage – slept for almost a quarter of an hour, and woke up just seconds before I had to sing again. That's how exhausted we can become!

Kirsten Flagstad sang Leonore in Beethoven's *Fidelio* for the first time at the Metropolitan on Saturday 7 March 1936. Lawrence Gilman, who reviewed the performance for the *Herald Tribune*, wrote:

> Perhaps yesterday's demonstrative audience had been a bit anxious to learn whether Flagstad could triumph in any other role than a Wagnerian one. They learned that she can. For this proved to be a Leonore conceived in that great tradition of simplicity and subtlety and restraint and eloquent repose of

style which Mme Flagstad herself had established in her Metropolitan performances. There were no mechanical and semaphoric posturings, no meaningless flinging out of arms and fatuous stridings to and fro. There was instead the constant use of pose and movement and facial change to indicate essential things in the simplest and most concentrated way. . . .

Her singing of the music was at all times nobly beautiful, thrilling in its sweep of line and fervor in such heroic outbursts as the concluding allegro section of the great aria, where (despite a momentary lapse of memory) she took us to the heights of Leonore's fortitude and faith.

The performance was conducted by Bodanzky, and the other principals were René Maison as Florestan, Ludwig Hofmann as Don Pizarro, Emanuel List as Rocco, Editha Fleischer as Marzelline, Hans Clemens as Jaquino, and Julius Huehn as Don Fernando.

The Metropolitan's 1935–6 season is also remembered for appearances by two other dramatic sopranos, one for the first time and one for the last. On 18 December 1935 the Australian soprano Marjorie Lawrence made her debut as Brünnhilde in *Die Walküre*, and on 29 February 1936 Florence Easton, the English-born Canadian soprano, a versatile artist who had been a regular member of the company from 1917 to 1929, returned at the age of fifty-one to make her farewell appearance in the same role.

Marjorie Lawrence was at the peak of her illustrious career in June 1941 when she was struck down by poliomyelitis. Her determination to surmount the disabling effects of the disease resulted in her return to the operatic stage, in North America and Europe, on a limited basis, from December 1942 to December 1946.

Kirsten Flagstad added two Wagner roles to her Metropolitan repertoire during the 1936–7 season: Senta in *Der fliegende Holländer*, which she sang for the first time in her career on Thursday 7 January 1937; and the *Siegfried* Brünnhilde, which she sang for the first time in New York on Friday 22 January.

Olin Downes reviewed the *Holländer* performance in the *New York Times* the next day:

This writer never heard the ballade presented so movingly and with such quality of imagination. There was the woman of Wagner's imagining, whose soul hovers between two worlds,

131

whose fate is known to herself alone; who waits, as one preordained, for the moment of her destiny.

The first call which ushers in the recital, that wild evocation associated with the thought of the accursed sea-wanderer, was sung, for once, as the composer intended: not as a whoop to the gallery, but softly, eerily in the opening phrases, almost in a disembodied tone.

Then commenced the tale of the ship with black masts and the blood-red sails which sweeps the ocean. . . . This was the wild preluding. Then came the change from the minor to the major tonality and the magnificently conceived contrast of mood and of the very sonority of the voice, with the 'piu lento' passage – the music which clothes the words of Senta that deal with her version of the one way to the Dutchman's re-demption. Word and tone, inflection and vocal mechanism in this lofty invocation were nobly one.

The cast included Schorr as the Dutchman; Kerstin Thorborg, the Swedish mezzo-soprano who had made her Metropolitan debut the month before, as Mary; Charles Kullmann as Erik, Emanuel List as Daland, and Hans Clemens as the Steersman. Artur Bodanzky conducted.

The *Herald Tribune* carried Lawrence Gilman's appraisal of the *Siegfried* performance in its columns on 23 January:

When Kirsten Flagstad sang her first *Siegfried* Brünnhilde last evening at the Metropolitan, she set before us one of the greatest of her numerous great achievements in the revelation of noble and heroic beauty. She sang the role more than a year ago in San Francisco, but her devoted New York public . . . was obliged to wait until last night to witness an impersonation which makes all possible comparisons seem futile and preposterous.

From the moment that she rose up on her couch and looked about her, raising her arms in greeting to the sun, the light, the day . . . she was the visual and aural image of Wagner's tonal poetry. The beauty and fidelity of the presented image – the noble loveliness of the radiant face, the gestures of touching simplicity, dignity, naturalness, and grace, the pealing splendor and purity of the matchless voice – these were living symbols of the rapture and majesty and tenderness of Wagner's creative thought.

Melchior appeared as Siegfried, Schorr as the Wanderer, Thorborg as Erda and List as Fafner, with Karl Laufkoetter as Mime, Eduard Habich as Alberich, and Stella Andreva as the Forest Bird. Bodanzky was again at the helm.

The nine Wagner roles and the Beethoven role that Kirsten Flagstad sang in her first three seasons at the Metropolitan were the only ones she sang there, or elsewhere in the United States or Europe, before her return to Norway in the spring of 1941.

On Monday 18 May 1936, she had made her debut at London's Covent Garden as Isolde, with Fritz Reiner on the podium, and she had gone on to sing the three Brünnhildes in a *Ring* cycle conducted by Sir Thomas Beecham. She had also presented a song recital in Queen's Hall, with Ivor Newton, the distinguished English accompanist, at the piano. After a combined holiday and study period in Sweden in the summer – Sweden, because she was having a dispute with the tax authorities in Norway – she had travelled to Vienna to sing Isolde and the three Brünnhildes, then to Prague to sing the *Walküre* Brünnhilde and Isolde. Critical opinion in all three cities had been, generally speaking, the same: her singing was glorious, but her temperament was phlegmatic. Only with her portrayal of the *Götterdämmerung* Brünnhilde had she roused the gentlemen of the press to enthusiasm.

In the spring of 1937, when England was celebrating the coronation of King George VI and Queen Elizabeth, Kirsten returned to London to take part in the gala Coronation Season at Covent Garden. She sang Isolde under Beecham, the three Brünnhildes under Wilhelm Furtwängler, and Senta under Reiner.

Her husband, Henry Johansen, and her daughter, Else, joined her in London. Else had returned to Norway in the summer of 1936 to see her father, Sigurd Hall, and had remained in Norway except for a brief visit to New York during the Christmas holiday season to spend some time with her mother. One of the sources of Kirsten Flagstad's strength was the happiness she had found in her second marriage. Johansen was a man on whom she could lean in all the vicissitudes of life. In her innermost soul she yearned to be just a good wife and mother. But, as we have seen, her great gift craved expression. Her husband understood this perhaps better than she did – at least at the beginning of her world career. He encouraged her to go on, and when time permitted, he accompanied her on her travels.

At the behest of the Oslo Journalists' Club, Kirsten agreed to sing in a concert with orchestra in the Frogner Park Stadium on 8 July 1937, four days before her forty-second birthday. More than ten thousand people had booked seats, and about three thousand more had purchased standing room. When the gates closed, the nearby streets were alive with people, and the 'free-seat-hill' overlooking the stadium was absolutely packed. On the shell-shaped stage sat the orchestra, eighty-five men strong. Kirsten's brother Ole, who was now a successful cellist, was the conductor for the evening. The royal family, who were warm admirers of Flagstad and had always attended her concerts in Oslo, were present on this occasion also.

The concert was a triumph. The enthusiasm of the audience increased with each selection. After the final storm of applause, there stood Kirsten Flagstad with the laurel wreath of the Journalists' Club around her neck and a mountain of flowers at her feet, visibly moved by the ovation, which simply would not abate. Finally she raised her hand, and said with deep emotion: 'I had looked forward with such joy to coming home this time and singing for all of you. But what has happened here tonight has exceeded all my expectations. A thousand thanks to all of you!'

King Haakon and Queen Maud rose and approached the stage, reaching up to Kirsten to thank her for the concert. Kirsten kept the telegram she received later from Queen Maud:

> Fru Kirsten Flagstad
> Tidemandsgate 6,
> Oslo.
>
> A thousand thanks for the beautiful flowers.
> I was so enthralled by your wonderful singing.
>
> Maud

Kirsten and Ole were to be the guests of honour of the Journalists' Club at a celebration in the Grand Hotel following the concert. The management had arranged a truly royal escort for them from the Frogner Park Stadium. With two mounted policemen in front of the car to lead the way through the tightly packed crowd, and two more behind, Norway's 'Queen of Song' and her brother were driven slowly through the streets of Oslo in the mild summer night. 'This is just about the most thrilling experience of my life,' she said to Ole.

A few weeks after the concert, Kirsten received a letter from the palace. His Majesty King Haakon vii had named her Knight of the Royal Order of St Olav, 'for meritorious artistic service'. The Oslo papers broke the news with bold headlines. Flowers, letters and telegrams streamed into Tidemand Street, where her family had gathered to celebrate the event. Maja Flagstad could not hold back her tears, so moved was she that such an honour had been bestowed upon a Flagstad. She thought how sad it was that Michael had not lived to see how far his 'little girl' had come. When he died in 1930, Kirsten was already a recognized singer but had not yet sung outside Scandinavia. 'This would have been a great day for your Father, Kirsten,' she whispered.

Less than a week after the Frogner Park concert, Else abruptly announced that she wanted to live with her father. She packed her things and left her stepfather's home. Kirsten was thunderstruck. While she was aware that her divorce from Else's father, her subsequent remarriage and the burgeoning of her singing career had imposed a strain upon her daughter, she had no idea that the accumulated effects of these events on Else's life had reached crisis point. Now she reproached herself bitterly for allowing the development of her career to assume precedence over her family responsibilities. She resolved to stop working as soon as her contractual agreements would permit, and to devote herself entirely to the needs and well-being of her family. 'I can no longer stand these goodbyes, having to leave my home and those dearest to me, having to live out of a suitcase and under terrible pressures for months and even years on end,' she said. 'I have already informed the Metropolitan that when my contract expires in 1939 I intend to retire.'

As she did so often in a crisis, Kirsten once again managed to display a more or less carefree countenance to the world. But she no longer found any joy in performing; she was no longer the hearty, open soul who took all obstacles in her stride. The artist's life had become a burden. Else had not written a word since she left home.

The deeply introspective facet of Kirsten's personality became predominant at this time. She withdrew into herself and shunned, as far as she could, all social life. Those closest to her found her difficult to get on with, and in artistic circles she was presumed to have taken on the airs of a prima donna. Nevertheless, she did not neglect her work; in fact, her unhappiness seemed to give her voice and her acting a new depth. On the stage and on the concert platform, she achieved the sublime. But when the performance was over, she sat alone in her hotel room and played game after game of patience, 'until the music stops in my head and I can fall asleep'.

> It was a shame for both me and my public that I felt such a need to be by myself, especially during those years when, as an artist, I was at my peak. I did finally realize that an artist is 'public property'. It really was part of my work to enjoy being the centre of attention, but I couldn't face it – not in the state of mind I was in then. I didn't want to be recognized in the street, at the opera or in restaurants. The only place where I felt secure was at the cinema. I went in when the cinema was dark, after the picture had started, and hurried out as soon as it was over. While I sat watching what was happening on the screen, I got rid of my gnawing thoughts. Films and patience were my best friends.

The year 1938 was a singular one in the life and career of Kirsten Flagstad, for in the course of it she appeared on the silver screen, welcomed her mother and her sister to New York, embarked on a concert tour of Hawaii and Australia from May until August, and celebrated the twenty-fifth anniversary of her debut on the operatic stage with a party for the entire Metropolitan Opera family.

The Big Broadcast of 1938, one in a series of musical extravaganzas released by Paramount Pictures, opened in New York on 9 March 1938. Kirsten appeared in a specially staged sequence, singing Brünnhilde's Battle Cry from Act Two of *Die Walküre*. The necessary work had been completed during a two-day stint in Paramount's Long Island studio, just before she sailed for England in the spring of 1937. She enjoyed it enormously:

> What a job it was, but what fun! Both days we started at seven in the morning. Since the sessions involved only me, there were, as far as I was concerned, practically no breaks. We worked until almost ten o'clock at night.
>   The first day the music was recorded. The orchestra played and I sang the 'Hojo-to-ho' over and over again, until

everything was right. Once in a while the orchestra took a break, because the brass players, especially, had to rest. Meanwhile, I was sent into another room where I listened to the playback. Then came more work with the orchestra.

For the film, Paramount had a magnificent Valkyrie costume made for me which I later received as a gift. The Battle Cry scene was filmed the following day. I mimed the action to the sound of the pre-recorded music, which was then dubbed in on the sound track. I received a very nice letter from the producer, Mr Harlan Thompson. He thanked me for being patient and cooperative. I also received a big bouquet of flowers, and with it the highest fee I have ever received for two days' work: $20,000. I thought that was an absurdly large amount in relation to my contribution – but of course, I accepted it.

Kirsten had asked the Metropolitan's costumier, N. L. Lanzilotti, to go with her to the Paramount studio on Long Island to help her with her costume. Lanzilotti knew all the stars' good – and not so good – features. He told a reporter in 1938:

Kirsten Flagstad is the greatest artist the Metropolitan has had in many years, and the easiest to get along with. There is never any fuss with Madame Flagstad. She is always pleasant and cheerful – a lady you are proud to know.

The film crew in the Long Island studio sat her up on a headless wooden horse, and two stagehands stood below rocking it while she sang at the top of her voice. I could name at least half a dozen singers who would have protested vehemently against such treatment, but Flagstad merely laughed. She had no idea what it was all about, but she thought it was fun. She laughed so hard she cried. They had to stop filming until she had laughed herself out. When they were all through, the director explained that there would be a double exposure so that Flagstad would appear to be on a real horse. There's no doubt about it, Flagstad is fabulous. She is kind and well balanced, and a really good person.

In the end, though, the horse idea was dropped and she sang standing on the Valkyrie rock.

Kirsten had long wished to bring her mother and sister over to America to stay with her for a while. So now, when she felt lonelier than ever before, she begged them to come for a month's visit. Maja and Karen Marie arrived in New York on 12 March 1938. Kirsten's spirits improved immediately. She looked forward to showing them round and having them present at her stage triumphs.

When the *Stavangerfjord* docked in New York, newspapermen were on hand to interview Kirsten's family. Karen Marie was shy about expressing herself in English, so she left the talking to her mother. Maja was like a fish in water, chatting away amiably with the newsmen in far from perfect English. Language difficulties never caused her any embarrassment. To Kirsten's delight, her mother, who had charm in abundance, talked and gestured her way right into American hearts.

The same day that her mother and sister arrived in New York, Kirsten was scheduled to sing an evening performance of *Siegfried* at the Metropolitan and had arranged for them to have tickets. As Maja and Karen Marie were walking down the aisle to their seats, people smiled and waved at them: they recognized Flagstad's family. Just as she was about to sit down, Maja realized that she had forgotten to get programmes. 'Please go out and buy them, Karen Marie, before the lights go down,' she said. But Karen Marie was bashful about walking up the aisle alone and asked to be excused. Resolutely, Maja turned to a gentleman behind her and said in her strong voice: 'Programme!' He jumped up, ran out, and hurried back with a programme which he presented to Maja with gallant courtesy. When she wanted to pay for it, as was customary in Europe, he smiled and shook his head. Maja beamed proudly at Karen Marie, who sank down as far as she could in her seat.

When Kirsten heard about the incident, she laughed, hugged her mother and said, 'Mother, you're a real character! Now that gentleman will probably think he knows me personally, just because he gave Flagstad's mother a programme. You really must be more careful. You don't realize that Americans feel they "own" an artist – and the artist's family, too, for that matter.'

She was right: everyone wanted to meet 'Flagstad's mother'. Invitations poured in, and as a result, during the visit Kirsten herself became a little more sociable. She went along to a few big parties where hundreds of people had assembled to greet the guests of honour. Maja soon learned that the magic words 'Flagstad's Mother', or, as she herself said with her heavy Norwegian accent, 'Flagstad Modder', opened all doors.

At one performance at the Metropolitan, Kirsten had arranged for Karen Marie to come backstage to her dressing-room during an intermission. Maja had said that she preferred to stay in her seat, but a few minutes later there was a knock on the door, and there stood Maja, smiling proudly. 'How did you manage to find your way here alone? And how in the world did you get past that giant of a man who guards the stage door?' asked Kirsten in astonishment. 'Oh, blah, that was nothing,' exulted Maja. 'I was shown the right way by lots of nice people, and when the man wanted to stop me, I just said, 'Flagstad Modder', and he opened both doors and gave me a big smile!' Karen Marie noted:

The Americans enjoyed Mother's personality immensely. She never put on airs for anyone. She was the same open, straightforward person in all situations. She talked on and on. When people praised Kirsten, Mother beamed like the sun: she could never hear too much about her 'little girl's' success. She treated both Kirsten and me like teenagers, and if we did something she didn't like, she let us know it.

Mother and I went along with Kirsten on one of her concert trips. It happened that I got the rather thankless job of keeping the fans out of Kirsten's dressing-room. Mother thought it was dreadfully wrong of Kirsten to be so strict. 'You really must let all those lovely people come in, Kirsten. They only want to tell you how wonderful you are. It's really a pity the way you treat them,' she said. 'Don't you think it's a bit hard on me, Mother, when I need to rest during the intermission?' asked Kirsten. 'Oh fiddlesticks! You can rest later,' Mamma snorted. But the reason Kirsten was so strict about people not coming into her dressing-room was, I know, because the gentlemen as a rule smoked cigars or cigarettes. The smoke irritated her throat, giving her bad coughing spells.

In Washington, I even had to make excuses to the Norwegian minister, Mr de Morgenstierne [Wilhelm Munthe de Morgenstierne]. That was really embarrassing, but Kirsten had a bad cold and had asked me to make sure that absolutely no one got into her dressing-room during the intermission. The minister also smoked, and I didn't feel I had the right to ask him to put out his cigar. So I had to say it was true that my sister had asked me to keep everyone away. I'm sure it caused bitterness and placed Kirsten in a very unflattering light as far as the Norwegian minister was concerned. Mother was so upset that she fled back to her seat in the auditorium.

'My love to Else if you see her,' were Kirsten's parting words as her mother and sister boarded ship for the return voyage to Norway. After they had gone, she felt as lonely as before, and only the preparations for an Australian tour kept her going.

Henry Johansen accompanied his wife on the Australian tour, together with Marks Levine, her manager, and Edwin McArthur, her accompanist. On 21 May they sailed for Honolulu from San Francisco aboard the SS *Matsonia*. Kirsten gave two concerts in Honolulu and enjoyed a brief stay with the Norwegian composer Alf Hurum and his wife, who lived there. On 30 May she and her party sailed for Australia on the SS *Mariposa*.

It was during this tour that the Johansens decided to sponsor McArthur financially in his ambition to become a professional conductor. He in fact made his conducting debut in Sydney, on 13 July 1938, with Kirsten Flagstad as soloist. Her subsequent zeal in promoting her talented accompanist as a conductor led to not a few misunderstandings, but it was quite in character for her. She never made a commitment that she did not follow through completely, even when such a course worked to her detriment.

Kirsten was always willing to further the careers of talented musicians. She helped when she could and in a manner she thought appropriate, be it through advice, personal influence or money. Her generosity stemmed from her gratitude for all the help she herself had received when she was a student. It would be difficult to determine how much money she gave to others during her lifetime, but a modest estimate would be $200,000. She always stipulated that her funds be given anonymously, except when she established the Marie and Michael Flagstad Scholarship Fund, in honour of her parents: the interest on the capital of $40,000 was given each year as a stipend to young musical artists, preferably children of professional musicians.

The tour was only a moderate success overall because of Kirsten's reluctance to observe the social niceties expected of a visiting celebrity. Her natural reserve was compounded by her continuing concern about her daughter, from whom she had not heard for a year. One of the memorable events of the Pacific trip took place during a stop-over in Auckland on the way back to the United States:

> We travelled to a Maori village quite a distance from Auckland, where the people had kept alive the traditional songs and dances of their ancestors. Our guide there was a real Maori princess, Princess Rangi. She was one of the most beautiful people I've ever seen. 'I shall have the women sing for you,' she said to me, 'but will you sing for them in return if they ask you to?' I said I would be delighted.
>
> We sat in the shade of the lovely trees while the Maori women danced and sang their unique songs for us, songs all in minor keys. When they were finished, they pointed at me. They wanted me to sing for them. I sang several Grieg songs, without accompaniment of course. The women smiled and nodded, but they didn't applaud when I had finished: they had no such custom for showing their appreciation. Nodding meant they wanted to hear more. I then sang a few Norwegian folk songs. Again there were smiles and nods, and they whispered among themselves. In spite of the difference in ways of living and art forms, I felt we understood each other remarkably well.

Marks Levine had booked a major concert for Kirsten in San Francisco on 27 August 1938, soon after her arrival back in the United States. McArthur was to conduct the orchestra, making his debut as a conductor in his homeland. The concert, which took place in the Civic Auditorium, was an important event in his young life (he would be thirty-one years old on 24 September).

It turned out to be a memorable occasion for Kirsten, too, for she saw there, for the first time, a young American teacher who, over the years, became one of her best and most faithful friends. Caryl Beckwith lived in New York but had travelled to the West Coast with a friend after she read that Kirsten Flagstad was scheduled to sing a concert in San Francisco. Caryl's brother, Robert, had heard Kirsten and had talked so much about her that Caryl could hardly wait to hear her. After the concert, the two friends made their way to the stage door to see Kirsten come out. She smiled at them as she passed by, and Caryl, quite by accident, stood in Henry Johansen's way as he was about to get into the car. He begged her pardon, but would she mind moving? Kirsten smiled at the incident, and as the car moved away she turned and waved to the two girls. A few months later, this scene was repeated at the stage door of the Metropolitan, where Caryl Beckwith stood with her brother and a group of Kirsten's fans as Kirsten walked to her car. When Caryl suddenly felt a hand on her shoulder, she said, without turning round, 'Of course, you want to get into the car with your wife. Excuse me!' Kirsten, who was sitting in the car, looked closely at Caryl, and then cried out, 'San Francisco!' Again she turned and waved as the car moved away.

'After that I heard Kirsten Flagstad as often as I could, and stood faithfully outside the stage door to catch a glimpse of her as she went by,' said Caryl. 'One evening Kirsten came over to my brother and me and said she would like to present us with several autographed photographs, if we were interested. I was asked to come to her dressing-room to pick them up. So began the friendship that has meant so much to me.'

When she was in San Francisco, Kirsten often stayed with her good friends Milton H. Esberg and his wife Caroline. Leading patrons of the arts in San Francisco, this unique couple had been the hosts at a reception held in Kirsten's honour following her debut with the San Francisco Opera in November 1935. An extraordinary friendship developed between her and Caroline Esberg. 'Caroline is like a breath of fresh air – she has a good influence on me,' Kirsten said.

Caroline Esberg was a warm and compassionate person. She was born in San Francisco in 1880, and in 1901 she had married Milton Herman Esberg, who was to become one of the city's most prominent financiers, political leaders, philanthropists and supporters of the arts. He was a founder and director of the San Francisco Opera Association. Caroline Esberg became a leader of the city's social and cultural life.

What began as a casual acquaintance between Kirsten and Caroline soon evolved into what was probably the closest and most significant personal relationship that Kirsten ever had with anyone outside the family circle. She became a regular guest in the Esberg home at Ross in Marin County, across the Bay from San Francisco. Her letters to Caroline, written over a period of twenty-seven years, reveal the intensely human side of Kirsten's nature, of which so few people were ever aware. She also became a devoted friend of the two Esberg children, Milton Jr and Ernest, and her letters contain frequent references to them.

Caroline Esberg, to whom music was first among the arts, was present at many of Kirsten's performances in America and Europe. Her collection of programmes, articles, photographs and other mementos relating to her friend, grew over the years, and after Kirsten's death, she gave it to the library of the California Historical Society in San Francisco, where it was established as the Kirsten Flagstad Memorial Collection. After several temporary homes, the collection – which includes several of Kirsten's costumes, vocal scores with her own notations in the margins, and personal keepsakes contributed by some of her other American friends – was finally housed in the War Memorial Opera House in San Francisco.

When I visited Arthur Dusenberry, I asked him if he had ever met Caroline Esberg. He had.

Kirsten was visiting us here in Phoenix once, and when she left she went on to San Francisco to visit Mrs Esberg and her family. I made the trip with her because I had business to take care of in San Francisco. I remember that we all had dinner together one evening, and I could see immediately why Kirsten was so fond of her. That's really an understatement. I think it would be accurate to say that Caroline Esberg was Kirsten's closest woman friend in this country, if not in the world. From the day they met in 1935 until the day Kirsten died, twenty-seven years later, Caroline Esberg was her true and loyal friend, her personal confidante, and the rock to which she clung when the turbulent waters in her life threatened to engulf her. What dignity that woman had, and how wise she was. I know you've seen the letters that Kirsten wrote to her over the years, and I'm sure you could tell from them what a unique friendship existed between these two unusual women. Of course, Caroline's devotion to Kirsten continued after her death in 1962 with the establishment of the Memorial Collection.

Kirsten's deep affection for Caroline was reflected in her close relationships with the other members of the Esberg family, but it was to Caroline alone that Kirsten revealed her innermost thoughts and feelings and those warm and tender qualities of character that so few realized she possessed.

When the controversy over Kirsten's proposed return to the stage of the San Francisco Opera erupted in the summer of 1949, it was Caroline's unwavering faith in Kirsten that helped to resolve the crisis in her favour. The Esbergs, of course, were Jewish, and many of their Jewish friends in the San Francisco area raised their eyebrows over Caroline's firm and un-compromising stand. But that didn't make any difference to Caroline. Of course, the opposition of the Jewish community in San Francisco was never as pronounced as that of the corresponding community in New York. First of all, the community in San Francisco was better informed; and secondly, its members were a safe distance from the primary source of infection, Walter Winchell [the New York newspaper columnist and radio newscaster].

Caroline Esberg died in San Francisco in 1976, at the age of ninety-five.

It is ironical that Kirsten Flagstad, whose dearest friend in the United States was Jewish, should, after the war, have been accused by many uninformed American Jews of anti-Semitism. It can be stated categorically that her liking or disliking of an individual was based not on his racial background or his religious affiliation but on what she perceived to be his character and motivation. She could be mistaken in her judgement, like anyone else, but she could not be faulted on the criteria by which she had arrived at that judgement.

Upon her return to Norway for a holiday in September 1938, Kirsten was happily reunited with her daughter. There was no need for words of explanation; their embrace erased for both of them the bitterness and melancholy of the past year.

There was time for several concerts in Oslo before Kirsten had to leave to begin another busy season – the one she had vowed would be her final one. She was the soloist with the Philharmonic Society Orchestra in a special concert in the University Auditorium on 26 September at which the king and queen were present. When it had been announced that Kirsten Flagstad would present a concert, the management had been besieged for tickets. They wished they had a hall that would hold several thousand – not just a few hundred like the auditorium. 'It is trivial to indulge in superlatives,' wrote the critic Reidar Mjøen of this concert, 'but what we have here is nothing less than a phenomenon of Norwegian vocal art.'

144

Then Kirsten agreed to sing at the Colosseum, so that more of her countrymen could hear her. She recalled:

I would have been delighted to sing many more concerts while I was in Oslo, but time was short, with appearances scheduled in Stockholm, Copenhagen and, for the first time, several places in Germany. In Paris, I was to make my debut at the Opéra. All this was to take place within the month before I was to board ship in England for New York, to be followed almost immediately by a long concert tour over a large part of the American continent.

No, don't come to me and say that a singer's life is to be envied, or is a bed of roses. The roses have been plentiful, that's true enough; they could easily have filled a Pullman car. But roses, as we know, have thorns. A performing artist of international repute has a life that is, I assure you, full of thorns. But there are compensations: to 'create' something is always an experience – one I could never have managed without.

Meeting the Paris audience for the first time on 13 October, as Isolde, was the high point of this European trip. My rapport with the French public was immediate, and I think I can say that the mutual affection has endured through the years.

At Kirsten Flagstad's request, the management of the Metropolitan scheduled Wagner's *Götterdämmerung* for the evening of 12 December 1938, the twenty-fifth anniversary of her operatic debut as Nuri in *Tiefland* at the National Theatre in Oslo. Following the performance, in which she sang Brünnhilde, Kirsten was the hostess at a gala party in Sherry's Restaurant on the grand tier floor of the venerable house for *all* members of the organization, from the general manager to the night watchman. Edwin McArthur, who was not on the staff, was 'permitted to come,' said the hostess, disarmingly, 'because he has taken care of all the arrangements so expertly'.

Kirsten's husband, who had sailed from Norway especially for the occasion, had to remain on board ship outside New York harbour that night because the port was fogbound. This took the edge off the festivities for Kirsten personally, but her guests never would have known it from her cheerful and gracious demeanour. Those who were required to remain on duty in the Opera House were sought out and served personally by the hostess, who greeted them with handshakes of thanks. No one who was present will ever forget that evening. Among the employees who attended the party arose a saying, used thereafter to establish dates: 'Was it before or after Sherry's?'

The German tenor Carl Hartmann sang the role of Siegfried on that special evening, but Kirsten's male counterpart in most Wagner performances from 1935 to 1941 was the Danish Heldentenor, Lauritz Melchior. He was the perfect partner for Kirsten in the late Wagnerian repertoire, particularly in *Tristan* and *Götterdämmerung*. They looked good together on the stage, his heroic figure and sturdy masculinity finely complementing her femininity and noble bearing. Their voices were well matched, although they did not really blend.

Melchior's voice, originally a high baritone, had developed into a Heldentenor of notable size. In quality, it was clarion rather than beautiful, and it sounded best when produced at a dynamic level ranging from mezzo-forte to fortissimo. Below mezzo-forte, it often took on a reedy, veiled quality which could be dramatically telling in passages such as Tristan's return to consciousness in Act Three of *Tristan und Isolde*, but which in slow, sustained piano phrases like those at the beginning of the Act Two Love Duet indicated lack of proper support, resulting in unsteadiness and pitch deviation. In sum, Melchior was primarily a declamatory singer, and in the heroic Wagnerian roles he was, and remains, without peer.

The Flagstad–Melchior years at the Metropolitan were a golden age of dramatic singing. And Flagstad and Melchior themselves are important historically, in that through their performances, especially those that were broadcast, they sparked a nationwide interest in the music dramas of Richard Wagner. The remarkable casts that they headed illuminated the German master's works, revealing to many for the first time their extraordinary dimensions.

A Flagstad–Melchior performance meant a sold-out house, but it was the Flagstad component that worked wonders at the box office. It is no exaggeration to say that her presence on the stage of the Metropolitan for seven seasons helped enormously to save that institution from bankruptcy. During the Saturday matinée broadcast of *Die Walküre* in February 1940, she even called upon the radio audience, during one of the intermissions, to send in their contributions to the Met's fund-raising campaign for that season.

As a result of that personal appeal, the Met received many thousands of dollars in the mail. That the Opera House saw fit to acknowledge its moral debt to her by turning its back in her time of need after the war, on shadowy and even spurious grounds, is hard to understand, if not inexcusable, and constitutes a distinct blot on its history. It is to Rudolf Bing's credit that, despite heated controversy, he brought Kirsten Flagstad back to the Metropolitan during the 1950–1 season, his first as general manager.

Arthur Dusenberry threw light on another aspect of the Flagstad–Melchior relationship:

> The largest floral tribute at Kirsten's funeral service was from Lauritz Melchior. It was a sincere gesture on his part, I'm sure, but it came, both literally and symbolically, too late. He and Kirsten had been the greatest team on the operatic stages of the world for over six years, from their first appearance together in Wagner's *Tristan und Isolde* at the Met on 6 February 1935 until their final appearance in the same work at the Met on 12 April 1941. They had had a tiff now and then, of course, but when he turned his back on her after the war – I'm sorry, but he did – he dealt Kirsten a blow more severe than most of those rained on her by some other former colleagues and 'friends'. She was so deeply hurt that no true reconciliation between them later was possible. I know that he regretted his attitude, because Else received a beautiful and moving letter from him after Kirsten died. But all in all it was a sad end to what had been one of the great musical partnerships of the century.

It was reported in the New York press on 14 March 1939 that Edward Johnson, general manager of the Metropolitan, had announced that Kirsten Flagstad had signed a contract for the 1939–40 season. She had made a fateful decision. 'If I had realized at that time how ominous the situation in Europe was, I would never have signed that contract,' she said later. 'I know it's a poor excuse, but I just didn't keep up with world events. I was far too busy, for one thing; besides, politics didn't interest me.'

In June 1939 Kirsten appeared for the first time at the Opera in Zurich. She made her debut there on 6 June, as Isolde. Her Tristan was Max Lorenz, who was to become a good friend and valued colleague. 'This year's performance of *Tristan und Isolde* takes place under a lucky star,' commented one reviewer. 'This star is named Kirsten Flagstad. Not only does she herself ascend to a higher realm in her portrayal; she also draws all her fellow performers with her, so that they surpass themselves.' Her appearances concluded with Brünnhilde in *Die Walküre*, which so moved the audience that the theatre reverberated with the final ovation.

When the manager of the Opera accompanied Kirsten to the station, he asked her if she would consider a return engagement sometime in the future. 'That I will gladly do,' she said enthusiastically. 'I feel very much at home here in Zurich.'

When you travel as much as I do, you discover which places have the atmosphere you like. I liked everything about Zurich.

Then I looked forward to a long, quiet holiday. First, I spent a few days in Oslo where I visited the Royal Palace to thank King Haakon for the Medal of St Olav, a third decoration, which had been bestowed upon me before I left New York. During the audience, the king referred to me as 'Norway's singing ambassador'. I can't tell you what it meant to me to be given that title by His Majesty.

For me the summer and Sørlandet, the southern coast of Norway, are inseparable. I couldn't imagine spending a summer anywhere but at Amalienborg, our home outside Kristiansand. I wouldn't exchange the shore of Sørlandet, its waves lapping the smooth, sloping ochre rocks, for the most luxurious beach in the world. Is there anything more wonderful than to dive into the refreshing, salty waves? I remember swimming in the famed surf at Honolulu – it was like swimming in warm bouillon.

As usual during all my holidays, I practised regularly. I had promised to sing with the Philharmonic in Oslo and the Symphony Orchestra in Trondheim before leaving for my last season at the Metropolitan. I was determined that it would be my farewell as a singer in America.

Lawrence Gilman, the music critic of the *New York Herald Tribune*, was one of the few in his profession to discern in Kirsten Flagstad's portrayals of Wagner heroines the depth of intuitive understanding that underlay and was reflected in the lustrous sound of the voice and the refined *plastique* of the acting. In his book *Wagner's Operas*, published in 1937, and in two articles in the *Herald Tribune* ('First

Lady of the Opera', which appeared on 20 March 1938, and 'Flagstad and the Metropolitan' of 12 March 1939), he paid uncommon tribute to the singer who, in his opinion, gave singular life to the great Wagner soprano roles. Gilman died in September 1939, and at a concert in his memory presented by the New York Philharmonic Symphony on 22 October, the soloist was the American dramatic soprano from St Louis, Helen Traubel, who sang Brünnhilde's 'Immolation' from *Götterdämmerung*. Miss Traubel, who had made her unofficial Metropolitan Opera debut on 12 May 1937, as Mary Rutledge in the world première of *The Man Without a Country* by Walter Damrosch (her official debut took place on 17 February 1938 in the same role), embarked on a relatively brief but significant career as the Metropolitan's leading Wagnerian soprano when she succeeded Flagstad in the heroic soprano roles from the autumn of 1941 to the spring of 1950.

On Thanksgiving Day, 23 November 1939, when Kirsten was in Chicago to sing five performances with the Chicago Opera (including one of *Tristan und Isolde* the following evening with the Italian tenor Giovanni Martinelli as Tristan), she received word from New York that her musical mentor, colleague and friend, Artur Bodanzky, had died. She was heartbroken. Their relationship had transcended the professional and become one of mutual affection, like that of a proud father and his devoted daughter. Erich Leinsdorf, the twenty-seven-year-old conductor from Vienna who had been one of Bodanzky's assistants – and who had made his conducting debut at the Metropolitan on 21 January 1938 with a performance of *Die Walküre* that had made people, including the critics, sit up and take notice – replaced his late chief on the podium during the 1939–40 season. Unfortunately, Kirsten's over-zealous efforts to advance the conducting career of Edwin McArthur were interpreted by some as a reflection on Leinsdorf's ability. When Lauritz Melchior, on 25 January 1940, aired in the press his feelings about Leinsdorf's lack of experience, it was intimated that Kirsten, who was ill at the time, agreed with him. There were newspaper reports that she had participated in a meeting with the young conductor about cues and tempi, and this was looked upon by some as her way of advocating McArthur's engagement by the Metropolitan. The so-called 'Melchior–Leinsdorf feud' – so-called because Leinsdorf maintained a public silence – was resolved, but Kirsten's ostensible involvement in it generated ill will towards her then and was misconstrued later as evidence of her alleged anti-Semitism. Leinsdorf apparently harbours no resentment towards her, although in his autobiography, *Cadenza: A Musical Career*, published in 1976, he relates that Flagstad 'had made it a pre-condition of her coming to San Francisco [in October 1939] that [McArthur] be engaged to conduct all *Tristan* performances and one *Walküre* repeat'. Nevertheless, he refers to her as 'the great soprano', and praises her discipline and musical integrity. He recalls:

> On a run-out (a term meaning that the company returns from a trip the night of the performance) from San Francisco to Sacramento [in 1939] with *Walküre*, the young soprano who was Ortlinde became suddenly afflicted by laryngitis and was unable to produce her battle cry, 'Ho-yo-to-ho'. She stood on top of the rock waving her spear while a helpful colleague backstage sang her few battle yells in a powerful soprano voice. That colleague was Kirsten Flagstad.

My respect and admiration for Kirsten Flagstad's art increased when I saw her Kundry twice in succeeding Good Friday performances of *Parsifal*, in 1940 and 1941. It struck me on the latter occasion more than ever before that here was an artist who continued to develop in an almost organic way. The vocal inflection and colouring of the text was even more penetrating than the year before, and the psychological perception of the conflicting personalities within the character had deepened.

The wild creature of the first act was like some elemental force struggling to free itself from unseen bonds, bringing to mind the words of St Paul in Romans 7:19: 'For the good that I would I do not: but the evil which I would not, that I do.' Her terrible cry when she was conjured up by Klingsor in the first scene of Act Two was fraught with anguish. Then came the demonic laughter: soft, low-voiced staccato at first, rising in pitch and increasing in volume to the brink of hysteria as she succumbed completely to her master's evil will. Transformed into the raven-haired enchantress of the second scene, she was subtly seductive, by turns caressing, cajoling, chiding and castigating Parsifal with her voice – her characteristic economy of movement pared to make every gesture, even a slight inclination of the head, a telling component of the drama.

In Act Three, she attained the ultimate in dramatic art. Although present throughout the first scene and at the conclusion of the second, Kundry sings only one word, repeated, in the entire act, 'Dienen, dienen'. Never have I seen the dramatic power of motionlessness demonstrated so eloquently. She sang only four notes, but by virtue of the spiritual calm that emanated from her, she was far and away the most riveting figure on the stage. Kneeling with her back to the audience, she washed Parsifal's feet and dried them with her hair, powerfully transmitting Kundry's emotional realization of her spiritual destiny. It was this scene at one performance that, according to Edwin McArthur, moved the renowned actor, Otis Skinner, to remark to Caroline Esberg, 'Caroline, what acting – marvellous!'

It was only a matter of time before my younger brother, Richard, became caught up in my musical life. On 19 December 1940, during the Christmas vacation, I took him to his first opera – *Tristan und Isolde*, no less. He was ten-and-a-half and I was sixteen. You might think that taking a ten-year-old to *Tristan* would stunt a burgeoning interest in music, but in this case it did just the opposite: it laid the foundation for a musical career. We stood through the first act and part of the second; then someone handed us two ticket stubs for a parterre box and we sat in regal splendour until the end.

The last two performances of *Tristan* with Kirsten Flagstad that I attended before her return to Norway in April 1941 were the one on 17 February 1941, at which Edwin McArthur made his conducting debut in the Metropolitan Opera House, and the matinée performance on 12 April, also conducted by McArthur, at the end of which she bade an emotional farewell to the audience.

A great deal has been written about Edwin McArthur's abilities as a conductor. There is no doubt that Flagstad, with characteristic stubborn determination, was unyielding in her advocacy of the young musician's talent. But allegations that her interest was motivated either by a decline in her breath control which he accommodated by his choice of tempi, or by a personal attachment, cannot survive scrutiny. The former is ludicrous; the latter is implausible. McArthur did possess talent as a conductor, but it was forced rather than fostered. The result was a classic example of too much too soon. For this, Flagstad, however well-meaning, must share the blame. Her own step-by-step development should have

151

told her as much. And McArthur himself should have resisted more than he did, if he was serious about establishing a significant career for himself as a conductor.

Be that as it may, his conducting of *Tristan und Isolde* on these two occasions was much more than competent. It was technically secure and revealed an intuitive understanding of the score. The orchestra responded well to his direction, giving him the sustained breadth of line and sonority he sought. His patroness sang as if inspired, and the other members of the cast, including Melchior, Thorborg, Huehn and List, outdid themselves.

By this time, I was a serious student of singing, spending much of my spare time on music. I continued to sing in the choir of Christ Episcopal Church in East Orange, where the weekly chanting of *Venite, Te Deum* and *Jubilate* kept me in practice.

My visits to the Met increased in the early 1940s. The revival of Mozart's *Le Nozze di Figaro* in 1940 awakened my interest in Mozart on the stage, and I frequently stood for performances of the opera in the next two seasons, which included my first opening night, 24 November 1941. The first cast assembled for this production was superlative: Elisabeth Rethberg, Bidú Sayão, Risë Stevens, John Brownlee and Ezio Pinza, with outstanding artists in the subsidiary roles and Ettore Panizza conducting. It was an altogether delightful evening in the theatre, especially memorable for the *esprit de corps* on stage and such magical moments as Sayão's rendition of 'Deh vieni, non tardar' in Act Four. Kerstin Thorborg's aristocratic Marina in Mussorgsky's *Boris Godounov* was another high point in my life at that time. Thorborg was an exceptional artist. She sang all the major mezzo-soprano and contralto roles from Orfeo to Klytemnestra with a moving intensity rarely encountered on the opera stage, and she possessed uncommon ability as an actress. I have often thought that Thorborg could have had a second distinguished career on the legitimate stage.

In March 1943 I was drafted into the Army, where I remained for the next two years and eight months. I spent two years of that time in Europe, moving from Northern Ireland to England, France, Belgium, Holland and Germany. I learned a lot about myself and about the world. The idealistic values that had been instilled in me by my parents, and that I had seen reflected in their own lives, were weighed in the balance and not found wanting. I sang whenever I could during the war years, and managed to keep my voice in shape. There was always a church that welcomed another choir member or soloist; and in England there was an opportunity occasionally to team up with a local pianist for a concert.

In 1947, after working for a while in a music shop in Newark, I applied for admittance as a voice major to the Eastman School of Music in Rochester, New York. I studied there for five years, earning Bachelor and Master of Music degrees and the Performer's Certificate in Voice. My brother followed me there in 1948.

It was at Eastman that I worked with the vocal coach Dr Herman Genhart, a scrupulous musician who made me describe and then analyse technically what I admired so much in Kirsten Flagstad's singing. He shared my enthusiasm; he described her as 'a great musician with a great voice. She has those qualities that distinguish the artist from the performer.' He pointed out that she consistently carried the vocal line through a phrase, intoning each consonant and vowel sound on its specified pitch. To illustrate, he played the passage in the *Tristan* Love Duet in which Isolde sings, 'Herz an Herz dir, Mund an Mund':

'How simple it is!' he said, with a mischievous twinkle. Then he spent half an hour explaining, word by word and note by note, how it should be sung.

All the sounds in each word belong to the note on which the word is sung. For instance, the unvoiced *H*, the voiced *e* and *r*, and the unvoiced *z* in the first word, Herz, are aspirated or sung on the *D*. You must hear that pitch mentally before you sing it so that you don't start the *H* on, say, an A-flat, and slide up to the *D* as you give voice to the *e* and *r* sounds after it. And you don't carry your final aspirated *z* sound down to the B-flat, so that you end up with a meaningless word, *zan*. You may think that that is what makes a legato line, but you're wrong – it makes hash! In a true legato, each word receives the full note value assigned to it; no more, no less. This takes practice, practice, practice; and discipline; and dedication. That's how a

153

Kirsten Flagstad comes to be, and not in a shower of gold from heaven.

Now take the last word, *Mund*. Most singers intone the *M* on the A-flat, not on the G-flat, as written, so that you get another nonsense word, *anM*, on the A-flat. There are only two sounds on the A-flat: *ah* and *n*. On the G-flat there are four: *M;u*, as in b*u*sh; *n*; and *d*. Try it sometime! And apply it to everything you sing.

Dr Genhart directed the Eastman School Chorus, in which all voice students had to sing. He was a taskmaster, but we respected him. His constant reminder to us fledgelings was, 'If you can't do it here, you can't do it as a soloist!'

Late in the afternoon of 9 January 1951, a group of us set out for Buffalo to hear Kirsten Flagstad in recital that evening in Kleinhans Hall, with Edward Hart at the piano. Genhart had told us to find out what she was singing and take the music with us, so that we could follow it and mark it. I did this with Schubert's song, 'Ganymed', which I had never heard before. Her singing of it was a revelation of the art of phrasing.

There were pickets outside the hall that night, and the auditorium was not full, but those who were there were friendly. I thought of how much those outside were missing because they preferred their own misinformation – that she had been a Nazi sympathiser – to the truth. It was sad, but I had no doubt that she would weather the storm. Two weeks later, she returned to the stage of the Metropolitan as Isolde and received a tumultuous welcome from the audience, with nineteen curtain calls after the first act alone.

7

The Fateful Years

On the night of 8 April 1940 Kirsten Flagstad was on a train bound
for Cleveland, where the Metropolitan was to present *Tannhäuser*
the following evening. Also aboard were the Melchiors, Lauritz
and Kleinchen (Maria, the tenor's wife) and Kerstin Thorborg and
her husband, Gustav Bergman. They were talking about Kirsten's
imminent trip home, which Melchior was very much against. He,
like all her friends, felt that she should stay in America until the
situation was clearer, for Scandinavia was now threatened. 'I am
suffering from a gnawing homesickness, Lauritz, can't you understand that?' answered Kirsten, in reply to his plea that she remain
in America for the time being. 'Norway is my homeland, and all my
loved ones, except Else, are there. I yearn for them so!' Melchior
understood perfectly well, but he had to point out that her country
– and his as well – could be occupied very soon by the Germans.
Kirsten was stunned. Recalling the incident later, she explained: 'I
was completely unprepared for such a development. Either I had
worked so hard that the outside world had not existed for me, or I
had run away subconsciously from the unpleasant truth. I know of
no other way to account for my unawareness of the dangerous
situation our countries faced. But his words prepared me for what
we would learn when we arrived in Cleveland the next morning.'

In thick black headlines, the American press broke the news of
Germany's sudden attack on Denmark and Norway during the
early hours of 9 April 1940. Kirsten remembered:

When the newspapers were brought to us, we all began to cry.
I'll never forget that our Swedish friends, Kerstin Thorborg
and her husband, whose country had not been invaded, cried
too out of sympathy for Lauritz and me.

My first thought was that perhaps the Germans would stop

155

me from going home. I had booked passages months ago for Else and me on the *Bergensfjord*, which was scheduled to sail on Saturday 20 April. I admit the thought was egotistical. I should have considered first my country and my countrymen at home. But it had been the thought of the coming trip home, and that thought alone, that had kept me going the last few months, so I was crushed when I suddenly realized that it might not be possible.

While they were staying in Cleveland, the two Scandinavians received letter after letter of sympathy. Friends from all over the country phoned that day to find out how Kirsten was, wondering how she could possibly get through the performance that night. 'I wondered myself,' she said. 'I felt completely dried up. I went through all the actions on stage like an automaton, while in my head rang over and over again the words, "You won't get home now, you won't get home now." When she and Melchior came out after the final curtain, the entire audience stood up and applauded, then remained standing in complete silence to express their concern for the two small countries that had been occupied by the powerful enemy.

Kirsten left for New York immediately after her last performance in Cleveland on 12 April. She still had one benefit concert to sing in Brooklyn before she and Else sailed for Norway. But it soon became apparent that the *Bergensfjord* would not sail:

In March I had sung a special farewell concert in Town Hall in New York. It was a completely Norwegian programme, with the *Haugtussa* song cycle of Grieg as the high point. The concert was meant as a farewell from a Norwegian singer to her American public, and it was a very moving experience for me. Now it seemed that it had not been a farewell after all. I had no idea what I would do now that my contract had expired. I felt quite desolate.

Kirsten's husband had cabled that she should stay where she was. Her family was safe. Her manager, Marks Levine, suggested that she continue to sing, since she appeared to have no choice but to remain in America. He would book concerts and Metropolitan Opera appearances. 'All right, Marks – if you think they want to hear me, I will sing. But first I must have two months' holiday. I am completely worn out, physically and mentally. And when the next concert tour begins, I want it to open in the Middle West where so many of my countrymen live. I will sing anywhere that Norwegian songs can bring hope and comfort,' she said to Levine. When he pointed out that her standard fee for a concert could not be guaranteed there, she said that that was not important. She wanted to be among her compatriots as often as possible.

Together with Else, Kirsten travelled to California, where it was almost like summer. Else celebrated her twentieth birthday in Santa Barbara on Norway's National Day, 17 May. It was a sad birthday, with thoughts of what might be happening at home. In San Francisco, Kirsten's good friends the Esbergs were waiting to make her stay as restful and comfortable as possible so that she could regain her strength. The peaceful days sped by all too quickly, and when the time came to return to New York, Else announced that she was going back to the Diamond J Ranch in Montana. Her mother's hectic life was not for her, she said, but the real reason was that Arthur Dusenberry was there. Kirsten knew this. She decided that she had to meet the young man who had made such an impression on her daughter. Her intuition told her that Else was in love. In June she visited the Diamond J Ranch. Arthur remembers that it was cold and rainy, and that Kirsten was badly affected by the altitude in Bozeman – 4,800 feet. Kirsten had liked him, even though at the time she was adamant that Else should marry a Norwegian.

Else wanted what her mother had wanted when she was her age: to marry and raise a family. She had studied singing for a time in Oslo with Kirsten's first teacher, Ellen Schytte Jacobsen, but she had no real interest in a singing career, although she was very musical and played the piano well. The outbreak of war in Europe in the late summer of 1939 had put a stop to plans for her to return to Norway that autumn to attend a school that prepared young women for marriage and motherhood – and besides, she had met Arthur Dusenberry.

Kirsten dreaded taking up her work again. She felt that being an opera singer was an onerous occupation – and now she no longer even had the incentive that had bolstered her earlier: thinking about the trip home. Recent events had also put an end to plans for her to sing Leonore in *Fidelio* and the *Walküre* Brünnhilde at the National Theatre in Oslo while she was there.

In New York, she was met by McArthur and Levine, who informed her of the engagements he had arranged.

> Before I saw the itinerary, I had no idea where Marks intended to send me, outside of the Midwest, where I had asked to sing. Marks was not only my manager; he was also my good friend of many years. I never had to worry about any of the arrangements he made. We had agreed that no contracts were to extend beyond April 1941. It was our firm belief that the war would be over by then, and that I would be able to travel home without difficulty.

Before she left New York, she received a letter from Else saying that, now that there was to be no trip to Norway, she and Arthur wished to marry and settle down as soon as possible. They would not think of having the wedding, however, without Kirsten's being present.

> Else's letter came as no surprise. I knew Arthur was the only man for her, and I thoroughly approved of her choice. I thought she was a bit young to marry – barely twenty – but the tone of her letter was so positive that I knew I mustn't protest. I telephoned her and told her I could be in Montana on Saturday 10 August. If she wanted me to be there for the wedding, it had to take place then. I was sorry that I had to give her such short shrift, but later I had to be in other places. Else replied that they would make all the arrangements themselves, even at such short notice.

Kirsten had asked Edwin McArthur if he, in place of Else's father, would escort her to the altar. She thought of him as her closest friend. He said he would be honoured to do so. They arrived in Bozeman, just in time, by train from Chicago, where Kirsten had sung in Grant Park before an audience of two hundred thousand on the 8th, and they left immediately after the wedding breakfast for San Francisco.

Kirsten had plenty of time to think on the long train rides between concert locales, and her thoughts were always the same: What was happening in Norway? What was it like at home? Her countrymen, her nearest and dearest – were they in need? She had had no word since the first cable from Henry. Then early in October, he sent a second cable. It had quite a different tone; he was waiting for her and wanted her to come home as soon as possible. A few days later came a third: 'What is delaying you? I am expecting you. Henry.' Kirsten was beside herself. What should she do? McArthur advised her to cable that she was bound by her engagements and could not leave. She must not, under any circumstances, write a letter or mention that she was earning money, he said. The Germans could force her to hand it over, threatening reprisals against her family if she said or did anything they disliked. With help from McArthur, she drafted a cablegram that they felt was a model of tact; she hoped her husband would understand the situation. He did not: a fourth cable arrived in which he bitterly upbraided her for not coming home.

She could take no more. She asked Marks Levine to release her from her contracts. She must go home. 'Of course I'll release you from your contracts, Kirsten,' answered Levine. 'But you must realize one thing. If you do this, people here in America will say you broke your contracts so you could go back to a country occupied by the Nazis.' Kirsten recalled later:

> It was blunt talk, and I understood it. I had never once in my entire life broken a contract, and I was not about to do so now – certainly not under such circumstances. I cabled my husband that I had to remain in America for the time being.
>
> I was deeply distressed to find myself in such a predicament. No one will ever know how despondent and unhappy I was. I was torn between two duties: to my husband, whom I had vowed to 'love and to cherish, in sickness and in health', and to my artistic conscience and my public. It was a dreadful struggle. That I lived through it was due to my good health and strong constitution at that time. I say 'at that time', because it became apparent later that I had suffered a severe emotional shock.

In September Kirsten learned that her younger stepdaughter, Annie Johansen, had fled from Norway through Siberia and Japan and was on her way to San Francisco. She arrived on 7 October aboard the *President Taft*. Kirsten became her guarantor until she could obtain a residence permit. With Annie she had her first direct contact with her family, and learned that, all things considered, they were reasonably safe and well. Annie brought a message from her father that Kirsten must come home as soon as her engagements were over – 'if only it is not too late,' he had said. 'Kirsten,' said Annie very seriously, 'you know how we look on people who travel to occupied Norway now, when everyone who can and wants to is trying to get out. On the other hand, I know Father well enough to realize that he isn't one to let himself be told what to do. Since he wants to remain in Norway, and asks you to come, there is nothing else for you to do but return.'

In a letter opening 'Dearest Caroline', Kirsten wrote to Caroline Esberg from Minneapolis on 13 and 14 October expressing deep affection as well as gratitude for the comforting days she had spent as a guest of the Esberg family during the summer and the previous week. Edwin McArthur had met her in Minneapolis after her train trip from San Francisco, she wrote, and they had given a concert in Duluth on the 11th and one in St Cloud on the 14th. They were to leave for Fargo, North Dakota, the following morning. It was freezing cold in Minneapolis, she said, and she was glad to have her fur coat. She asked Caroline to do her the favour of asking Dunn and Pringle's, a store in San Francisco, to send her a double skein of yarn like the sample enclosed in her letter, together with the bill, care of the Blackstone Hotel, Chicago, so that she could finish the sweater she was knitting for the Esbergs' elder son, Milton Jr. She added that she had just received a letter from Annie Johansen, who 'raves about all your kindness'.

In the autumn and winter of 1940–1, Kirsten Flagstad gave as many benefit concerts as she could for Norway. When she had to say no because of lack of time, she contributed large sums of money anonymously, or did anything else to help that was within her power.

In 1940 she was engaged to sing several concerts in Washington, DC. The final one, in Constitution Hall, which took place on 27 November, was presented under the auspices of the National Symphony Orchestra. The Norwegian minister, de Morgenstierne, and his wife were present as invited guests of the chairman of the Orchestra Board. De Morgenstierne's impression of the concert was reported in Oslo's *Aftenposten* on Monday 17 August 1953. The newspaper had approached the ambassador (who had been elevated to that rank in 1942), in connection with allegations of his animosity towards Kirsten – allegations made in the book *The Flagstad Manuscript: An Autobiography Narrated to Louis Biancolli,* published in the United States in 1952 and subsequently published in England in 1953.

My wife and I were at the concert presumably in acknowledgement of the singer's Norwegian nationality. Official Washington and the Norwegian legation and colony had turned out in full force. The concert was looked upon as a tribute to fighting Norway.

My wife and I had not seen the programme beforehand. . . . It was in disappointment and sorrow that we returned home that evening, *without having heard a Norwegian word or a Norwegian melody*. To the large, representative gathering of friends of Norway, it seemed like a slap in the face. Especially at that time, we, and all Norwegians, had a greater need than ever to hear Norwegian music.

I can produce a copy of the concert programme at any time, if the *Aftenposten* or anyone else should wish to see it. Or perhaps Madame Flagstad herself would prefer to produce it? She must, in that case, not forget to mention that the two encores were also German songs. It must be understood that this unpleasant episode necessarily disturbed the friendy relationship which, until then, had existed between Madame Flagstad and myself.

Kirsten defended herself:

It is true that I sang only German music during the concert, but I was not in charge of the programme. I had been engaged by the Orchestra as soloist. The programme, including the encores, had been arranged by the Orchestra management.

I think it is very unfortunate that the selections on a programme can give rise to such an unpleasant situation. Perhaps I should have persuaded the Orchestra to change its programme, but that is something I have never done. In my whole career I have never taken issue with arrangements made for me by professional colleagues. What I was asked to sing, I sang, unless it was beyond my ability.

The German chargé d'affaires was also present at the concert in Constitution Hall. It was stated in the press that he was there at my request, but I had not the slightest knowledge of his presence until long afterwards. One thing I certainly know:

it was not my purpose at any time to give offence to my countrymen in any way. I trust they will believe that this is so.

At my own concerts I sang as little German music as possible; I sang Norwegian and English music instead. And I was criticized for this, too, particularly by my countrymen in the Midwest. I thought they were longing to hear Norwegian music, but I learned later that they were very disappointed that I hadn't sung Wagner.

Kirsten had been asked to sing a benefit concert for Norwegian Relief in Chicago in January 1941. 'With the greatest pleasure,' she had replied. The concert took place in the Civic Opera House before an overflow audience and at benefit prices. Afterwards, she was presented with a gold locket on which was engraved: 'A token of gratitude to Madame Kirsten Flagstad for the Norwegian Relief Concert, Chicago, 17 January 1941'.

In February she was again at the Metropolitan: Bruno Walter was to make his debut there on Friday the 14th, conducting Beethoven's *Fidelio*, with Flagstad as Leonore.

I was honoured that Bruno Walter wanted me for the part. We worked together enjoyably and fruitfully. This preparation led to a warm friendship between Bruno Walter and me, a friendship that has stood the test of time. My good friend and benefactor, Alexander Kipnis, also sang in the three *Fidelio* performances. The *Parsifal* on Good Friday, 11 April 1941, was the last time we sang together in opera. For me, the three Beethoven performances were the high point of my first Metropolitan career.

Over the years, there were other eminent conductors to whose musical understanding and leadership she responded. Not the least of these were Fritz Reiner and Sir Thomas Beecham. Strangely enough, she never appeared with Arturo Toscanini. Why this was so was a matter of speculation, even rumour, for years. The explanation from people who knew them both rather well was that Toscanini would not share top billing with any other artist, which would have been obligatory with a singer of Kirsten Flagstad's stature. (The most prominent musician ever to appear with him was probably his own son-in-law, the pianist Vladimir Horowitz.) Before she left America, Flagstad sang Isolde for the one hundredth time, on 17 February 1941. It was an especially significant occasion for two other participants as well: Lauritz Melchior, who celebrated his fifteenth anniversary with the Metropolitan, and Edwin McArthur, who was making his first appearance as conductor in the Opera House.

In the meantime, NBC Artists Service, her management firm, was trying to devise a way of getting her home. A trip to Norway via the Pacific and Siberia, as Annie had travelled to the United States, would take too long. There was only one possibility: to fly to Lisbon, then travel via Berlin to Scandinavia. 'My original plan was to go to Stockholm, where my husband would meet me; then we would decide whether or not to return to Norway,' said Kirsten. 'When I finally realized that I would be flying over the Atlantic, I was beside myself with fright. I had flown only twice before and had been scared out of my wits.' Her management's representative contacted the Norwegian legation in Washington to ask for help in obtaining the necessary visas, but help was denied.

In the *Aftenposten* interview mentioned earlier, Ambassador de Morgenstierne commented:

> It was, of course, out of the question that we, at that time, could help a Norwegian citizen to travel to an enemy country. But on the basis of the request submitted, we cabled the government-in-exile in London, which, of course, was totally in agreement with us. . . . In spite of appeals from the Washington legation, the Consulate General in New York and outstanding leaders in the Norwegian–American community, Madame Flagstad held fast to her plan to travel to Norway, and with the enemy's help succeeded in April 1941 in travelling from America by way of Berlin – where she stayed for several days – to Norway.
>
> One must think back to the climate in America at that time to fully understand how harmful this trip was to Norwegian interests. Norway's Washington legation and Bureau of Information had pointed out to the American press and public from the first invasion day that Norway *was at war* with Germany. We spoke of the Home Front Battle, of the contribution of the merchant marine and of all the young people who set out, some in open boats, to join the forces abroad. The current was going *out* from Norway. . . . Then suddenly

America sees the most famous Norwegian person in America nonchalantly going *against* the current to the enemy's country, and to that Norway tortured and occupied by him. It had a most disturbing effect, and weakened the trust in the Norwegian Bureau of Information.

It has been maintained that Madame Flagstad should have been allowed to go home to her family in Norway. But one forgets the thousands whom the war compelled to live separated from each other. What would have happened to the Norwegian merchant fleet, and to Norway, if our thousands of married seamen who, during the war, were sailing to foreign ports, had suddenly said, 'Now we must go home to our families'!

While one can readily understand the intensity of de Morgenstierne's feelings, his innuendoes are not acceptable. Edwin McArthur sets forth in detail the facts concerning the arrangements made for Kirsten Flagstad's trip home in his book *Flagstad: A Personal Memoir*, first published in 1965 in the United States and Canada. The fact is that all original travel arrangements were handled by the NBC Artists Service, Kirsten's management in America, and it was they who made the plane reservations to *and from* Europe.

Many prominent Americans tried to dissuade her from making this trip, among them former President Hoover, who lived in the Waldorf–Astoria, where Kirsten was staying. He invited her one afternoon for tea, and during their talk, Hoover referred to the coming trip and pointed out how dangerous such a journey was in wartime, and what difficulties she would encounter in occupied Norway. 'What my countrymen can endure, I also can endure,' was her firm reply.

She had agreed to sing a Norwegian Relief benefit concert at Carnegie Hall in March 1941, but the committee in charge came up with several stipulations that she found unreasonable. For one thing, they wanted the ticket prices lowered so that as many Norwegians as possible could afford to attend. Her manager argued that, since it was a benefit, Americans would gladly pay even higher prices in order to raise more money for Norway. 'Only if we can get the crown prince and princess to attend,' persisted the committee, adding that they also had to put their stamp of approval on the programme. 'That really annoyed me,' said Kirsten. 'They seemed to be questioning my right to plan my own programme. Perhaps it was unwise of me, but I said that I could not participate under such conditions. I offered to pay the rental fee for Carnegie Hall if the concert had to be cancelled. It was cancelled, and I regret that Norwegian Relief was the loser.'

This unfortunate episode, which created anger and bitterness on both sides, forged another link in the chain of circumstances that led to a misreading – in some instances thoughtless, in others deliberate – of Flagstad's character, motives and actions by many people in the United States and Norway during and after the Second World War. Ignorance and spite would in time bear the unwholesome fruits of slander and persecution.

Kirsten Flagstad sang in the Metropolitan Opera House for the last time, until her belated return after the war, on Saturday 12 April 1941. McArthur conducted. Even standing room was sold out, as friends and admirers flocked to hear her Isolde. When the curtain fell, no one would leave. The audience stood shouting, 'Flagstad! Flagstad!' Hand in hand with Melchior, she came out time after time to receive the tribute of the crowd. Then Melchior raised his hand for attention: 'Madame Flagstad will in a few days leave for Norway to see her husband and family for the first time in one and a half years. I think we all should wish her a good journey home and a good journey back here to us!' From all sides came the cry, 'Safe journey! Come back! Come back!' Then, 'Speech! Speech!' When she came out alone again, she said hesitantly: 'My dear friends, I am very happy I am going home, but I know that on the day I come back I will be even happier. Thank you – all of you.'

'After these few words, I walked quickly off the stage and burst into tears at the thought of leaving these marvellous people who had given me so infinitely much,' said Kirsten. She had every intention of returning to the United States in the autumn.

Early on the morning of 19 April 1941, Kirsten, accompanied by Annie Johansen and McArthur, was driven to La Guardia Airport. There she was to board Pan American Airways' *Dixie Clipper*, bound for Lisbon. A number of her closest friends were waiting to say goodbye. Right up to the time she boarded the plane, everyone was trying to believe that she was only going home for a few months' holiday, but they felt that the separation could turn out to be a long one. The last her friends saw of her was a waving hand and a smiling face. At 9.55 a.m., the 'flying boat' was airborne.

McArthur could no longer restrain himself. He wept openly. He who through all her years in America had done so much to make her life easier, by taking care of all the details, in matters large and small, professional and personal, was overcome by the realization that she was now completely on her own on a long, hazardous trip in wartime. Kirsten noted:

McArthur's anxiety proved later to be well founded. All travel reservations from America had been seriously neglected. Travel was bogged down in an endless chain of problems, delays and inconveniences. The only exception was the flight from New York to Lisbon that I had dreaded the most. The trip over the Atlantic Ocean was really an adventure that cured me for ever of my earlier fear of flying. In fact, I became a flying enthusiast.

To the question of why Kirsten Flagstad met with ill feeling in Norway after the war, most Norwegians respond along the lines of:

Because she came home. We understood her personal motives, but we did not consider them a justifiable reason for her to travel to an occupied country in wartime. Kirsten Flagstad allowed herself to be ruled by her emotions, forgetting that she was one of Norway's greatest artists and, as such, one of our most outstanding cultural representatives. We felt that, first and foremost, she had obligations to her country in the unfortunate circumstance of the German occupation. It certainly did not help the situation that she came home to a husband who was a member of the NS.

Henry Johansen had been a member of the Nasjonal Samling Party since 1934. Kirsten knew this, but that the party was now illegal and that it had been declared unpatriotic to be a member of it after 9 April 1940, she first learned in Lisbon from some Norwegian travellers, who condemned her husband's membership of the party as well as the fact that he had allowed himself to be appointed a member of the Board of the State Liquor Monopoly – a clearly unpatriotic enterprise.

Because of travel complications, I had to go from Lisbon to

Madrid and from Madrid to Barcelona. From there I flew to Berlin where I had to pick up my Swedish visa, which was supposed to be ready for me. Things didn't go as planned, and for a couple of days I had to run around from office to office to make further travel arrangements. I didn't receive permission to travel to Stockholm; the Swedish legation would issue only a transit visa. I had to go straight to Oslo, whether I liked it or not. On Sunday 27 April the train rolled into the Eastern Railway Station in Oslo, where my husband was waiting for me.

Kirsten then telephoned her mother, who almost collapsed when she heard that her daughter was in Oslo. She went immediately to Tidemand Street. Later Kirsten's relatives and friends arrived to greet her after the year-and-a-half separation. Kirsten sat with her hand in her mother's and looked at all the dear faces.

We talked and talked, far into the night. There were so many questions to ask, so many answers to give. The first evening home, we had almost no time to eat. My first impression was that everything was better at home than I had been led to believe by the American newspapers. When I asked about Kate, I received a vague reply. 'Kate is married,' they said, 'and lives out of town.' Then there was an awkward silence, and I asked no more. Not then.

After a few days in Oslo, Kirsten went to Amalienborg. There she found a letter from Kate, who wrote that she was coming for a visit. She commented later:

I was much opposed to Kirsten's coming home during the war. I had hoped she would remain in the States to work for Norway's cause there. But I was aware of her total lack of interest in politics, and knew that she genuinely loved Father, so it didn't really surprise me at all that she came home. My reason for visiting Kristiansand was to urge Kirsten to use her influence to persuade Father to resign from the NS. To my relief, she promised to take this up with him at the first opportunity. With that, my mission was over. I saw neither Kirsten nor Father during the whole of the war after my short visit to her. I don't know if she regretted coming home, but she had no easy time of it here, during or after the war. No matter how much she maintained that she really only wanted to be a housewife, she was born to sing. To sit there in Kristiansand with almost nothing to do, without any artistic contacts, and without being able to sing in public, was a terribly nerve-racking experience for her. She became restless, and that affected Father; it was not easy for anyone. I'm sure Kirsten often felt herself a prisoner. Father had his factory to go to, so for him it was perhaps easier. They saw no one at home, except Leif Stake when he came from Oslo.

Calm, amiable and soft-spoken, Leif Stake was Henry Johansen's right hand. He had come to the firm as a very young man, as a driver, and had become Johansen's chauffeur. It was during the long car trips during the war that Johansen and Stake really got to know each other. Stake disclosed a thorough knowledge of everything that pertained to the running of the factory, and revealed himself to be the most loyal of employees. From his position behind the wheel, he was moved first to one of the factory offices outside Kristiansand, and later to a subsidiary company's office in Oslo, until – after the war and Henry Johansen's death – he became the Oslo office's manager. No problem was too big or too small for Stake to tackle and he always seemed to come up with the right answer. He took on many responsibilities to spare Henry and Kirsten unnecessary worry. Kirsten looked forward to his visits. As time went on he undertook assignments concerning her career, and in her 'second career' after the war he was her indispensable secretary and good friend, and her best adviser in all practical matters.

When she first arrived home she was exhausted, and wanted only to rest. But when her strength returned, she discovered that she missed her career. She missed rehearsals and performances and concerts – even all the difficulties and pressures that went with them. Through the years, Kirsten had had sent to her all press clippings, reviews and articles about her career. She now began to put them in order and place them in portfolios – 'just to get it done,' she said. She would not admit to herself the real reason – that through these clippings she felt closer to the world she had left, and now, in this time of inactivity during the war, longed for.

Yes, perhaps that was one of the reasons I thought it was fun to sort out clippings from all the places I'd sung. I knew there could be no singing for me in Norway during the war: I would sing for neither the Germans nor their Norwegian followers. Before I left America, Marks Levine had asked me straight if I would sing for the Germans if they asked me to; he thought I might be forced to do so. I remember what I answered: 'A singer can always be ill, Marks.' I was 'ill' several times during the war, and just ignored several other inquiries. I think they knew only too well which way the wind was blowing; whom they could count on, and whom they could not.

My husband resigned from the NS and from the Board of the State Liquor Monopoly less than three months after I came home. Henry thought it best that he stay away from Oslo for a while after his resignations, and we lived almost like hermits the rest of the summer in our home outside Kristiansand.

Marks Levine had asked me to let him know if I would return to America in the autumn of 1941, as had been my hope when I left. The deadline for my answer was the middle of June. As time went on, I realized that to return then was out of the question. I wrote and told him that I was staying in Norway for the present. . . . I already had my return ticket from Lisbon to New York, bought before I left America. And my immigration papers for the States were in my purse, where they remained until I finally went back in 1947.

Perhaps some people expected Flagstad to turn into a veritable Brünnhilde, donning breastplate, helmet, shield and spear and charging down the streets of Oslo impaling every German in sight. No doubt they thought, in their naïve fantasies, that her *Walküre* role on the stage was but a reflection of her own personality.

While she was in Norway Kirsten received an inquiry from the Zurich Opera asking if she could appear at the 1942 June Festival.

It gave me such pleasure to be asked. I realized then that I had really missed singing before an audience. I asked Stake to find out if there was any possibility of obtaining a passport to Switzerland, and I started immediately to work on my voice. As part of a daily regimen, I sang through *Oberon* of Carl Maria von Weber, studying it in earnest. In my answer to Zurich, I mentioned *Oberon* and asked if it would be possible for me to sing the role of Rezia there.

169

Both requests, for passport and opera, were granted. In addition, I had to brush up on Leonore in *Fidelio* and Brünnhilde in *Götterdämmerung*, which they wanted me to sing in Zurich. While in Switzerland I would try to get in touch with Else and Edwin McArthur.

Early in May 1942, accompanied by her sister, Karen Marie, she arrived in Zurich, of necessity by way of Berlin, where they had had to secure their Swiss visas. She immediately sent cablegrams to both her daughter and McArthur, telling them that she would be there for over a month and that she was staying, as usual, at the Dolder Grand Hotel.

One night she was suddenly awakened by the ringing of the telephone. 'Transatlantic call from New York,' said the operator. A moment later she heard McArthur's voice, faintly but clearly. It was a moment of great emotion for both of them. The conversation was stiff and unnatural, for they had been told that it was being recorded and that they must talk only about commonplace things. McArthur, who had hoped to hear that she had fled from Norway and was en route to America, was dismayed to hear instead that she planned to return to Oslo after the Zurich performances. 'Take good care of Else and Arthur, and write about all my friends there,' were her last words before the call was abruptly cut off.

Her debut in *Oberon*, in which she portrayed the caliph's daughter, took place on Saturday 30 May 1942, and was a formidable success. Kirsten was almost forty-seven, approaching the age that can be dangerous for a singer, but here she was singing with a voice as fresh as ever. Both the vocal and the acting style were completely different from anything in Wagner. Yet she found, in the critics' opinion, the expressive key to the character of the role. Both her singing and her stage portrayal received unqualified praise.

Kirsten relished this stay in Zurich with Karen Marie and all the good friends she had made at the Opera. She received a long letter from McArthur saying that Else and Arthur were fine, and that all her friends were well and longed to see her. More contented than she had been for many a day, she returned to Norway after the successful guest appearances.

In November 1942 she made plans to present a concert in Stockholm. This would give her another opportunity to cable and write to Else and McArthur – which was the main reason for the trip to Sweden. It seems incredible that she did not realize what a frosty reception she could expect from the many Norwegians who were living in the Swedish capital after having fled from occupied Norway – Norwegians who looked upon her as a traitor. Determined to boycott her concert, they picketed the box office on 5 November, the day of the performance.

When Kirsten walked on stage, she faced a half-full hall and an audience obviously inclined to be cool. She had never been a success in Stockholm. Even in 1938, when she stood at the height of her career, she had not convinced the public there that she was the world's greatest Wagnerian singer. Had she sung Isolde then instead of Elisabeth in *Tannhäuser*, in what was her only appearance at the Royal Opera, the impression she made would perhaps have been different, and many friends and admirers might now have been waiting in the concert hall to hear her again. Instead, she met only coldness. It made her nervous, and she began off-form with four short arias from Handel's opera *Rodelinda*.

My voice stuck in my throat, and I could hear that I wasn't singing well. When I started the second group, seven of Grieg's *Haugtussa* songs, I suddenly felt a change of mood. The listeners grew more and more enthusiastic, applauding after each and every song in spite of the programme note stating that the seven were to be sung without pause.

As a rule, I'm irritated by such interruptions, but that night in Stockholm I wasn't bothered at all. I had finally reached them and given them something! It was stupid of me to give such a concert – I can see that now. It was the first time I realized that anyone had anything against me personally. I had perhaps been too naïve, but it had never dawned on me that I would be considered a traitor because I had come home to Norway during the war. Never for one instant had I felt guilty in thought, word or action of anything that could have been considered a traitorous act.

'That's exactly what we criticized about Kirsten Flagstad,' said several of those who were opposed to her. 'She was more naïve than an adult has any right to be in a war situation. We were against her not for what she did, but for what she did *not* do for Norway during the war.'

Again there came an invitation from the Zurich Opera, this time for the June 1943 Festival. She accepted with pleasure, but wrote that everything hinged on her receiving the necessary travel permits. She also wrote that she had been studying the title role in Gluck's *Alceste*, which she wanted very much to sing if the theatre could produce the opera. The Opera was overjoyed at the prospect. As she immersed herself in Gluck's music, and the noble character of Alceste was revealed to her, she became more and more caught up in the role.

In 1943 the Finnish conductor, Georg Schnéevoigt, wrote to Kirsten from Malmö, Sweden, where he was in charge of the Malmö Symphony Orchestra. (Before the war he had been a conductor of the Philharmonic Society Orchestra in Oslo.) Schnéevoigt knew of Kirsten's desire to help musicians, and asked her if she would sing a Wagner concert with the Orchestra as a benefit for its pension fund. He received an affirmative reply.

The concert took place on 28 March, and was a much happier experience than the one in Stockholm five months earlier. The poor reviews she had received there, together with newspaper articles about that performance, kept some people away from the Malmö concert. The house was not full, but those who were there were friendly.

The atmosphere in Malmö was almost Latin in warmth. I could feel it the moment I stepped out onto the stage, and it had its good effect on me. It is so much easier to sing when you have the public with you from the beginning. I'd like to have returned to Malmö after the war, but unfortunately that never came to pass.

In May I set out once more for Zurich and had two heavenly summer months there, together with good colleagues and friends. America had been in the war for over a year now; both my son-in-law, Arthur Dusenberry, and McArthur were now on active duty. I received a letter in Zurich from McArthur's wife Peggy, who assured me that all my friends were fine, under the circumstances. The only disappointment in the letter was that I learned I was not yet a grandmother. I had longed so much for a grandchild.

Kirsten Flagstad's debut in *Alceste* was a triumph, as were all her

172

With her characteristic curtsey, Flagstad acknowledges the ovation of the Metropolitan Opera audience after the opening night performance of *Tristan und Isolde* on 29 November 1937. Background, right: Kerstin Thorborg (Brangäne), et al.

Kirsten points out a landmark to her sister, Karen Marie, and her mother, from the balcony of her suite at the Hotel Dorset, New York, March 1938.

Flagstad as Brünnhilde in Wagner's *Die Walküre* in *The Big Broadcast of 1938*. The scene is the opening of Act II, the famous 'Hojo-to-ho' Battle Cry.

Henry Johansen and Kirsten Flagstad in their hotel suite in Sydney, June 1938.

Flagstad as Brünnhilde and Herbert Janssen as Gunther in Act II, Scene iv of Wagner's *Götterdämmerung*, Metropolitan Opera, 1940.

Act I Scene iv of Wagner's *Tristan und Isolde*, Metropolitan Opera, 1940, with Flagstad as Isolde and Kerstin Thorborg as Brangäne.

Lauritz Melchior as Parsifal and Flagstad as Kundry in Act II of *Parsifal*, Metropolitan Opera, 1940.

Brünnhilde (Flagstad) accuses Siegfried (Lauritz Melchior) of treachery in Act II, Scene iv of *Götterdämmerung*, Metropolitan Opera, 1940.

Conductor Victor de Sabata lectures Flagstad, who had complained about having to wear Brünnhilde's heavy winged
helmet during rehearsals for *Die Walküre* at La Scala, Milan,
April 1949. Background: Maria Reining as Sieglinde and Max
Lorenz as Siegmund.

Pickets outside Carnegie Hall in protest against
Kirsten Flagstad's first post-war appearance in
New York, 20 April 1947.

Flagstad's first post-war appearance in London, 6 February
1947, with Karl Rankl conducting
the London Philharmonic
Orchestra in the Albert Hall.

other appearances in Zurich that summer. After the first performance on 29 May, the newspaper *Die Tat* reported:

> The production's tremendous impact is due in large part to the
> memorable portrayal of the title role. Madame Flagstad's
> Alceste far surpassed the performances of all her colleagues,
> and not only because of her magnificent voice. Almost more
> impressive was her artistic understanding of the difficult role.
> As Alceste she had royal bearing, while at the same time she
> made the character's human greatness come alive for us. It was
> a sublime interpretation.

It was almost taken for granted, wherever she appeared, that she
would sing Isolde. In Zurich, she had a worthy Tristan in Max
Lorenz, whose voice and dramatic ability had made him one of
Europe's most sought-after singers. Kirsten recalled:

> They wanted me to sign a contract for the 1944 Festival, but I
> preferred to wait and see how events unfolded. When the spring
> of 1944 arrived, I certainly didn't want to travel. The war had
> reached such a pitch of intensity that performances in Zurich
> were out of the question. Even in our own family the war had
> taken its deadly toll. Kate, my stepdaughter, who was then
> married to Dr Johan Bakken, lost her brother-in-law, who was
> taken hostage and executed. As active Resistance workers, both
> Kate and her husband were in constant danger. We supported
> them with money in their work against the enemy. Stake was the
> go-between.

On 8 February 1945, while he was in Oslo, Henry Johansen was
arrested by the Gestapo and taken to the Victoria Terrasse prison.
He was questioned day and night for a week. Leif Stake barely had
time to telephone the news to Kirsten before he, too, was picked up
for interrogation. At the same time members of the underground
were being taken as hostages, then executed. When her husband
returned to Kristiansand, Kirsten asked him if he knew why he had
been held for questioning. 'That I can't tell you now, Kirsten – not
until the war is over. And I don't believe we will have long to wait,'
he replied. Three months later the Allies won a complete victory.
Norway was again a free land. Peace brought unbounded joy to
millions of homes, and for most Norwegians the celebrations lasted
the whole summer of 1945.

On 13 May Henry Johansen was arrested for the second time, this time by the Norwegian home guard. Kirsten remembered:

We were enjoying a walk around the garden, admiring the first blossoms while we discussed plans for my fiftieth birthday party. Henry had just asked if we should celebrate in Oslo or here at Amalienborg, and I had said that we had plenty of time to decide, as it wasn't until 12 July. Then we saw a car in front of the house, and suddenly three men came running towards us. They had machine guns pointed at my husband. It all happened so fast that I didn't realize what was going on until he was put in the car and driven away.

I remained standing there as if paralysed. After a few minutes, which seemed like hours, I dragged myself up to the house where Berit Stabben, our housekeeper, met me at the door. She was as white as a ghost and had tears in her eyes. She knew what had happened. The men had been inside the house first, looking for my husband. I went straight to my room and stayed there for several days, numb with fear and despair.

A few days later, Kirsten learned through her lawyer that her husband was imprisoned in Ilebu, the former German concentration camp called 'Grini', now used by the Norwegians as a camp for traitors.

She felt as if turned to stone. For two months she heard nothing from or about her husband. Then a postcard came – a double one for a return message – assuring her that he was as well as could be expected under the circumstances. His message ended with good wishes for her fiftieth birthday. 'Just seeing Henry's handwriting made me easier in my mind,' said Kirsten. 'When he was first taken away and I heard nothing, I had the feeling that I was encased in ice. During the summer, letters from friends and colleagues streamed in. Concert bureaux asked if I would soon be resuming my career. The very thought of answering such a quantity of mail made me ill.'

The Compensation Directorate appointed a lawyer to administer the Henry Johansen estate, and Kirsten was notified to appear in court in Torridal on 16 July 1945, to establish the extent of their combined resources. Her husband was charged with doing business with the enemy, or 'economic collaboration'. His firm had sold timber to the German military forces during the war. Johansen had built up his timber business from scratch, and entirely single-handed. When Norway was occupied by the Germans, he chose to cooperate rather than have the industry confiscated. There was no official complaint against Kirsten, but their assets were so intertwined that the court laid claims on both their fortunes and forbade her to leave the country.

Arthur Dusenberry later told me that he truly believed that Johansen was the victim of circumstances beyond his control. The Nazis had given him two alternatives: either to retain control of his business enterprises himself, with security for his employees, on condition that he manufacture equipment for the occupation forces; or to face the confiscation of his property and the dispersal of his workers. He chose the former. Kirsten was loyal to him to the end, stoutly defending his decision and maintaining that what appeared to be a choice of actions was really no choice at all, since Henry's first concern was the welfare of his employees. Arthur did not believe that Henry Johansen was an opportunist who sold out to the Nazis for personal gain, as his detractors would have us think. Johansen was a very wealthy man long before the Nazis invaded his country. No doubt he would not willingly have handed over his business enterprises to the Nazis and seen everything he had worked for all his life crumble before his eyes – but that is a long way from being a traitor. It is important to realise, too, that Johansen, like many Norwegians, was very concerned about the spread of Communism from the East. At the time, he may well have looked upon the Occupation as the lesser of two evils.

Frédéric Horwitz, Kirsten's European representative, now wrote offering to arrange appearances for her. He reminded her of the successful guest appearances in Switzerland during the war which he had been instrumental in bringing about. Would she not consider taking up her career again? Her public longed to hear her, and he was confident that he could plan an interesting schedule for her. Kirsten said later:

I felt so miserable those first months after my husband's arrest that I couldn't bear the thought of singing again. My first impulse was to answer categorically 'no' to every offer. I delayed replying to Horwitz' first letter, but he was not one to give up so easily. Letter followed letter, and as I gradually regained my strength the thought of resuming my work did not seem so inappropriate. No one could say at that time whether my husband and I would be able to keep what we owned. Perhaps it should now be I who earned our income, I thought.

When the next postcard from Henry arrived, I asked on the return card for his opinion: 'Should I begin to sing again?' After two months, his answer came. 'Leave Norway as soon as you can and resume your career. I am all right, but can do nothing as long as I am here.'

I felt my will to live returning, and wrote to Horwitz that he could explore the possibilities of engagements in Europe. He telegraphed his answer: 'Can arrange all the engagements you wish. When will you begin again?'

Kirsten turned to the appointed estate lawyer for permission to leave the country; her old passport had expired, and she needed it renewed. She was told that she had to remain in Norway as long as her husband's case was in the courts; she was needed as a witness. How long would this go on? No one could answer that – she had to wait and see. She wrote to Horwitz that she could not get a passport, and that he must not count on her.

All through that autumn, winter and spring of 1945–6, Horwitz continued writing, ending each letter with, 'How goes it with your passport?' He would try to hold open all the dates he had tentatively booked for her.

The first Christmas of peace brought no news to relieve her anxiety.

Then one day in mid-February 1946 the family lawyer visited her. She could tell at once that he was the bearer of bad news: 'I have visited your husband in prison, and he is not well. He has been put in the infirmary for observation. Neither he nor the doctors can say with certainty what is wrong with him, except that he has a constant fever.' Kirsten asked if Henry could not be taken to a private hospital, but the prison authorities would not hear of it. From the infirmary, Henry managed to have a letter smuggled out to Kirsten. 'I don't feel so bad,' he wrote. He thanked her and Stake for all they had done for him, and concluded, 'If I live, all will be well, Kirsten, believe me!' She did not know how to interpret his words: he was either more ill than he knew, or it was just a passing indisposition. Weeks went by without a word.

I tried to console myself with 'no news is good news', but deep down in my soul I was aware of what lay ahead. I was therefore not surprised when, one night in late April, Leif Stake called from Oslo saying that he had reason to believe that Henry had been taken to Ullevål Hospital. I begged him to find out for certain at once. As soon as I heard from Stake that my husband was in Ullevål, I left for Oslo.

Kirsten tried to find out what was wrong with Henry. She received unexpected help from the composer Arne Dørumsgaard, who knew the head doctor at Ullevål. It was Dørumsgaard who brought her the news that her husband was seriously ill; barring a miracle, he would die within months. His daughter Kate had been given permission to visit him in the hospital. It was an agonizing meeting for both of them: he was very weak and had difficulty speaking. After that, he told his lawyer that he would see no one, absolutely no one.

While Kirsten was in Oslo she received notice that the Agder Court of Appeal, in a unanimous ruling on 20 May 1946, had upheld the decision of the Torridal magistrates' court that both her property and Henry's estate should be confiscated on the grounds that the two were really one and the same, and that she had to remain in Norway to testify during the continuing investigation. So she stayed in Oslo for the whole of May, and asked their lawyer there to try to have Henry moved to a private hospital. Then she called together her whole family, at Vinderen in her brother Ole's home, and told them that Henry was dying and that the doctors gave him barely a month to live. Outwardly she was, as always, calm and composed, revealing her innermost feelings to no one. But the pained expression around her mouth, which could not be concealed even when she made the effort, betrayed the inner struggle.

Without her knowledge, their lawyer asked if it would be possible for her to visit her husband in the hospital. 'Yes, under police guard,' was the reply. Such a condition was not specified when Kate had asked to see her father. But the authorities were afraid that if husband and wife were left alone with each other, financial matters might be discussed. Kirsten asked the lawyer to find out if Henry would agree to a meeting under police surveillance. 'Certainly not,' he told the lawyer.

177

I know that both my family and friends were astonished and, indeed, very critical of me for failing to visit my husband in the hospital. To the world it looked hard and cold – yes, callous and unfeeling, I understand that. But incredible as it sounds, it was precisely because our feelings for each other were so infinitely deep that we could not bear to meet in the presence of a gaoler. During our entire marriage I had respected my husband's every wish. Had he wanted to see me, I would have been at his side in an instant.

And it was not that I did not *want* to see him, as many have surmised. They can think what they like. My husband and I knew each other's innermost feelings. He knew – and I knew – that a meeting under such circumstances would be so harrowing, so heart-rending, that it would have been a hateful memory for us both. Henry was such an unselfish man that he wanted to spare me such an ordeal. That is the truth – and the only reason that we never saw each other again after our abrupt leave-taking in the garden on that beautiful but so sorrowful May day when he was arrested.

When Kirsten, through her lawyer, had received permission to transfer Henry to a private hospital, she returned to Amalienborg. She tried to fulfil all her husband's wishes. She sent him the very first strawberries from the hothouse. When the magnolias that he had had planted in the garden were in full bloom, large branches were cut off and sent to Oslo to be placed in his sick room. She wrote to Else and McArthur that Henry was gravely ill and that there was little hope that he would recover.

At this very time there was a hate campaign against her going on in the American newspapers: they were writing that she had proclaimed herself a Nazi performer, and that she had sung for Hitler in Berlin and for the German occupation forces in Norway. Those who knew her refused to believe such falsehoods; those who chose to turn their backs on her believed every word. McArthur was bewildered. He realized what was being written about her would whip up public opinion to such an extent that it would be difficult later to reverse it. He was never in doubt that she would return to America to sing. He was also sure that she had a new and greater career ahead of her, despite what the war years might have done to her voice. It was his hope that Kirsten would be spared the reading of these hate articles, at this moment when she was experiencing such personal grief and despair. 'The only ray of light was Else's letter telling me she was expecting a child,' said Kirsten. 'If everything went as it should, she would give birth sometime in October. She knew how I yearned for a grandchild, and how impatiently I had waited to become a grandmother.'

On Midsummer Eve, 23 June 1946, Kirsten stood at her window and looked out over the rolling lawns and the sea which she could glimpse through the trees. She thought of all the people who later in the evening would sail out from Kristiansand in boats large and small to spend the night in the open air, on islets or reefs, with open fire and coffee pot. Suddenly a thick fog rolled in from the sea. It was so dense that the trees in the garden were completely hidden. 'How sad for them all,' she thought, as, with a shiver, she stepped back from the window. The telephone rang. She knew at that moment that her husband had died.

When the housekeeper came in to say that Leif Stake wished to speak with her, she had no need to ask why he called. 'He slipped away, quietly and peacefully,' said Stake. 'I sat with his hand in mine, and felt nothing until it was all over.'

The flag at Amalienborg was lowered to half-mast. Mechanically Kirsten got ready to travel to Oslo. Mechanically she accepted the condolences that poured in, and gave the necessary instructions. On Saturday 13 July, the day after her fifty-first birthday, she wrote to Caroline Esberg from Kristiansand, thanking her for her 'dear letters', and saying how much she longed to see her again. 'It has been a hard time for me, and I am sure you know how I feel now,' she wrote. 'I am very quiet as I know my beloved husband would have wished me to be. I have not been left alone yet, so I have not been able to cry out as I feel it would be good to do.' Her husband had cancer in both lungs, she told Caroline, 'so I must be grateful that he was released so soon.'

A week earlier she had written to McArthur about Henry's funeral service, telling him that it had been simple and dignified, as Henry would have wished. The pastor who had officiated was the same one who had presided at her own confirmation in 1911. He had spoken sensitively and beautifully on the text, 'God is Love.' 'If I am to be blamed for something, it must be this: that out of love for my husband I journeyed to an occupied country in wartime,' she said. 'I loved Henry more deeply than I can ever say.'

McArthur knew that he could help to explain Kirsten's financial affairs if he could be present during the trial. He implored her to let him come to Norway; in late August 1946 she gave in, and cabled: 'You are more than welcome!' He packed a suitcase full of gifts from her friends in New York, and took an overnight flight to Oslo on 7 September. After several days of meetings in Oslo with her lawyer there, Kirsten and McArthur then drove to Kristiansand and began day-long conferences with her lawyer there. McArthur had a fantastic memory for figures as well as for music. He remembered day-to-day details throughout the many years he and Kirsten had worked together. She began to see the case in a clearer light after he arrived in Norway.

The twenty-fourth of September was McArthur's birthday, and they took the day off from work. Kirsten had planned a festive dinner for him. When early that morning, before he came downstairs, she shouted for him, he knew instantly from her excited voice that something special had happened. He took the stairs two at a time. There she stood below, waving a cablegram and unable to utter a word. He grabbed the cable from her hand and burst out laughing as he read, 'Sigurd born 22 September. All our love, Else and Arthur'. Kirsten's eyes filled with tears: one of her dearest wishes – to become a grandmother – had been fulfilled. It had long ago been decided that Else's first child, if a boy, would be named after her father, Sigurd Hall.

Writing to Caroline Esberg, three days later, about her grandson's birth, she went on to say: 'Edwin is here with me now and I am sure he will be of great help to me. . . . I use the opportunity to sing very much and it certainly is a treat to make music together with Edwin again. We are singing through all my opera parts and lots of songs.' McArthur's presence in Norway also speeded up the case concerning Kirsten's passport. Her lawyers' several attempts to resolve the issue had been unsuccessful; they had been told that she was needed as a witness. Now that they had McArthur's clear explanations of her personal finances, they thought that the time was ripe for another try. The prominent lawyer Annaeus Schjødt, who practised in the High Court, would be, in their opinion, the one who could best advance the case concerning a new passport for Kirsten Flagstad. Having heard how the case stood, Schjødt said firmly, 'Madame Flagstad shall have her passport.'

At the court session in Kristiansand on 10 October, McArthur was called as a witness and all his documents produced. Many matters were clarified, but the counsel for the prosecution found that there were still so many obscure financial details to be resolved that the confiscation decision was upheld. When an appeal was filed with the Court of Appeal of the High Court, it was rejected. A few days after the last court session in Kristiansand, McArthur had to fly back to New York.

In November 1946, Kirsten received word that she would be granted a new passport. Finally she could leave. When she was convinced that she had both the voice and the stamina to resume her operatic and concert career, she wrote to her agent Frédéric Horwitz and asked him to arrange whatever engagements he could in Europe.

> It was quite remarkable to discover that the voice was really still there. I hadn't sung a note in months, and I was fifty-one years old. In direct contradiction of the time-honoured dictum that a woman's voice is in its decline at fifty, mine was apparently just as strong and solid as before the war. All I'd gone through didn't really seem to have had any effect on it. Perhaps some brilliance in the high tones was missing, and it was harder to take the high C, but this was compensated for by a much darker timbre. Even when judging by my own strictest artistic standards, I didn't have the slightest hesitation in resuming my public career. Need I say how grateful I was that the voice had been spared?

With passport and immigration papers for America safe on her person, Kirsten left her home in Kristiansand and was driven to the Swedish border; the ever-faithful Leif Stake was at the wheel. At the border, Henry Johansen Jr, her stepson, was waiting to drive her to Stockholm, where she stayed for two weeks before flying to Switzerland to spend Christmas at the Dolder Grand Hotel in Zurich.

The Oslo magistrates' court had appointed certified public accountants to examine the financial records of Henry Johansen Ltd. On 31 January 1947, the following statement was issued:

> After a thorough study of the material at our disposal, it is our opinion that the financial accounts of husband and wife are so intertwined that it is next to impossible to separate them. The

wife was not directly involved in the management of her considerable fortune. She left the handling of all financial transactions to her husband, whose judgement in such matters she trusted implicitly. There is apparently no separate record of the husband's disposition of his wife's funds.

Kirsten was not in Norway when the auditors' report was submitted. The case against Henry Johansen Ltd for alleged war profiteering proceeded in her absence.

After serving during the war as an active member of the Resistance, Henry Johansen Jr had fled with his whole family to Stockholm. During the court proceedings against his father's firm, it was recommended by the prosecution that he be imprisoned on grounds of his ostensible involvement. High Court lawyer Schjødt had undertaken his defence. Towards the end of 1949, the newspaper *Dagbladet* ran a series of controversial articles on the case. In the issue of 7 December, Schjødt wrote:

> The prosecution demanded a five-and-a-half-year prison sentence for Henry Johansen Jr, but he was acquitted by unanimous vote. The court concluded that, from the outset, he had taken an unequivocal patriotic position, and at all times had been totally opposed to any business connections with the Germans. The judges further stated that, far from helping the enemy, he had joined the work of the underground and, at great personal risk, had carried on a number of dangerous underground activities, including forgery of passports, arrangement of escapes and dissemination of news, until he fled to Sweden in February 1944.

While in Stockholm in December 1946, Kirsten spent many happy hours in her stepson's home. Being with his three children was just what she needed to regain her equilibrium. As the time drew near for her journey to Zurich, she asked eleven-year-old Henry if he would like to celebrate Christmas with her there at her favourite hotel. He was keen to do so, and on a cold December day she and the boy flew to Switzerland.

When she had arrived in Stockholm, Kirsten had had with her only a few kroner. When she boarded the plane for Zurich, she had $US 2,500, thanks to a new friend whom she had met that summer:

a Norwegian-born American, Captain Thorkild Rieber, who had visited her at the Grand Hotel in Oslo, offered her his condolences, and told her that whenever he could be of assistance, in Europe or in America, she should not hesitate to contact him. In the first difficult years after the war, Rieber and his daughter Ruth proved to be her faithful friends. Before the Christmas flight to Switzerland, Kirsten had cabled McArthur from Stockholm for money. McArthur in turn had telephoned Rieber in New York, and within a few days his representative appeared at her hotel with twenty-five hundred-dollar bills. When Kirsten wanted to repay Captain Rieber some years later, he said no, it had been meant as a gift, a gesture of thanks for all he had experienced through her art.

She was met in Zurich by Frédéric Horwitz, who had a long list of tempting offers, among them guest appearances at La Scala, Milan. 'The only place in the world where I had really longed to appear was La Scala. I couldn't end my career without singing there at least once,' she said.

After a joyous Christmas with young Henry, 'a little gentleman', as she wrote to his mother, Kirsten was again in fine physical and mental condition and looked forward to her 'second' singing career. The first concert was at Cannes, on 18 January 1947.

It was a strange experience to stand once more on a concert platform. I had really dreaded this moment, when I would be alone on the stage with hundreds of staring eyes in front of me. The difficult years I had just lived through had really taken their toll: the mirror told me that. Now the public would see how much I had aged. Of the voice I was more confident; but would it last for a whole concert? It was a fearfully tense moment.

The audience's warm reception gave me the stimulus I needed to get through the first few minutes. Then, as I sang, I became completely calm. And I discovered as I went on that the voice not only held out, but seemed to have benefited from its long rest. This made me so happy that I felt like throwing my arms around each and every one who had come to hear me. What was this gift that had been given to me? And how grateful I should be that this voice, this instrument that gave me the means to support myself, had survived those last few nerve-racking years.

183

Grace Moore, the famous American soprano and film star, and her husband, Valentin Parera, watched from a box at the second Cannes concert. Miss Moore nodded to Kirsten as she bowed, and later invited her to supper at the Casino. The invitation was welcome, for Kirsten needed sympathy and understanding at this time.

I shall always be grateful for Grace Moore's warm and genial manner towards me. We had such a delightful supper, we three. And the orchestra honoured us in a charming way, playing an aria from *Louise* for Grace and a song by Grieg for me. I was so sad when I learned of Grace's sudden death, barely one week later, in the tragic plane crash at Denmark's Kastrup Airport that also claimed the life of Swedish Crown Prince Gustavus Adolphus. I cannot understand why such a vibrant person, so glad to be alive, so attractive and so gifted, had to die so young. It was cruel and incomprehensible.

In Paris Kirsten sang two concerts with the well known Paris Conservatory Orchestra, to warm and friendly audiences. After this, she no longer hesitated to accept the invitation to sing Isolde at La Scala. She realized that she had both the voice and the physical stamina to undertake the strenuous role again. From Paris she travelled to London, her beloved London. It always gave her a special pleasure to revisit this city, but she was shocked in January 1947 to see what devastation the bombings had caused. Only a few blocks had been completely rebuilt. The Albert Hall had survived almost unscathed, and there, in that marvellous auditorium in which it was such a joy to sing, she sang again.

There was a festive atmosphere in the Albert Hall as she walked out onto the platform for the first time in almost ten years. The entire audience rose to its feet and greeted her with an ovation. It was reminiscent of the days before the war when she was at the height of her career. This spontaneous outburst was the public's way of saying, 'Kirsten Flagstad is an eminent artist. We remember her fondly, and we welcome her back to our musical life.' The warm reception made her cheeks glow and her eyes shine. She sang Isolde's 'Liebestod' and Brünnhilde's 'Immolation' from *Götterdämmerung* with effortless mastery. Kirsten remembered:

To come from the enthusiastic public in London to the cold and

184

reserved public at La Scala was a great shock. And especially so, since I had looked forward to singing in Milan. Fortunately I had had a preview of this typical La Scala audience behaviour. I had attended three performances in February while rehearsing for Isolde on the 26th. The paid claque applauded wildly, while the audience could barely lift their hands to clap. As we say in the theatre, 'They kept their gloves on.'

Nevertheless, it was heavenly to stand once more on an opera stage, in costume, and to sing grand opera. I had waited so long for this! I relished each moment of it, even though the response for me, as for the others, was slight. 'I can't go out to say thank you for applause I haven't heard,' I insisted. 'That doesn't matter. You have to do it,' was the answer. And I was pushed from the wings. I felt like an idiot, and realized more acutely than ever before what applause means to an artist. I had been spoiled. I had always been fortunate in hearing, through applause, that the audience had appreciated my performances. No doubt I, like most others, should have arranged to have a paid claque sitting around in the theatre. I know it sounds pretentious, but I have never had to use one.

Kirsten experienced no public demonstrations against her while she sang in Europe during the first few months of 1947. The one protest came from the conductor, André Cluytens, who was to lead her first concert in Paris on 25 January 1947. But his protest concerned the public as well. She observed:

I didn't understand until later that his whole attitude was a demonstration. For example, he did not appear at all at the first rehearsal, while the orchestra and I waited. We were then told to return for rehearsal at eight o'clock in the morning. The final rehearsal was scheduled for 10 a.m., with the concert at three that afternoon. It was difficult, but no one said a word. The conductor was there for both rehearsals, and all went well. The opening selection was the prelude to *Tristan und Isolde*, followed without pause by the 'Liebestod', which I was to sing.

I sat dressed and ready offstage when the conductor came up to me and, without any explanation, said that he would conduct the entire 'Liebestod' without me. 'Oh, he wants to spare me,' I thought, and I answered softly, 'I can sing, I'm not tired.' 'You misunderstand,' he said, 'I *prefer* to conduct without you.' I merely shrugged my shoulders and sat quietly as before, offstage, with my hands folded. He was the director; I could only follow his orders. When I didn't appear, the public became restless. But he continued, and there I sat.

Afterwards the reporters stormed backstage asking question after question. 'Were you late? Were you sick? Nervous?' 'Nothing like that,' I replied. 'I was right here, waiting. But beyond that I have nothing to say.' The conductor, standing a few feet away, turned crimson. But he let me take the blame for that rudeness towards the public – not giving them what they had paid to hear. It was not his concert alone, after all.

On Saturday 8 March 1947, Kirsten sailed from Southampton for New York aboard the United States Lines flagship, *America*. On board she sent McArthur a telegram saying that she was on her way. When he received it, he immediately contacted all those friends who had remained loyal despite all that had appeared about her in the American press. The ship docked in New York on 14 March. She was to have a taste of what was to come even before she set foot on land.

Kirsten had come to the United States primarily to visit her daughter, son-in-law and grandchild in Bozeman, Montana. News of her arrival had leaked out to the press, and no sooner was the gangplank in place than reporters streamed aboard, and subjected her to a veritable crossfire of unpleasant questions. A great many Americans had still not forgiven her for allowing herself to be guided by personal considerations and returning to Norway during the war. Completely stunned by this onslaught of questioning in what she called 'a third degree manner', she greeted her friends waiting on the pier to welcome her back. She knew McArthur dreamed of a comeback for her in America, but after this harrowing reception, she wished for no such thing. After a few days in New York, she flew out West to see Else and her family.

This reunion made up for all the unpleasantness. When little Sigurd was placed in her arms, she burst into tears. She remembered her own mother's words when Else was a baby and Kirsten was completely obsessed with her: 'Wait until you have a grandchild. You will find yourself even more captivated.' She realized how wise her mother had been, in this as in so many other things. Sigurd came to hold the firmest place in her heart, and he held it as long as she lived.

On 28 March she wrote to Caroline Esberg from Bozeman, thanking her for her welcome and her repeated invitation to visit: 'I am sure you know how much I long to see you again, but I am afraid Bozeman is as far west as I am going this spring. . . . My grandson, six months old, was baptized today. He is a lovely baby and we are already great friends. It will be so difficult to leave tonight, I am sure. Else and Arthur are fine and send their love to you all.'

In the warm family atmosphere, and with little Sigurd a daily joy, the memory of that frightful first press conference had begun to fade. Her courage returned, and she began to think seriously again about a new American career. She would make a decision about that after she had sung the recitals booked for April and May. One thing was certain: she had to earn money to live. The war years and her consequent enforced idleness in Norway had eroded her savings, and her family assets in Norway were still tied up in the litigation over her husband's estate.

It had not been easy for her management to arrange concerts for her; many places did not wish to book Kirsten Flagstad. Boston was the city chosen for her first post-war concert in America: the Boston public was known to be dignified, courteous, friendly and just. McArthur felt it would be a good testing ground for future concerts, and although he was not altogether right about that, the Boston performance gave Kirsten the good start she needed to strengthen her for what lay ahead.

The concert, her first in America for six years, was presented on the afternoon of Sunday 6 April 1947. Kirsten and McArthur drove there from New York, followed by detectives, hired to forestall any trouble. From the moment she left New York until she was back in her hotel after the performance, she was surrounded by guards, except when she was actually on the stage. Police ringed Symphony Hall and parted only for her as she went though the stage door. Plainclothes men were stationed everywhere throughout the hall, which had been thoroughly searched beforehand for bombs. When she came on stage, followed by McArthur, she received the most enthusiastic reception Boston had ever accorded an artist. The hall was not full, but from the audience's greeting she knew she was welcome.

She sang Beethoven, Brahms and Wolf, as well as a selection of Norwegian songs, ending with a group of American songs. At the end of the concert the audience stood as one, shouting, 'Wagner! Wagner!' Wagner had been deliberately left out of the programme. Kirsten turned to McArthur, whispered to him, and he nodded. Then the introduction to Brünnhilde's Battle Cry rang out over the audience. But just after she began to sing the famous 'Hojo-to-ho!' cries, she suddenly stopped and looked at McArthur in consternation. He jumped up and addressed the public: 'It's all my fault; I haven't played this in six years, and I've forgotten how to play it from memory.' Kirsten had become scarlet and hidden her face in her hands. Now she smiled apologetically, and the audience went wild. This human error only added to her success and endeared her further to her listeners.

Next day the papers assured their readers that Flagstad was still at her peak and, heartened, she and McArthur travelled to the Midwest for a recital in Milwaukee on 9 April and one in Chicago on the 11th.

> Milwaukee was just the opposite of Boston. Pickets carried signs saying that I was not welcome, that I had lived in luxury while my countrymen starved and died, and that the best I could hope for was to go home.
>
> I faced a half-full hall, but those who came were most friendly. It wasn't easy to start. For the first time in my life I was unnerved. During the intermission, I could hear the voices of the demonstrators outside. The same thing happened in Chicago, but the house was full, and the mood warmer and more congenial. I grew accustomed to the ever-present police, and wondered if I would also get used to the demonstrators. George Engles, my manager at the time, and McArthur did what they could to spirit me in and out of the concert halls without my being seen. I had always arrived long before concert time, but now I arrived at least two hours in advance to avoid the demonstrators.

Critics were unanimous in their opinion that the Flagstad voice was as remarkable as before the war. But several declared it was puzzling that so great an artist had preferred to remain passive while so many of her colleagues had committed themselves to the Allied cause during the war. They could understand people's resentment, but did not agree with the protesters who accused her of Nazi collaboration. 'Had this been so, the Norwegian authorities would not have cleared her, and the American authorities would not have granted her an entrance visa,' they said.

Kirsten Flagstad's first post-war Carnegie Hall concert took place on the afternoon of Sunday 20 April 1947. The New York press was divided into two camps, for and against. Veterans' organizations demonstrated *en masse*, causing commotion outside as well as inside the hall.

I dreaded this concert. No one could foresee the consequences. I learned in advance that it was sold out: three thousand people would be there. But were they coming to show me goodwill – or the opposite?

The reception that awaited me was the last thing I expected. The whole vast audience arose, applauded, stamped and shouted, 'Welcome back! Welcome! Welcome!' I was more overwhelmed than if they had booed me, accustomed as I now was to unpleasantness and raw feelings. The unexpected enthusiasm almost caught me off-balance. But how it boosted me! I think this concert became one of my best at Carnegie Hall, and it further immunized me against the indignities I encountered later.

Only two days after the concert in New York, she and McArthur experienced in Philadelphia the worst of all the protests mounted against her. Demonstrators shouted not only outside the Academy of Music, but also inside during the concert. Four or five interrupted her singing; other troublemakers screamed, 'Nazi!' and threw stink bombs and rotten vegetables. Each time an interruption occurred she stood quietly at the piano while police removed the demonstrators. Then, nodding to McArthur, she continued from where she had left off. The programme was given in its entirety. When she walked off the stage at the end, a policeman stationed there exclaimed, 'You sure have guts, lady!' 'Thank you, officer,' she replied. 'It must be my Viking blood.'

Afterwards, she and McArthur drove to New York in utter silence. When they reached her hotel, she took both his hands in hers and said, 'Edwin, I'm sorry to have placed you in this position.

But I am determined to win. People cannot continue to treat me in this way!'

Before the next concert, on 27 April in the friendly little city of Charlotte, North Carolina, the police chief announced that no demonstrations would be tolerated. He said that should there be present any of the persons who had threatened to come from Philadelphia to repeat their performance, woe betide them. In the event, there was no disturbance whatsoever, and the concert proceeded as planned, with only the pleasant disturbance of applause after each group. Now the tone of the press shifted in Kirsten's favour. The well known conductor, Dr Walter Damrosch, wrote that the persecution of such an artist was reprehensible. He would, with the greatest pleasure, accompany her in a song at her next concert. Other former colleagues, including Geraldine Farrar, Gladys Swarthout and Paul Althouse, also spoke out against the disgraceful conduct to which she had been subjected.

With a Cleveland concert on 10 May, the first post-war season ended – if it could really be called a season. She who before the war drew the largest crowds and was in constant demand for opera or concert appearances, had had to fight her way through several violent demonstrations. In addition, the 'season' had been an economic fiasco. Had she not had good and well-to-do friends who willingly lent her money, her financial situation would have been jeopardized. Also, she had certain incomes assured in London and in Zurich, where she was again the guest artist at the Opera during the June Festival.

While she was in Zurich, she received a copy of the *Aftenposten* for 17 June. It carried a statement entitled 'The Persecution of Kirsten Flagstad', which was signed by many of her fellow artists in Norway:

It is now more than two years since the liberation of Norway, and those of our fellow artists who were not allowed to perform after the war because of their 'wrong sympathies' are by now back at work.

This fact makes the continued persecution of Kirsten Flagstad biased and unjust. There has been absolutely no accusation against her in Norway by the police or the government department dealing with collaborators. The public reports about her have generally been torn from their context and slanted in a false light, not conforming in the least to the actual facts. Moreover, the floodtide of human sympathy and appreciation for her art rushing towards her from the world press has been systematically repressed here in Norway.

We propose to our countrymen a halt to this unworthy attempt to bury the name and reputation of Kirsten Flagstad.

Oslo, 13 June 1947

The Board of Directors of the Norwegian Music Association Bjarne Brustad, Chairman. Rigmor Norby, Egil Nordsjø, Arvid Fladmoe, Rolf Karlsen.

On behalf of the Norwegian Opera Association . . .

There followed the names of nearly forty Norwegian musicians, headed by Eyvin Vedéne, the chairman. Kirsten commented:

It was heartwarming to find so many artists supporting me in the belief that I had been unfairly accused. I sent the article to my friends in America, and McArthur had it translated and tried to place it in the American papers. But the time was not yet ripe for a change of heart in that country. Several years were to pass before I was fully 'rehabilitated' there.

Kirsten returned to America later that summer to spend more time with her 'little family' in Bozeman. Arthur Dusenberry remembered:

She was as close to being unnerved as I ever saw her. She was very tired, and very upset, naturally. In fact, that was the only time that she actually broke down in my presence and wept. It was so sad. Soon after that, Else and I decided to rent a cabin at Whitefish, Montana, not far from Glacier National Park. It is an area of spectacular natural beauty. We felt it would be good for Kirsten to be in such a healthy atmosphere for a while. Our cabin was right on Whitefish Lake. One beautiful summer night, when there was a full moon, we were down at the lake shore sitting around a campfire when suddenly, without a word, Kirsten stood up and began to sing some of her Grieg songs. The sound of this unbelievable voice filling the vast open space enthralled everyone who was there. Among the songs she sang, I remember especially 'En Drøm' and 'Jeg elsker dig'. It was as near perfect an experience as one can

191

hope to have in this life. I will never forget it. It was magical.

It was also during this time that Kirsten decided to honour us with her 'bankebiff', the Norwegian equivalent of our Swiss steak. This was a production not to believed. Kirsten was no cook; she could boil an egg, and that was about it. But she had a few favourite recipes that she would prepare on special occasions. First of all, we were all thrown out of the kitchen. Else was highly amused. Kirsten had tied a towel completely around her head, and the next thing we knew there was all this pounding coming from behind the closed kitchen door. It was all very operatic, very Wagnerian. Always the diva! And the result? Fit for the gods, one might say!

She began another season in America in October 1947. No opera company wanted her back, so she had been advised to appear in concert and recital. Nevertheless, heartening news had reached her towards the end of the summer: she had been invited to appear, in the summer of 1948, at the Teatro Colón in Buenos Aires, where Erich Kleiber was the music director and conductor of the German repertoire; and the Chicago Symphony Orchestra, with its conductor Artur Rodzinski, wanted her to appear as guest artist in a special performance of *Tristan und Isolde* in November 1947.

The performance took place in the Civic Opera House on 16 November, without incident, and before a distinguished audience which greeted her and her Tristan, Set Svanholm, with an ovation. At the final curtain, flowers were presented to her in honour of her one hundred and tenth performance of Isolde. For fifteen years this loveliest of all Wagnerian roles had been in her repertoire. There was never a thought that she might be too old or 'sung out' to give a fine performance: quite the contrary.

It must not be forgotten that Chicago was the first city in the United States to welcome Kirsten Flagstad back to the operatic stage after the war. Of that performance, music critic Claudia Cassidy wrote in the *Chicago Tribune*:

Who says the great days of opera are gone? None who sat transfixed in the Civic Opera House yesterday and hovered between tears and cheers as the just tribute to the blazing incandescence of a magnificent *Tristan and Isolde*. . . .

But when, at the end of the opera, after a 'Liebestod' that tore the heart to tatters, Kirsten Flagstad stepped out un-expectedly to take her first bow alone, why then there was no question. Tears and cheers came out together in a half-choked roar that seemed to shake the huge house before it fell at her feet in tribute. In that roar was the pent-up admiration, the trust, and the love the public has for this great singer, and in it, too, was the great sigh of relief that she has come back to us not just as good, but better than ever. . . .

But do not think that the deeply emotional tension felt through the opera was contingent merely on Mme Flagstad's return. Nostalgia is potent, but it is no match for the dynamic reality of such a present. That tension was born not of something remembered, but of something experienced. It was born of her performance, of the distinction of her colleagues and of the molten splendor of the score as it poured from the pit, lifting performance and audience alike into a heady world of musical experience, deeply shared.

If I seem to dwell on Mme Flagstad, it is not to exclude the extraordinary Tristan of Set Svanholm, which touched a whole world of qualities I had not known he possessed. . . . It is just that never before in my life had I heard such an Isolde, and I am rich in its memory, should I be so luckless as never to hear it again.

It had been my experience that when Mme Flagstad first came to America her Isolde was matchless in the first act, and that it tapered off to the calm glory of a 'Liebestod' I could not accept as the opera's culmination. Yesterday it was no less glorious, but it was a glory that knew the depths, and the heights, of human suffering and pain.

The beauty of the woman, the wonder of that great voice so golden in tone, so burnished in shadows, the way she came alive in the music, so that her voice, like the throat from which it poured, was flooded with color – surely these were more than enough. But there was, too, the infinite wealth of phrasing, of seemingly instinctive gesture. Did you see the way her arm on the garden bench suddenly captured the crest of Brangäne's darkling song in the dusk? . . .

And on 30 November Miss Cassidy wrote further:

I wish I could print all the mail that poured in after *Tristan and Isolde*. It was extraordinary mail, almost white-hot, and it came not just from Chicagoans but from those who had traveled long distances and had been rewarded. There was mail from those who had not heard it, too. A man in Boston, a bit confused as to its sponsorship, wanted the address of the opera company, so he could engage it. A man in Batavia, who could have come, wrote, 'I realize I have probably missed the greatest musical treat of our times.' And a woman in an Evanston hospital, who could not come, wrote a letter I will keep when she said, 'This morning I sat On the Aisle [the name of Claudia Cassidy's *Chicago Tribune* column] with you, listening to *Tristan and Isolde.*'

But those who did go – well, once in a blue moon you get letters written after a performance because the writers are too wrought up to go to bed. One of them begins, 'It is midnight and I am still shaking from the emotional impact of this afternoon's magnificent *Tristan and Isolde*. In a sort of help-lessness I am trying to think of a way to say "Thank you" to all who made this production such an unforgettable experience.'

I told you people were worked up, so don't be surprised that this man goes on to say how happy he was to have Chicago restore Kirsten Flagstad to opera in America after her return had been ignored by the Metropolitan, 'this in spite of the fact that she had, during her first season in America, practically single-handed saved that miserable institution from total financial collapse'.

Still another, 'Yes, I was there. Now it was no small thing for me to travel 500 miles to spend the afternoon at the opera. I am a small town music teacher and you can easily understand how $15 seats would strain the pocketbook. But for Mme Flagstad I would have gone twice as far and paid twice as much.

The big town on the lake has taste – and heart. Claudia Cassidy, whose book *Lyric Opera of Chicago*, a twenty-fifth-anniversary commemorative volume, was published in 1979, was one of Kirsten Flagstad's staunchest supporters in the immediate post-war period in America. On Wednesday 31 October 1945, she devoted her regular *Chicago Tribune* column, 'On the Aisle', to excerpts from the letter that Flagstad had written on 5 September, less than four months after the war in Europe, to Mrs E. Payson Clark, a friend in

Rochester, New York, who had written to her when the war ended to express her loyalty and that of her son John, whom the singer had befriended in 1936 when he was nine years old:

It is so good to know that you believe in me and that you do not believe the lies and gossip about me. I have not sung other places than in Zurich twice and in Sweden twice. I have kept quiet at home with my husband and family. The only crime I have done is to be loyal to my beloved husband. He never was a politician and he was only a paper member of the NS from 1933 to 1941, three months after my return from America. He has been arrested since 13 May, accused of membership in the NS and of profiteering.

He has the biggest lumber business in Norway and naturally the enemy came to him for collaboration. He was forced, as so many other people, and he preferred to keep his business in his own hands instead of letting the Germans take it, and fly to Sweden or England as so many others did. He felt responsibility for his labourers, and he thought it better to stay at his post than to leave and live in safety as a refugee. I know that he tried to do his best. It seems that his case will not come up soon, so you can imagine how I feel. The treatment the prisoners get is very bad and has been criticized in the papers.

My husband is sixty-two years old. I hear that he is well and in good spirit and helpful and encouraging to his fellow men. He is the kindest and best man I have ever known. All his property is taken hold of; and so is mine as his spouse. For me it is likely to be cancelled, as the law has been changed. Our house in Oslo is now on hire and there is done as much harm to us as possible, and this *before* any sentence has fallen. It seems to be politics only that dictates everything here now. I write you frankly all this and I hope you will understand what I try to explain.

I am sorry to have to answer with only bad news. Thank you for all the information about the music life, which interests me immensely. As you probably do not know, I intended to stop singing in America in 1940, but had to continue for one more year. I was fifty years old in July and I think I have worked long enough, having been an active singer since I was eighteen. I may sing in Europe, though. I have offers from England,

France, Spain, Belgium, and from Switzerland. I have not decided yet. It is so difficult at the moment to know what to do, as you can imagine.

I am in very good health, and I do practise quite a bit, mostly learning new songs. I have practised the piano, too, which I had not done since I was fourteen. My younger brother, who is a pianist, is my teacher. I like to accompany myself and have given daily concerts for my husband, who loves music. Since 1941 our radios were taken away, but we had a gramophone and quite a lot of good recordings. I have done a lot of reading, too, and have tried to keep up my English by reading English literature. Please excuse me for all mistakes, as I do not take time to look up every word. Later on, when time is better and I have better news to tell you, I will write again.

Postscript: My husband was arrested by the Germans in February, and accused of having given money to the home front. American papers stated that it was for black marketing. He never did any such thing, of course. He was released after eight terrible days.

Kirsten Flagstad Johansen

In October, Kirsten had received a cablegram from London asking her if she could appear on 24 November at a benefit concert by the Royal Philharmonic Orchestra, to be led by Sir Thomas Beecham, for the English War Nurse Memorial Fund (whose patron was Queen Elizabeth). To Kirsten this invitation represented the vindication of her honour, and she insisted on flying to London, despite her straitened circumstances. She felt that the London appearance would help to alter the general American attitude towards her, making her professional future brighter in the United States.

It came, therefore, as a blow that two important and potentially lucrative concerts in Georgia, previously scheduled, had to be cancelled because of new onslaughts of hatred in the press. Two completely sold-out concerts at Carnegie Hall late in December helped both her and McArthur financially. The demonstrators paraded on 57th Street in front of the hall in an attempt to prevent those with tickets from entering.

But the number of demonstrators was dwindling, and the intensity of their shouts and chants was diminishing. It was one more sign that the climate in America was gradually changing.

It grieved me to think that my colleagues in America had turned against me, refusing me membership of organizations to which I had once belonged. Even my former manager, Marks Levine, who had now started his own agency, did not represent me when I first came back to America. We were finally in contact in late December 1947, when he became my manager again. After that, things began to happen. He got in touch with the San Francisco Opera; I had been a regular guest there before the war, but up to now they had refused to have anything to do with me. Before I left for Europe in mid-January 1948, Marks Levine told me there was the probability of an engagement in San Francisco.

My two short seasons in America had been strenuous, and very unsuccessful financially. Now the prospects seemed brighter. On 17 January I sailed for England aboard the *Queen Mary*.

Kirsten was overjoyed at the prospect of a South American tour, having been unable to accept an invitation to appear in South America in 1935. She looked forward to singing at the Teatro Colón after she had fulfilled her commitments in Europe.

Concerts in London, Paris, Brussels and The Hague were followed in February and March 1948 by ten performances of *Tristan* and six of *Die Walküre*, all sold out, at Covent Garden in London. She received a warm welcome from the London opera public.

At a party given in her honour while she was appearing at Covent Garden, Kirsten was introduced to the English theatrical producer Bernard Miles, who had wanted to meet her for a long time. Although usually very reserved with strangers and reluctant to make new friends, she felt immediately drawn to Bernard Miles. He invited her to visit his home in St John's Wood and to meet his family: his wife, the actress Josephine Wilson, and their three children, Sarah, Biddy and John. After dinner one night at his home, Miles told Kirsten he had something to show her outside. He suggested she wear a coat, for the air was cold, and it was raining. Later, she recalled:

197

I was taken by surprise, and slightly annoyed at being dragged out into the drizzle after a good dinner. Bernard led me through the garden to a dark, odd-looking building. He opened a huge door which looked like the entrance to a barn; it squeaked on its hinges. Then he ushered me into a large, empty, musty-smelling room. When he asked me to sing a few tones, I thought he'd lost his mind. I didn't know him then as I did later, when he became a welcome annual guest at Amalienborg. I discovered that he could dream up the most wonderfully bizarre things just for fun.

Very reluctantly, I sang a few notes. 'Not so bad,' he said; 'not bad at all.' Then he closed the door, took me by the arm, and led me to the house, all the time smiling the most mysterious smile. Some time later I was told of his plans to build a theatre in that deserted schoolhouse which I had thought was a barn! Moreover, he had it in mind to engage me to sing in the little opera *Dido and Aeneas* by Henry Purcell, which he had chosen as the first production at his Mermaid Theatre. He realized this dream of an 'Elizabethan theatre' in 1951.

I have often marvelled at the unfolding events of life that lead to new situations. Months before my appearances at Covent Garden in 1948, I had been asked if I would learn and sing *Die Walküre* in English. I had replied that I would have to experiment a bit before I could answer; actually I doubted I had the fortitude to learn a role in another language. But language has always interested me, so it was much easier than I had thought. I agreed.

I could never have mastered *Dido* had I not already sung an opera in English. It is no easy thing for a foreigner to sing a demanding role before an English public in their own tongue. But I must have done reasonably well in my first attempt with *Die Walküre*, for I received special praise for my diction.

An article entitled 'Flagstad' in the drama section of the 8 April 1948 issue of the *New English Weekly*, written by the British drama critic P. L. Travers, gives the perspective not of a connoisseur of opera, but of a devotee of the theatre:

How wonderful it is, after the drops of water and the grains of sand that make up our modern drama, to come to the great ocean of Wagnerian opera and receive the full force of that tremendous theatrical wave. This is the art of the romantic theatre *in excelsis* – grandiose, uplifted, superlative in histrionics. . . .

Acting in Wagner – and it is only of the acting that I can speak – has its own special technique, traditional and formal, which includes a system of athletics as rigorous in its way as the athletics of ballet. . . . In this present season [at Covent Garden] (specifically the productions of *Tristan* and *The Valkyrie*) the acting is full of freshness. There is hardly any of that overwrought ham playing that so often makes grand opera appear to burlesque itself, and, so served, the ancient magic upsurges with new force much as mature wine throws a crust when the vineyards flower.

This fresh atmosphere is due in great measure to Mme Flagstad, whose serenity of singing and tranquility of acting seem to lift up, as on a clear wave, every other performer into a world of rapture and precision. Her Isolde is nobly conceived and beautifully performed. Here is a large woman, largely filling a great rôle and adding to it a thousand simple graces, as the big broad earth adds to herself the small flowers of spring. Her acting is intense but without anxiety, everything about it has simplicity and depth. Above all, it is continuous. She does not halt and wait when her song for the moment is over but, actively living the music, she carries forward the vital thread of the story until she sings again. Whole-hearted and unself-conscious, she gives a plus to every traditional gesture. When she waves her veil to signal her lover she does it with energy and joy enough to bring to her side not one but a dozen Tristans. She is not a *prima donna* acting a rôle, she is a woman rapturously in love and entirely self-forgetful. At the same time, with all this enthusiasm she never makes a thoughtless or unnecessary gesture. She sits beneath that same veil through Marke's upbraiding and Tristan's protestations making no movement, quiet as stone. But her silence is all ears and her stillness full of action so that when she springs up at Melot's sword-thrust her gesture is but the end movement of a single leap from happiness to disaster. From then on every move she makes is heavy with fate. An actress with more melancholy in her makeup could never so make plain, as

199

Flagstad in her serenity makes plain, the truth that emotional love has desolation at its core and in death alone its hope of consummation. Even at the end she makes no effort to mime Isolde's sorrow. She merely sings her song of ecstasy, and sorrow breathes itself out to her; she is its willing instrument.

This submissiveness to score and script is still more pronounced in her performance of Brünnhilde. In the second act of *The Valkyrie* throughout Wotan's long recital of the fortunes of the Ring, it is she, with her silence and active listening, who makes the scene dramatic. It is through her, rather than the god, that we learn of the fateful gold; watch it rise before us, so innocent in its natural element, but gathering fate and terror and power as it is drawn up through waters and earth of instinct into the cunning mind. When she sings again, it is not with words alone – not even with music alone – that she unfolds the story's meaning further. For, disobeying Wotan's command, she defies without defiance, and thus serenely brings the saga to that point where the feminine principle takes over. Her acting makes abundantly clear that in defeating the immediate will of the god she is making possible the fruition of his deepest desire – the giving up of security and the willing of his own downfall in order that, with power broken, the reign of love may begin.

This Valkyrie of Mme Flagstad's is quite without ego and at the same time extraordinarily personal, even intimate. Largely benign and simple, she packs the Warrior Maid with all the ardours of youth – selflessness, love, courage, prophecy. With what eagerness she appeals against her punishment, and with what triumph – as of one lovingly embracing his shadow – does she accept her fate. In the last scene where she stands motionless, her back to the audience, listening to Wotan's song of reconciliation, her Brünnhilde reminded me forcibly of Cordelia. In both characters there is the same filial compassion, the same ardent forgiveness. . . . As one watches Flagstad, head bent before her father, all daughterly and submissive, it is she again in her revealing silence who foreshadows for us the rest of the Nibelung saga – Siegfried killing the dragon and climbing the magic mountain; the shattering of the spear, the death of the gods and at last the triumph of love.

This is a performance in the grandest sense of the grand style. With such acting, at once so heroic and so simple, its detail all filled in by the music, one drinks at the theatre's Pierian spring. After so heady a draught one has to make the transition from there to here very gradually. As I made this journey recently, down Long Acre with Valhalla behind me and the Leicester Square tube ahead, I looked into the future and heard one of my possible grandchildren praising some Brünnhilde of his day and myself insisting with the smug superiority I always detest in the old, 'Ah, but you should have seen Flagstad!'

Hans Hotter, the great German bass-baritone who sang the role of Wotan, had an amusing story to tell about this production of *The Valkyrie*. When asked by Alan Blyth, the English music critic, in an interview in March 1976 (parts of which appeared in the July 1976 issue of *Opera* magazine) if singing Wotan in English had been to his liking, he replied:

Well, no, but it came about like this. I was looking forward to meeting Kirsten Flagstad, with whom I had never yet sung. After the pitfalls of singing *Meistersinger* in English [in 1947], I went to see David Webster [the general administrator], and asked him if it would be possible to sing *Walküre* in German, not because it was so hard to learn a role in English but because it *is* hard to forget the original, with which the music is so closely connected. He said he would like to help but his dear Kirsten had learnt it all in English. She would be most offended if we now did it in German. So I left it at that. Then the rehearsals began. Kirsten came. We soon became good friends. One day we were sitting together, and she suddenly asked, 'Can you tell me why *you* had to insist on singing this work in English?' We then realised that Webster had played her off against me, and vice versa!

The spring of 1948 brought a very important development: Kirsten was asked by the United Jewish Relief Appeal in London to sing a benefit concert in July for Jewish children who were refugees from the war. She certainly wanted to help, but how would her detractors interpret such an event? Some of the hate literature in America had painted her as an enemy of the Jews.

At my first meeting with the chairman of the committee, a Mr Schusterman, I said I feared that many Americans would interpret my acceptance as an attempt on my part to buy a reputation. Mr Schusterman admitted that such a reaction was possible, but he said he could not give me any advice; I would have to make the decision. When I said I would take part no matter how it was interpreted, a warm smile spread over his face. Then he confided to me that even within his own organization there had been opposition when my name was first mentioned. They had subsequently undertaken a confidential screening of my actions during and just after the war. The investigation had proved to their satisfaction that I was not guilty of any of the charges made against me. 'And this result of our inquiry we would like to make available to the American press,' Mr Schusterman concluded, adding that such a declaration would be a great help to me. I was deeply moved by this spontaneous gesture. He proved right. When this declaration was made public in the American press, many who had sided with the opposition suddenly changed. From then on my treatment by the press became humane, and I was gradually accepted as an artist and as a person even in America.

One year after the first concert for Jewish refugee children, held in Central Hall, London, on 7 July 1948, Kirsten Flagstad accepted an invitation to sing a second benefit concert for the United Jewish Relief Appeal.

The offer she had received from the Teatro Colón resulted in an extended concert and opera tour of South America. From August to November 1948, she sang in the capitals as well as in the smaller towns. She was greeted with friendliness and enthusiasm at all her appearances. At the Teatro Colón she sang *Tristan und Isolde* with her old friend from Zurich, Max Lorenz. They were soon heralded as the 'ideal Wagnerian lovers', just as she and Melchior had been at the Metropolitan before the war. Max Lorenz and his wife, Lotte, became Kirsten's constant companions during their stay. As a widow far from all those she held dear, she needed the consolation of loving friends. 'I don't see how I could have lived through that lonely time without Max and Lotte Lorenz,' she said. She wrote to

202

Caroline Esberg from New York on 8 December, telling her that she would be singing in Oakland on 11 January and could visit her for a few days: 'My accompanist and I will go to the hotel in Oakland and if you find it convenient I could come with you after the concert. I can hardly wait to see you and yours.'

Her annual Carnegie Hall concert took place on 12 December 1948, the thirty-fifth anniversary of her stage debut. She was saddened to find that demonstrators still appeared. And the Met remained silent: general manager Edward Johnson did not want Kirsten Flagstad back.

When she arrived at Else's for the Christmas holidays, little Sigurd, who had celebrated his second birthday in the September, rushed to meet her. Sigurd was beside himself with delight whenever 'Mormor' came; he soon discovered that he had her completely in his power. They played together until she was ready to drop. At night, she sat by his crib and sang lullabies until he fell asleep. 'To think this is really true!' she said to herself, looking at her grandson. 'And especially now, in these difficult days. How can I ever be hurt again when this wonderful thing has happened to me?'

After a few concerts in the United States in January 1949, and another visit to her daughter's family in Montana, Kirsten flew to Europe for appearances in London, Paris, Brussels, Amsterdam, Milan and Zurich. In mid-May she was back in London to sing at Covent Garden, where she was engaged for the three Brünnhildes in the *Ring*, and for Isolde, which she would sing for the one hundred and fiftieth time on Saturday 28 May.

> I'd never have thought it possible to sing Isolde so many times. And I rather think it's a world record! I was to sing it thirty-two times more. I couldn't celebrate this one hundred and fiftieth jubilee at the Metropolitan, so I was glad it was to take place at Covent Garden. The occasion was as festive as one could imagine. After the final curtain there were speeches and congratulations, and it was an added joy for me that my Tristan was the Swedish tenor Set Svanholm, a dear colleague and friend.
>
> Some of the critics were surprised that I had any voice left for Isolde after three Brünnhildes in one week. I was no less amazed myself! It was most astonishing that both voice and body held up despite my age and all I had gone through.

203

Before the war, Kirsten had received many invitations to sing at the Salzburg Festival in Austria. She had been unable to accept because of other commitments. Now, in the summer of 1949, she was finally able to appear on that renowned stage, as Leonore in *Fidelio*. The first performance, on Saturday 30 July, was conducted by Wilhelm Furtwängler, who also led the subsequent performances. 'It was harrowing to sing this moving role so soon after my own personal sorrow. I found it difficult and distressing, for my fate and Leonore's were so inextricably bound together. But she had triumphed, and I had been vanquished. Somehow I had to rise above it all, and I succeeded better than I would have thought possible,' she said.

After the first performance, the reviews were somewhat mixed. Some wrote that it was unfortunate that she had not come when her star was at its height. There was a hint of strain in the voice, they said. But there was unanimous praise for her deeply affecting portrayal of Leonore. 'It is not often that one is so moved by Leonore's fate,' wrote one critic, expressing the sentiments of many of his colleagues. The public was strongly affected by her portrayal, too. And when the Begum Aga Khan visited Norway a few years later, she said she had been eager to see Kirsten Flagstad's country, having heard her in Salzburg – one of her loveliest memories, she said. Kirsten sang at the Salzburg Festival again in the summer of 1950. It was then that Wieland Wagner asked her to appear at the first post-war Bayreuth Festival, in 1951. She declined, saying that she planned to retire, and suggesting that he give younger singers, especially Astrid Varnay, a chance.

While Kirsten was in Salzburg in 1949, she had received a surprise cablegram from her manager, Marks Levine: 'Will you consider singing at the Metropolitan next year?'

It went without saying that I would consider singing at the Metropolitan again, but I was not free to go that year. It disturbed me that Marks should ask: he knew that my engagements for 1950 were already booked. 'Sorry, not available,' was my response. It never occurred to me that my manager might not have had a definite offer from the Metropolitan. But such was the case. He had only sent up a trial balloon. This placed me in a very difficult position.

The minute word was out in New York that Kirsten Flagstad had

Hans Hotter as Wotan and Flagstad as Brünnhilde in Act III,
Scene iii of *Die Walküre* at Covent Garden, March 1948.

A *Fidelio* rehearsal at the Metropolitan Opera, February 1951. From left to
right: Bruno Walter, conductor; Herbert Graf, stage director; Kirsten Flagstad,
Leonore; Deszo Ernster, Rocco; Nadine Connor, Marzelline; and Peter Klein,
Jacquino.

Conductor Karl Böhm, mezzo-soprano Constance Shacklock, Kirsten Flagstad, and tenor Set Svanholm, after recording the Love Duet from *Tristan und Isolde* with the Philharmonia Orchestra, London, in June 1949.

Four generations – from right to left: Maja Flagstad, Kirsten's mother; Kirsten; Else Hall Dusenberry, her daughter; and Sigurd Hall Dusenberry, her grandson, at Amalienborg, Kristiansand, Norway, summer 1952.

Flagstad (Fricka) listens intently as Set Svanholm (Loge), left, and George London (Wotan) rehearse for the first stereo recording of *Das Rheingold*, Vienna, 1958.

The music room at Amalienborg, 1957. On the piano are photos of Else and Arthur Dusenberry, Wilhelm Furtwängler, Geraldine Farrar and Bruno Walter. Above the mantel is the 1936 portrait of Flagstad by Brynjulf Strandenaes, now in the Metropolitan Opera House, New York.

Flagstad about to sing a Grieg song at the memorial concert on the fiftieth anniversary of the composer's death, 7 September 1957. Sir Malcolm Sargent conducted the BBC Orchestra in the Albert Hall, London.

At the dedication of Joseph Grimeland's statue of Kirsten Flagstad, in Oslo on 5 May 1982 – from left to right: Arthur Dusenberry, Flagstad's son-in-law; Karen Marie Flagstad, her sister; Berit Stabben, her housekeeper; and Sigurd Hall Dusenberry, her grandson.

declined what everyone thought was a gracious offer from the Met, the New York papers made the most of it. Just think of her being so ungrateful after all the Metropolitan had done for her, they said. Then the winds of fury were once more unleashed: hate articles reappeared, and some angry New Yorkers poured out their rekindled wrath in letters to the press. Edward Johnson added fuel to the fire by stating that the Metropolitan had made no such offer, and that he did not want Kirsten Flagstad back at the Met.

With this turn of events, much of the goodwill she had earned evaporated. In San Francisco, the Board of Trustees of the War Memorial Opera House refused to allow the San Francisco Opera Association to produce any opera in which Kirsten Flagstad might appear; to which the Opera Association Board retorted that there would be no opera in San Francisco that year, should she not sing. The Memorial Board reconsidered.

My first thought when I saw the papers was, 'Oh, God, shall I never have peace?' And I asked myself, 'Why do you subject yourself to all this in America when you can sing anywhere in Europe, where you are always welcome?' But it was tremendously encouraging to know that the San Francisco Opera Board supported me. Then my Norwegian stubbornness took over, and I determined to fight on until I won.

After the performances in Salzburg, I travelled home to Norway to enjoy a few months' well earned summer holiday. It was my first visit to my homeland since I had left before Christmas in 1946. How wonderful it was to be home again! Time is the healer they say it is. I found that most of my bitterness had vanished.

When Kirsten arrived in San Francisco in September 1949, a tense opera management awaited her. Threats poured in from both named and anonymous sources; there were threats of sabotage if she should sing. Her friends the Esbergs, with whom she was staying, did not know how best to protect her, should these threats be carried out. She herself was unconcerned: she had been through all this before and was hardened to it.

The only thing that disturbed me was the fact that it is so easy in the theatre to arrange an 'accident'. If someone is determined to harm you, there are a thousand ways, on or off stage.

205

The first night, Friday 30 September, I had to go through a police cordon to get in, and, moreover, I had to produce identification. Once inside, I wasn't permitted to take a step without police protection. On stage, I was literally ringed by police stationed solidly around the backstage area. Nothing happened, either because of tight security or because the threats were in fact harmless.

What did take place was a stunning success for Kirsten Flagstad as Isolde in her first appearance in the San Francisco War Memorial Opera House since the war. Her Tristan on this occasion was again Set Svanholm. In his review of the performance, Alfred Frankenstein, music critic of the *San Francisco Chronicle*, wrote:

No *Tristan* in local history seemed so intense, so totally absorbing, so completely overwhelming in its impact. The main reason for this, of course, was the return of Kirsten Flagstad after ten years' absence from the roster of the San Francisco Opera Company. Nothing has happened in that decade to dim Flagstad's luster as the supreme Wagnerian of our time. . . . Her voice remains an instrument of incomparable golden glory supported by the most unfailing perfect ear in opera and by reserves of strength and power which belong in the realm of the fabulous. . . . But when you have accounted for everything – beauty of tone, richness of phrase, tireless vitality, impeccable musicianship, splendor of presence – there remains a certain magic over and above the describable factors which is the product of their sum and the personality behind it all. . . .

For the rest, one was delightfully reminded of certain turns of phrase, gestures and mannerisms one had forgotten, including Flagstad's way of taking a curtain call as if she had wandered out more or less by accident and wasn't quite sure that this was the place where she belonged.

In December Kirsten went to New York for her annual Carnegie Hall recital. She was met at the airport by McArthur and Marks Levine, who had much to tell her.

Marks had barely said hello, when he asked if I would mind discussing the Metropolitan, after all the trials of the rightly named 'trial balloon'. Without waiting for an answer, he burst out with the news that Rudolf Bing, the newly appointed general manager, had asked for a meeting with me. Although I felt cheered and happy about it, I told Levine I wasn't sure I wanted to go back to the Metropolitan after all I'd gone through on that score. But I would see him.

When I met Rudolf Bing, I was charmed at once. He was friendly, most courteous, and very positive in manner. 'Will you come back to the Met, Madame Flagstad?' he asked after we sat down. 'Yes, Mr Bing, I will,' I replied. We agreed very quickly on which roles I would sing, and we also agreed that that information should be kept confidential until he decided it was time to let the bombshell drop. He added that he had his reasons for this. There was nothing more to say. I had full confidence in Mr Bing.

In February 1950, while Kirsten was in Barcelona where she had been engaged by the Opera, she received a cablegram from America saying that Bing had let the bombshell drop and that it had gone off with a mighty bang. The repercussions included the temporary defection of Helen Traubel, the resignation of Lauritz Melchior and the personal harassment of Rudolf Bing. Sir Rudolf – he was knighted by Queen Elizabeth in 1971 – gives a succinct account of this episode in his book *5000 Nights at the Opera*, published in 1972. He stood his ground, and he hoped that Kirsten Flagstad would be strong enough to weather this latest storm. He was certain that all the scurrilous attacks would stop long before her first scheduled appearance in January 1951, and that she would then be received as the great artist she was.

During those first three years of concertizing in America after the war, I experienced extremes of both good and evil. I had become well acquainted with malicious newspaper articles and demonstrators, and I hoped I was finished with them. But as the time approached for my first appearance at the Metropolitan, the whole thing flared up again. When I sang at Carnegie Hall in December 1950, the place was surrounded by demonstrators, larger in number and uglier than ever before. I could hear the shrieking even in the quiet of my dressing-room. Through the curtain I could make out their placards, and I can assure you that what was printed on them was not pleasant. But when I went on stage, the greeting of the more than three thousand people in the audience struck me with the force of a tidal wave. I had evidently not lost all my friends in New York.

Each day many letters were brought up to my hotel suite. Most of them were warm and friendly, but there were also some threatening and abusive ones – anonymous, of course. Those unsigned letters told me in no uncertain terms what would happen to me if I ventured onto the stage of the Metropolitan. The most horrible of all was a letter from a woman who declared she would circumvent the security and lie in wait for me backstage. She would hide in a dark corner, and when I went by to go on stage she would throw a whole bottle of acid in my face. I know I would never have read those horrible letters had I not been instructed to hand over to the police all those containing threats, so that the necessary safety precautions could be taken.

On the night of my first appearance, Monday 22 January 1951, as Isolde, I was smuggled into the Opera House through a side door. While I sat fully made-up and in costume, I heard the police covering every inch of the passageway outside my door. Bright lights illuminated each entrance to the stage. The management dared not take a single chance of anything untoward happening. I must confess I was in a highly nervous state, and to calm myself I played one game of patience after another. I knew I would be fine as soon as I walked on stage. I heaved a sigh of relief when I was told the Prelude had started.

She was not told, however, that Fritz Reiner had conducted the opening measures of the Prelude with the house lights on. Nor was she informed that the chief of police occupied a centre box from which he had a view of the entire auditorium. The police escorted her on stage, and not until she reclined on Isolde's couch were any lights dimmed. Then the curtain slowly rose, and the audience saw Kirsten Flagstad. There was a roar of recognition and thunderous applause that went on and on. Then someone cried out, 'Welcome back!' and the cry was picked up by hundreds of voices. Reiner put down his baton and simply waited for the clamour to subside. 'I thought, mistakenly, to myself, "they only think I'm nervous and need help. I wish they'd stop so I can begin to sing." Nearly ten years had passed since I had sung at the Metropolitan. It surprised me that I wasn't happier to be back – I felt more triumphant than happy. The most important thing to me was that I had been asked to come back.'

Happily there were no incidents – only demonstrations of enthusiasm and devotion. In the history of the Metropolitan, no artist had ever experienced such a tribute.

Her Tristan on that historic night was the Chilean tenor, Ramón Vinay. Before the third act, Kirsten liked to arrange the bearskin covering Tristan's deathbed.

This precaution was habitual with me. It had nothing to do with superstition, but rather with common sense. I had a secret dread that sometime, while bending over the dead Tristan, I might slide down from the bearskin before standing up to sing the 'Liebestod'. Therefore, each time I sang Isolde I went on stage before the last act to make sure the skin was secure, with the pile facing upwards towards the head of the couch. If the pile went the opposite way, it was slippery, and both Tristan and I had a good chance of landing on the floor. My habit of inspecting the pelt was known on every stage on which I sang. Many laughed at my caution, but they were all helpful and sweet about it. Not until I had made sure everything was right did I feel at ease.

The New York critics, with one accord, called her 'the world's greatest Wagnerian singer', likening to spots on the sun a certain lessening of fullness in the high notes, as compared to ten years before. One reviewer mentioned the new cello sound of the lower notes, saying that if she ever tired of singing as a soprano, she could start a new career as a mezzo-soprano.

Kirsten had invited Else, Arthur and Sigurd to attend her first performances in the four roles she had been engaged to sing at the Metropolitan in 1951: Isolde, the three Brünnhildes, and Leonore in *Fidelio*. Sigurd had turned four in the September, and was allowed to stay with 'Mormor' backstage when she sang matinée performances:

Whenever Sigurd went with me to the theatre, I asked Else to dress him in his sailor suit. It had white cuffs, and sometimes when he stood in the orchestra pit, I could see his white cuffs and imagine those small hands applauding. When I took a curtain call I blew him a kiss. He was permitted to be in my dressing-room between acts and to help me dress. The most fun of all for him was powdering my face with the very largest of powder puffs before I went on. He was an enchanting little boy. Is it any wonder that my heart beat faster every time I looked at him?

When Kirsten had a night off, she would baby-sit for Sigurd, so that Else and Arthur could have some fun in the Big City. Sigurd received the most lavish gifts from complete strangers, which was a puzzle to Kirsten. 'Don't be so naïve, Kirsten,' said her son-in-law. 'Don't you realize that many people send Sigurd presents so that they can be on speaking terms with "Mormor"?'

The agreement with Rudolf Bing was that Kirsten would sing eleven times in 1951. It would be useless to ask her for more, she had said.

I was satisfied to be back, but I was not interested in singing night after night as I had done before the war. I was no longer able to do that. Mr Bing understood completely and respected my wishes. One thing for which I am deeply grateful is that I had the opportunity during that time to sing again under the direction of Dr Bruno Walter. I was a great admirer of Dr Walter, and we were good friends, even though we saw each other socially very seldom. We were both much too busy to lead social lives. I was, therefore, very surprised one afternoon when the doorbell of my hotel apartment rang, and there he stood. 'I have come to rehearse,' was all he said. He took off his hat, but kept his overcoat on. He went straight to the piano and played the opening bars of Leonore's aria. 'Would you be so kind as to sing through it, Madame Flagstad?' he asked.

We had made no appointment for any rehearsal, but he acted as if we had, so I obediently sang. He got up, bowed and said, 'Many thanks'. Then he took his hat, bowed once more, and left without another word. I stood in the middle of the room, completely flabbergasted. Dr Walter never explained why he had come that day and asked me to sing. I can think of no other reason than that he just wanted to hear me sing that aria.

The last performance of that Metropolitan season for Kirsten was on 26 March 1951. It had to be as Isolde, the role with which she was so identified in America, that she said farewell. At the mere mention of Flagstad as Isolde, there was standing room only. She had requested that Set Svanholm sing opposite her on that last night. The applause at the end went on and on. Even when the asbestos curtain was lowered, the public made it clear that they had no intention of leaving. So the heavy curtain was raised again, and Kirsten appeared time after time.

She lunched the next day with Rudolf Bing. 'Is it quite out of the question that you will sing at the Metropolitan next year?' he asked. He knew she planned an extensive farewell tour to take leave of her American public. 'Oh, absolutely! I will have sung all the roles in opera I intend to, after my commitments in London.' Bing continued: 'What about *Alceste*? The Metropolitan is willing to stage Gluck's opera, if you will sing the title role.' The pause that ensued convinced Rudolf Bing that he had won. Kirsten simply could not resist singing in *Alceste* a few more times.

There were to be five performances, in English, in March and April 1952. Her manager was upset over this sudden change of plans, because he had arranged the next season down to the last detail. Like a departing queen, all she said was, 'You'll manage, Marks,' and set off for Europe.

Kirsten Flagstad had determined that the spring of 1951 was to be her final Wagner season. She felt she no longer had the physical stamina the roles required. Though she moved on the stage with surprising agility and grace, she had gained weight over the years. She had not been feeling well, and in the opinion of the doctor she had consulted in New York, she had a form of arthritis of the right hip, for which he suggested therapy. She never mentioned this to anyone, but there are many appointments for treatments listed in her diary for 1951. Public and press received with sadness the news that she had dropped Wagner from her repertoire, but they understood the reason for her decision. They also realized that she wished to be remembered as a Wagner singer in her prime.

In the spring and summer of 1951, she made farewell appearances in Paris, Zurich and London. Saturday 30 June at Covent Garden marked her one hundred and eightieth performance of Isolde, with twenty-one curtain calls and a few words to the audience: 'This is the last time I will sing Wagner at Covent Garden, but not the last time I will sing opera in London. I hope to take

211

things a little easier from now on, so please try to understand.'
While in London, she stayed with Bernard Miles and his family in
St John's Wood. Miles could see his dream of building a small
theatre taking shape: work on this first Mermaid Theatre was in
progress, with the grand opening scheduled for September 1951.

Kirsten looked forward to singing Queen Dido, which would be a
far less taxing role than any Wagnerian one. But she had to study
Purcell's music all summer, as well as perfect and polish her
English. At the same time she had to learn *Alceste* in the same
language for next season at the Metropolitan.

Oh, how overjoyed I was to come home each summer – and
home, that was Amalienborg near Kristiansand. I became as
excited as a child as we neared my house. When the car arrived
at the gate, the chauffeur honked twice. My housekeeper
rushed to the front door and flung it open wide.

The gardener had made a paradise of the garden: it was so
beautiful to look at. Inside, everything was in order. I walked
through the rooms to see if they were as cosy as I remembered
them. Miss Stabben had put fresh flowers in every vase. It was
indescribably lovely to come home.

Speaking later of these visits, Berit Stabben said:

And if Madame Flagstad was happy, we were no less so! It was
a joy to see her go around and actually touch everything,
saying, 'But how wonderful it is to be home; how cosy it is!'
She was usually quite alone the first few days; then the guests
would arrive from far and near. Those who had been guests at
Amalienborg before always asked if they could come again.

Madame Flagstad was very hospitable, and a wonderful
hostess, so that it was always gay and lively in the house when
she had guests. But she also liked to be alone, make herself at
home, and enjoy her own company. Then she would sit down
to embroider, to read a book or to listen to music. And of
course practice was always necessary, holiday or no holiday.
'There is no place on earth where I relax as well as I do here at
Amalienborg,' she often said.

When Kirsten Flagstad was at home in the summer of 1951, she
received greetings, letters and flowers from many fellow countrymen wishing to express their friendly feelings towards her. And

they wanted to hear her sing again in Norway, but she had had no desire to let her voice be heard in her homeland after she had resumed her career following the war – certainly not while the case against her husband's firm was still pending in the courts.

The case of the State versus Henry Johansen Ltd lasted from April to November 1949. On 30 November the jurisdictional Court of Appeal ordered the firm to pay 1,085,000 kroner to the State Treasury from profits made during the occupation. Two subsidiary companies were exonerated, as was Henry Johansen's estate. Henry Johansen Jr, as mentioned before, was declared innocent of any complicity in the firm's business dealings with the occupation forces, and received only commendation for his tireless and dangerous work in the underground during the war until he had had to flee to Sweden in 1944. His twin brother, Frederic, had to pay half a million kroner in reparations, and was given a six months' prison sentence. The compensation directorate appealed against the judgement, but waived later appeals. There had been no evidence to support any case against Kirsten Flagstad. She was named only as the widow of Henry Johansen, whose estate she was permitted to inherit when it was declared free by the courts.

Arthur Dusenberry commented:

I should mention the case of Frederic Johansen, Henry Johansen Jr's twin brother. Frederic was a charming man, by far the more affable of the two. He was also very naïve. His wife Helga was German, and many of their friends were German. This made the wartime situation in Norway a very difficult one for him. Both men worked with their father in the business, but Henry Jr and his family managed to get out of Norway and into Sweden in early 1944. They remained there until after the war had ended. Frederic stayed on in Norway and continued to work with his father. I'm sure he was used by the Germans for their own purposes, partly because of his wife's background. In 1949 he was tried on charges of economic collaboration with the Nazis and found guilty. This struck at the core of his being, and it was not long after that that he died. We have to be careful when we make judgements about people. Frederic was no more a supporter of the Occupation regime than was his brother, who was a member of the Resistance. But their responses to their situations were different, because they were individuals living entirely different lives. Henry Jr was also brought up on charges of economic collaboration with the enemy, but his record of activity in the underground proved decisive in his defence. Dear Kirsten, who was Mrs Henry Johansen, and the step-mother of these two men, was not a political person in any sense. It cannot be repeated too often that her decision to return home to occupied Norway in 1941 was based on two overriding concerns: the fate of her besieged homeland, and the well-being of her husband, who had asked her to come home if only for a short time. As a result, she found herself caught up in the tangled web of Occupation politics and had to cope with the situation as best she could. She certainly knew right from wrong, and her actions throughout the rest of the war and after reflected that awareness.

Americans have never been forced to live their daily lives under the gun of a cunning and ruthless enemy. Yet many Americans, *without a shred of solid evidence*, took it upon themselves to pass judgement on the actions of people they did not know and on a sequence of events totally beyond their comprehension. This defies rational analysis, but I learned something from it: to beware of the self-righteous, and to shun the person whose mouth is the master of his mind.

I'd also like to say a word about Kate Johansen, Henry Johansen's elder daughter. Of the four Johansen children, it was Kate I liked the most; she was Else's favourite, too. I believe it was Kate who understood the members of her family best, and she was devoted to her father, which should say something about Henry Johansen's character. Kate died in 1982; only her sister Annie is still living.

Now Kirsten considered the invitations to sing in her homeland, and discovered that she had so many offers that she had to think seriously about whether she should resume her concert career at all, even in Norway. She did find the time and the strength, before the coming *Dido and Aeneas* première in London, to appear in Oslo, in a benefit for the pension fund of the Philharmonic.

The concert was set for 5 September 1951, in the Calmeyer Street Mission House, a hall holding three thousand. Following the announcement that Kirsten Flagstad was giving a concert in Oslo, requests for tickets came in from everywhere. Cabled reservations arrived even from people in America, who intended to fly over to hear her. The day before the box office opened, the first hopeful took his place in the queue. There was a veritable festival atmosphere as the queue lengthened, with people spending the night in sleeping-bags or sitting on camp stools, in real carnival spirit. 'Nothing like this has ever happened in the whole history of Norway,' said the astonished box office attendant. 'People were almost crazy. The house was sold out before we could turn round. We could have used the Colosseum!'

At the dress rehearsal, Maja Flagstad sat in the front row, white-haired and wearing thick-lensed glasses. The imperious face was unchanged, her small figure ever regal. As the first notes of Grieg's 'Ved Ronderne' filled the hall, she smiled contentedly. Kirsten's voice was as powerful, rich and pure as she had remembered it. The minute the rehearsal was over, Kirsten left the stage, went down to her mother, and hugged her. Maja took Kirsten's face in her hands, and embraced her.

The night of the concert was warm and balmy. Before the appointed hour of eight, the summerclad crowd converged on the hall. A long line of cars drove up to the entrance as if for a Metropolitan opening, but the bare brown benches and faded grey-green walls of the mission house were in sharp contrast to the red velvet and gold leaf of the Met. Nonetheless the flower-encircled platform and the musicians in full dress gave the auditorium a festive atmosphere. And when Kirsten entered in her evening gown of ivory lace, Norwegian medals at her shoulder, everyone rose and greeted her with applause and shouts of joy. She had never had a more tremendous reception, even at the Metropolitan.

While she waited during the intermission in the old kitchen that served as a dressing-room, Maja held court outside. Everyone wanted to shake hands and offer congratulations. Proud and moved, she accepted the tribute, but when the excitement became almost too much for her, she said in her forthright way, 'But it's Kirsten's victory, not mine!' Not a little of the glory, however, belonged to her. Kirsten would never have been what she was, had it not been for her mother, and Kirsten herself admitted it. 'I am lazy,' she would say, 'but Mother is a bundle of energy.' The truth was that, although she would allow nothing to interfere with her artistic development, in matters that did not pertain to her career she could be a great procrastinator. She would sit playing patience by the hour, saying over and over again, 'Why am I doing this when I should be writing letters? I have so much mail to answer.' Then the day would come when she finally decided to get down to business, and everyone and everything else would be banished.

There was a great public demand for more concerts. 'I would gladly have sung had I not had to leave the following morning for London to attend the final rehearsals at the Mermaid Theatre,' she said.

Had Bernard Miles succumbed to advice, he never would have built his first little theatre (only 176 seats) at his St John's Wood home. His insistence on building an Elizabethan theatre met with some opposition, but fortunately Miles and his fellow workers swept away all obstacles in their enthusiasm. The Mermaid Theatre was completed on time and stood ready for the scheduled opening.

The cooperation and friendship surrounding Bernard Miles at this time inspired Kirsten. She threw herself wholeheartedly into bringing ancient times to life in the person of Queen Dido of Carthage. In her fifty-seventh year, and at the end of an extraordinary career, she made her debut in an English opera, the music and style of which were quite foreign to what she had known in Wagner. She said later:

It was great fun, and everything was just as it should be. Bernard himself was the stage director. With consummate ease he instructed soloists, chorus and dancers. The orchestra played from a small balcony, far back, above the rear of the stage. Geraint Jones, England's fine harpsichordist, conducted the orchestra from his place at the keyboard, playing all the recitatives himself.

So that we could see the orchestra and conductor without turning our backs to the audience, Bernard, who is both a magician and a wizard, had hung three enormous mirrors at the back of the hall. We could then see all that transpired, as well as watch for our cues from the conductor.

I must confess that it hadn't been at all easy to learn Purcell's music. Its rhythm and style were at first quite strange to me. But I loved Purcell's little opera from the first to last note, and I'm glad to have taken part in something as exquisitely perfect as *Dido and Aeneas* proved to be at the Mermaid. Memories of that, and of working with the fine artists Bernard had assembled, not to mention my friendship with him and his family, are some of the happiest I have.

The Mermaid Theatre opened to a specially invited audience on Sunday 9 September 1951, to honour its sponsors and all who had helped to make it a reality. Upon presentation of his card, each guest took a ticket from a large hat. In this way there were no privileged seats: the chief carpenter might sit in the first row, while the industrial tycoon sat in the last. Since the opera lasted only an hour and a half, two performances were given each evening, with half an hour in between. This, too, was a new experience for Kirsten. After the nervousness of the first few days, and when the production was 'set', her calm was restored and she found it exhilarating. That she was praised for her voice and her acting was not surprising; but what she herself was most proud to hear was that she had sung in faultless English.

She gave several Lieder recitals of Grieg, Strauss and Brahms at the Mermaid before leaving London. It was a daring experiment, since her voice seemed too large for singing Lieder in such a small hall. Much to everyone's surprise, she instinctively modulated the volume to fit the hall. When asked how she did it, she answered truthfully, 'I really don't know. There's nothing magical about it. I don't try to do it. It just happens. That's all there is to it. I can't explain it otherwise.'

After London, she was off again to Europe. Following the war she had won a large and enthusiastic public in Spain, and concerts in Barcelona became a regular part of her schedule. From there, she went on to several German cities. Everywhere she was greeted with acclaim. Then, suddenly, she was tired from all the travelling: 'I told myself I should retire, but that was easier said than done. I still had to earn my living and prepare for later years when I couldn't work. When people asked why I kept on, I said it took time to shut down a factory.'

The Norwegian Music Association, of which Kirsten had been made an honorary member in 1949, was to celebrate its fortieth anniversary with an orchestral concert in Oslo's National Theatre on Sunday 16 December 1951. When she was asked to participate, her answer was an immediate 'yes'. All proceeds were to go to the

Founders' Fund, and so she donated her services. She did this twice in Bergen when asked to aid their Philharmonic, paying all her own expenses.

After spending Christmas at Amalienborg for the first time since 1945, she left for America for her last season in that land of her greatest triumph.

8

A Long Farewell

Within three months, Kirsten Flagstad visited every American state in which she had appeared during the previous seventeen years. Everywhere it was the same. The public was sad and disappointed that she was leaving: 'Flagstad, we won't let you go!' they shouted wherever she went. After every concert there was a standing ovation, with stamping and shouting. It was very moving for her, but she knew it was time to say goodbye.

She dreaded singing for the last time in her beloved Carnegie Hall, on Friday 1 February 1952. She knew it would be hardest of all to say farewell to the audience she loved best. When she walked on stage hand in hand with Edwin McArthur, everyone rose, shouting, 'Flagstad! Flagstad!' When she came on with McArthur after the concert, she addressed the audience: 'This is a sad moment, because, after long and serious consideration, I have decided that this will be my last recital in Carnegie Hall.'

'No! No!' they shouted.

'Seventeen years ago tomorrow, on 2 February 1935, I made my debut at the Metropolitan as Sieglinde in *Die Walküre*. Last season I made it clear that it was to be my last, but I was tempted by Mr Bing into singing five performances of Gluck's *Alceste*.'

'Bravo! Bravo! Thank you! Thank you!'

'Because of the anniversary, I will sing "Du bist der Lenz" from *Die Walküre*.'

After singing Sieglinde's aria, she continued:

The Carnegie Hall concerts have been for me, always, the high points of each season. I must say thanks for them, and to my accompanist and good friend, Edwin McArthur, who has given me such great support through all these years in America. We have given more than a thousand concerts

219

together. Besides that, he has also often conducted my opera performances and orchestral concerts. He has most certainly earned the title of friend, true and loyal, particularly in these last years when I have been so alone.

With the last song I will sing tonight, 'When I Have Sung My Songs', I take my leave of you, my dearest audience. Three times more I shall stand here, when next month I sing with the New York Philharmonic Orchestra with Bruno Walter as conductor. But tonight is my *own* very last concert in Carnegie Hall. Thank you all.

The encores lasted as long as the concert; the audience just would not leave. But finally the hall was emptied. One of the last to leave was a young man who jumped up on the stage to pick up a single red rose that lay there.

Kirsten Flagstad's diary reveals that she was far from well at this time. At every opportunity she had sought medical help for the troublesome skin disease, psoriasis, which had already afflicted her for some time. (Arthur Dusenberry thought that the psoriasis was probably a physical manifestation of the tremendous mental and emotional stress she had experienced, and was still experiencing, as a result of the scurrilous attacks made on her by unscrupulous or ill informed people, and that the emotional upheaval in her life following the war was a contributing factor to her final illness.) She also had almost constant pain in her right hip. Her two doctors did everything they could to relieve the symptoms, which in the beginning were comparatively mild. She was able to keep to her schedule of concert and opera appearances, but the gnawing discomfort affected her general health. She did not like to talk about her ailments, and so those closest to her were surprised that she who had always been so calm and composed was now often irritable. Only Sigurd could do as he wished, without any protest from her. Arthur Dusenberry recalled:

When Kirsten visited us early in 1952 (we were living then in Madison, Wisconsin), she was working on the role of Alcestis with which Mr Bing had enticed her back to the Metropolitan for another season. Sigurd used to come in from play, bringing his friends with him, and there would be 'Mormor' at the piano practising her part. His friends were absolutely entranced by Kirsten's voice. There wasn't a peep out of them while she was singing. Sigurd, on the other hand, paid no attention whatsoever. That was just Grandma singing.

On Tuesday 4 March, she sang her last opera role, Alcestis (Alceste), at the Metropolitan. Olin Downes wrote in the *New York Times*: 'The revival of Gluck's *Alcestis* . . . last night at the Metropolitan Opera House was memorable, indeed unique, for the performance of the name part by Mme Flagstad. . . . No artist could take a nobler farewell of the public.'

Of her final performance at the Opera House, on Tuesday 1 April 1952, Kirsten said:

It felt almost like a ceremonial occasion to appear at the Metropolitan for the very last time. I wasn't the least bit sentimental about it, but that night everything seemed to take on a special meaning. It was somehow uncanny to be sitting at the same make-up table, because I realized I was sitting there for the last time. Uncanny, too, to hear so distinctly the usual backstage sounds outside the dressing-room. All my senses seemed to be heightened. Jennie Cervini, who had for so many years faithfully helped me with my costumes, walked around in tears the whole time she was helping me. It affected me so much that I too began to feel downcast.

But oh, how satisfying it was to say farewell with so lovely an opera as *Alcestis*. The Metropolitan's production was perfect in every detail: scenery, costumes, and all my colleagues, not to mention the lovely ballet. I had asked McArthur to buy some little thing for all the children in the production. That last evening they all came into my dressing-room to receive a farewell present – together with a good hug, of course!'

Else, Arthur and my closest friends attended. They said they felt quite emotional, and I felt the same reaction in the audience the moment I stepped onto the stage. But what happened at the end came as a complete surprise. After I don't remember how many curtain calls, the golden curtain went up behind me, and there in a great semi-circle at the back of the stage stood the entire cast, the opera's managers and directors, and everybody who had taken part in the production. In the very centre of the stage stood a table covered with a cloth. 'What in the world is going to happen now?' I thought to myself. The Chairman of the Board, Mr George Sloan, took my arm and led me to the table.

Mr Sloan then said:

Madame Flagstad, we have here on the stage a group of your friends in the Metropolitan Opera and the Metropolitan Opera Guild. We are just a few of the countless thousands of music lovers in America who are deeply grateful for your glorious singing here at the Metropolitan Opera House. Tonight we are overwhelmed by the realization that we have seen and heard you on this stage for the last time. From your first Sieglinde on 2 February 1935, until this evening's Alcestis, we of the Metropolitan have enjoyed a wealth of magnificent artistry from you that will never be forgotten.

In our gratitude we wish to leave with you a small token of our admiration and affection. We hope this will serve to remind you of those great days at the Metropolitan Opera House that will be recorded in opera annals as so much the greater because of you. May this silver cup and tray serve as a memento of all your friends of the Metropolitan Opera. The inscription reads:

> To Kirsten Flagstad from her friends of the
> Metropolitan Opera in profound gratitude
> for her magnificent performances: Sieglinde –
> Isolde – Brünnhilde – Elsa – Elisabeth –
> Kundry – Fidelio – Senta – Alcestis
>   1935   1952

On behalf of all of us we wish you, Madame Flagstad, the full reward of enjoyment in your retirement that you have so richly merited through the happiness you have given the world.

Very moved, Kirsten accepted the gifts.

The United Nations Secretary General, Trygve Lie, representing her countrymen, now appeared, carrying a large bouquet of flowers. From everywhere in the house came the cry, 'Flagstad, we will not let you go!' Kirsten only bowed her head and smiled. Trygve Lie, interpreting her smile, said to the audience, 'It looks as if she's made up her mind. And is she *stubborn!*'

Five of us who were at the Eastman School of Music in 1951 have fond memories of Easter that year. On the evening of 25 March we piled into musicologist Ernest Livingstone's rattletrap with him and his wife and set out for New York to attend Kirsten Flagstad's last Met performance as Isolde, the next day.

We travelled all night, the drivers among us taking turns at the wheel while the rest of us huddled in blankets against the cold. Everything went well until, at dawn, we found ourselves on a hill outside Moscow, Pennsylvania, with no petrol. It was a beautiful, clear morning, but very cold. My singer friends, Ed Willson and Cliff Snyder, went off in search of petrol and came back triumphantly with a US Army can full of the precious liquid. We had got as far as Verona, New Jersey, just a few miles from my parents' home in Upper Montclair, where we were headed on this first lap of our journey, when suddenly the brakes gave out and we went sailing through a red light at a major junction. We crept the rest of the way, thanking God that the early morning traffic was so light. When we arrived, in hilarious mood, my mother declared we were all crazy, but served us a fine breakfast, all the same. Ernest phoned a local garage, who sent a mechanic up to mend the brakes. He did what he could, and the Livingstones set off for the city. My father had succeeded in getting the other three of us seats for the performance, so we had time to spare. We took showers, and stretched out for a nap; but we were much too keyed up to sleep.

A glorious performance that evening was our reward. Flagstad was in superb form, sending one brilliant top C in the second act, ringing though the house. We looked upon it as a special gift to us. Flagstad set all her colleagues afire that night. The result was one of those unforgettable nights in the theatre when everything comes together to transcend greatness. When the curtain fell on the final tableau, there was a twenty-two minute ovation.

I took the next train back to Rochester and my job at the Sibley Music Library. In 1944 Congress had passed a law authorising financial assistance to veterans of the Second World War. The education benefits received under this act had run out at the end of my junior year, so I had had to find work in order to stay at the school. Fortunately, I had been offered a Fellowship, which meant that in return for working thirty-eight hours a week in the Sibley Music Library, the school would underwrite my academic tuition and pay me a modest salary to boot. It was a godsend, even though it meant working full time while carrying a full academic load. Dr Ruth Watanabe, head of the library, understood how hard-pressed we Fellowship students were and allowed us the maximum of flexibility in our work schedules. On this occasion, I had promised to work the rest of the Easter vacation if I could make the trip to New York.

Another KMF, the great English contralto Kathleen (Mary) Ferrier, came into my musical life at this time through her recording of Schumann's *Frauenliebe und -leben* and Brahms' *Vier ernste Gesänge*. Ferrier and Flagstad had much more than their initials in common. Ferrier's singing, like Flagstad's, was like the over-flowing into sound of a noble and generous spirit. It too seemed to emanate from an inner core of rock-like integrity, giving life to the saying that 'he who sings prays twice'. And Ferrier's voice, a true contralto of rare quality and richness, also had a unique timbre. Her untimely death in 1953 at the age of forty-one left the world a poorer place. I have often imagined how magnificent Flagstad and Ferrier would have sounded in the great duet 'Mira, O Norma', from Bellini's opera. Their voices were especially persuasive in music of a classical mould, and they would have blended to perfection.

In June 1951 I received my Bachelor of Music degree with distinction from the University of Rochester. I began to study for my Master's that summer, and continued working in the Sibley Music Library.

Knowing that Kirsten Flagstad would probably be making her last appearances in the United States in 1952, some of my Rochester friends and I made three trips to hear her early that year. The first was to New York, to hear her Carnegie Hall recital on 1 February. Luckily, we had a short break then, so we drove down in time to hear the première of the new production of Bizet's *Carmen* at the Metropolitan Opera House on 31 January. Fritz Reiner was the conductor, and I remember being fascinated by the sound of the Basque drum he was using in the orchestra for the first time.

Flagstad's recital gave further evidence of her continued growth as an artist. She had obviously heeded the opinions of some critics, who in years past had found her song recitals somewhat bland. The songs by her countrymen which made up the first half of the programme were sung with that singular understanding that comes from an affinity and a complete identification with the music and the language. She was never more eloquent, even on the opera stage, than when singing the haunting songs of Grieg in Norwegian. But the remarkable achievement of the evening came with her performance of Schumann's *Frauenliebe und -leben*, which she was singing for the first time in public. It revealed a new depth in her understanding of German Lieder. With no loss in quality or projection, she scaled down the volume of her voice to match the intimate mood of the songs, as if she was confiding in a close friend. And she allowed the text to make its own effect through the music, never indulging in the overemphasis and sentimentality which have often marred performances of this most personal and feminine group of songs.

Three songs by Richard Strauss concluded the official programme, but they now became the prologue to a series of moving events which brought this memorable evening of music to a close. After acknowledging the applause that followed the singing of 'Heimliche Aufforderung', Kirsten Flagstad announced that as the next day, 2 February, would be the seventeenth anniversary of her American debut, as Sieglinde in *Die Walküre* at the Metropolitan Opera House, she would like to commemorate the occasion by singing 'Du bist der Lenz'. Her voice now in glowing form after more than an hour of masterly use, she gave it free rein in the great declaration of love. It was then that she told us that she had just sung her last recital in New York. She asked Edwin McArthur, her colleague at the piano, to stand, and told us how much his professional excellence and personal friendship and loyalty had meant to her through the years. Her tribute clearly moved McArthur. She closed with three songs by American composers – songs with which she had long been associated – McArthur's 'We Have Turned Again Home,' 'Morning' by Oley Speaks, and Ernest Charles' 'When I Have Sung My Songs'.

At the end we all stood up, applauding and shouting 'Bravo!'; we realized that someone who had enriched our lives beyond measure was taking leave of us.

One wintry March day of the same year we made our way to Cleveland to hear Flagstad in concert with the Cleveland Orchestra in Severance Hall. The programme was Strauss and Wagner, with George Szell conducting; Flagstad was to sing three of Strauss' *Vier letzte Lieder*, the 'Liebestod', and the 'Immolation Scene'. She had introduced the *Four Last Songs* to the world at a concert in the Royal

Albert Hall in May 1950, with the Philharmonia Orchestra, conducted by Wilhelm Furtwängler. It had been the composer's wish that she sing them in their first public performance.

There can be no doubt that between Flagstad and Furtwängler there existed a musical rapport that was tantamount to spiritual affinity. They were both intuitive artists, and people said that her singing was never more glorious than when she sang with him. They shared a sense of form and phrasing which allowed the music to breathe and pulsate organically in accordance with its own structure. Of all the great conductors with whom Kirsten Flagstad worked, Wilhelm Furtwängler was indisputably the greatest and the one that she most respected and admired, and it was under his direction that the extraordinary scope of her powers was fully revealed.

My guess is that, in Cleveland, the first song in the Strauss opus, 'Frühling', was omitted because at this time in her life Flagstad found the tessitura too high for her to sustain as an opening selection. She was almost fifty-seven, and she had learned to husband her resources in order to meet her own exacting standards of performance. It now took more time for her voice to warm up, and she was aware of it. The three songs she sang – among the most profound that Strauss ever composed – were projected with an ease and vocal splendour that took our breath away.

Later, as the orchestra played the last notes of the *Tristan* Prelude, she rose from her chair, and with that remarkable, almost telepathic power she possessed, transported us to Kareol, to the side of the dead Tristan. Like Isolde, we were oblivious of all around us. The golden voice amid the orchestral sound evoked the image of the radiant orb of the sun embraced and then enveloped by the great expanse of the sea, leaving a golden afterglow.

Although she was identified in the public mind with Isolde, the *Götterdämmerung* Brünnhilde was Kirsten Flagstad's greatest role. Its epic sweep struck the taproot of her Nordic heritage, the reverberation rousing the mythic consciousness within her, and transforming her into a hieratic figure of unfathomable mystery. Every nuance of her phenomenal vocal art was revealed, in a portrayal of such heroic grandeur that it left its hearers stunned. Anyone who had seen her in this role on the stage looked upon the 'Immolation' not as an excerpt when she sang it in concert, but as the monumental climax of the entire drama, the sublime conclusion of an epic tragedy. That night in Cleveland, I felt more than ever before that I was in the presence of a singer whose greatness was akin to genius.

After the concert we waited inside the stage door to catch a glimpse of her as she was leaving. When she came down the stairs with Dr Szell and a group of friends, we applauded, and she smiled at us. She was radiant.

Flagstad was not as tall as most people imagine; she stood so erect that she appeared to be taller than she actually was, which was between five feet six and five feet seven inches. Her hair had been light brown, but it had darkened over the years until now, in 1952, it was medium-brown flecked with grey; she never tinted it. Her eyes were blue with a hint of grey, and she had a fair complexion. Arthur Dusenberry told me that her skin was sensitive: she could not take the sun, and avoided it as much as possible. When she was emotionally stirred the colour would rise in her neck until it became deeply flushed, almost red. This often occurred after performances when she was exhilarated, or on other occasions when she was angry or excited, Arthur said. There were no wrinkles to be seen in her face as she got older, because of the extra weight she put on over the years. Arthur also told me that she had the most beautiful legs imaginable. Else's father, Kirsten's first husband, used to say to Else, 'My dear, you have beautiful legs, but they're not nearly so beautiful as your mother's.' More often on view were her exceptionally fine, expressive hands, which, Arthur noted, seemed always to be in motion. And how eloquently and to what great dramatic effect she used them on the stage. Arthur said that as she grew older, her hands never seemed to age: they were always soft and white, with skin like a baby's.

We had decided to drive to New York to attend Flagstad's farewell performance at the Met, as Alcestis, on Tuesday 1 April. But before that, I embarked on my singularly unillustrious career as a recording engineer.

I spent the afternoon of Sunday 23 March in a second-floor seminar room of the Sibley Library taping the broadcast of the New York Philharmonic concert from Carnegie Hall. Bruno Walter was conducting, and Flagstad was the soloist in an all-Wagner programme, including the *Five Wesendonck Songs*, with Walter at the piano, and the 'Immolation'. I had to have absolute quiet, so the library seemed like the logical place. I had armed myself with my radio, a borrowed tape recorder and two tapes. I have to laugh when I recall with what professional seriousness I went about setting up my 'studio'. I placed radio and recorder on a sturdy table, plugged them in, turned them on, threaded the tape, and positioned the microphone in front of the radio speaker. Of course I had heard about using a jack to record directly from the amplifier, but I didn't trust anything so technologically sophisticated. When the broadcast began, I used the *Parsifal* Prelude and *Tannhäuser* Bacchanale to experiment, quietly but frantically, with microphone position and volume levels, first recording, then rewinding, then playing back – all at a frenetic pace more appropriate to the fanfare finale of the *William Tell* Overture than to either Monsalvat or the Hörselberg. Then, just in time to catch the ovation greeting Flagstad and Walter as they walked on stage, I pressed the 'record' lever, switched on the tape reels, and engaged in silent prayer.

I closed my eyes, and there was the stately auditorium filled to capacity with eager listeners. The conductor–pianist seated himself at the piano, and the singer took her place in the curve of the instrument, letting her right arm rest lightly on the slightly raised lid. He was seventy-five, and she was fifty-six. It seemed incredible that we were about to hear two musicians who between them had logged ninety years of public performance. The opening notes of 'Der Engel' rose from the piano, and then came the voice. 'In der Kindheit frühen Tagen. . .'. The lower tones, almost contralto-like in timbre, were fuller and richer than ever. In the 'Immolation', the runic utterance beginning 'Alles, Alles, Alles weiss ich' descends to the low A-sharp on the last syllable of the second 'Alles': the note was awesome in its evocative power. It spoke of a world veiled to the physical senses, a world of wholeness and inviolability. And at the end of the prescient passage, with the compassionate valediction, 'Ruhe, ruhe, du Gott!', the voice took on an unearthly quality at one with the majestic yet mournful tone colour of the muted pianissimo horns. In this masterful matching of vocal tone colour to both the word and the predominant instrumental sound, Kirsten Flagstad revealed the ultimate refinement of her art. It was this consummate musicianship, as much as if not more than her glorious voice, that earned her the respect and admiration of conductors, instrumentalists and discerning musicians in every branch of the profession.

William Barry Furlong, in his book *Season with Solti: A Year in the*

Life of the Chicago Symphony, published in 1974, records the rather similar experience of Margaret Hillis, conductor of the Chicago Symphony Chorus:

> Since young Margaret loved to sing and was fascinated by the radio broadcasts of the Metropolitan Opera on Saturday afternoons – 'I wouldn't miss one, or of the New York Philharmonic on Sunday afternoons' – her parents were willing to give her more exposure to music. 'My mother brought me to Chicago just to hear the opera,' she remembers. 'On one Christmas vacation, my mother and I went to New York – I was about fourteen, then – and I remember that in ten days we went to eight concerts, four recitals, and six plays.'
>
> On one such venture, she heard Kirsten Flagstad in *Tristan und Isolde*. Given a miniature of the score, Margaret tried to follow the performance right to the point where she heard a microtone shift in the midst of a long-spun note: the orchestra changed chords and, accordingly, Kirsten Flagstad had changed from a D-flat to C-sharp. *That*, to Margaret Hillis, was great musicianship, and attention to detail as well as to volume. It established Flagstad forever in her private Valhalla. 'I just adored her,' she says today. 'She's still my heroine.'

By some miracle, the recording turned out well. I considered it a triumphant vindication of my primitive methods, although I had to concede to the friend who had advised me to record at seven and a half inches per second instead of three and three quarters that his advice had been a positive contribution to success. I still have the tapes, and I play them every once in a while, happily reliving that Sunday afternoon almost thirty-five years ago.

The following Saturday afternoon, 29 March, I recorded the first and third acts of *Alcestis*, with Flagstad in the title role, from the stage of the Met. My piano teacher at Eastman, Zillah Halstead, had said that I could use her radio and set up the tape recorder in her apartment, which was in Swan Street, right next door to the library. Zillah was an excellent musician and teacher, and she had a droll sense of humour. She used to say that she went right back to the beginning, and could cite Scripture to prove it: Genesis 4:19. I loved her dearly. She accompanied me at my Master's graduation recital on 7 April. I felt honoured, because she very rarely agreed to play for anyone in public.

I managed to record everything but the final section of the ballet music at the end of the opera. The results were not very distinguished, but I've kept the tapes, and, like the others, I play them occasionally for old times' sake, or in remembrance of Zillah Halstead, who died tragically four years later.

After work on 31 March, five of us Flagstad enthusiasts set off for New York and Flagstad's farewell performance at the Metropolitan the following evening. We knew we could only hope to buy standing room, so we drove straight there, shaved and took showers in the Port Authority Bus Terminal, had a quick breakfast, and headed straight for the Opera House to get into the queue. The day went by quickly, and before we knew it the workaday hustle and bustle of the city had given way to the stir of early-evening excitement. Our queue got longer with every passing minute, and we were glad we hadn't dawdled in the morning.

At 7.30 the queue began to move, and in less than ten minutes we were in the great auditorium and had found good places along the railing behind the orchestra circle seats. A few minutes later the asbestos curtain went up, revealing the famous golden curtain, and by 7.50 the house was completely filled. The air of suppressed excitement in the auditorium was palpable. A few stragglers hurried down the aisles to their seats. Then the magic moment came: the house lights dimmed; the footlights cast a soft glow on the golden fringe of the curtain, and applause greeted the conductor, Alberto Erede, as he made his way through the musicians to the podium. He shook hands with the concert-master, bowed to the audience, turned to the orchestra, raised his baton to signal attention, glanced quickly from left to right to catch the eyes of his players, and gave the downbeat for the solemn D minor arpeggio with which the majestic Overture of *Alcestis* begins.

I, who had been caught up since youth in the Romantic outpourings of Verdi and Wagner, found myself strangely stirred by the classic nobility of this music. It was sombre, even stark in its effect, and yet it had about it a grandeur that was movingly human. It seemed to touch both the mind and the heart with equal force. As the performance progressed, I became increasingly aware of the marvellous architecture of the work, its symmetry, and its cohesiveness as a musical drama. I realized how much Wagner was indebted to Gluck for laying the groundwork for the *Gesamtkunst-*

werk, the 'total art work' which Wagner envisioned and ultimately forged in *Der Ring des Nibelungen*.

In one of her greatest performances, Flagstad brought to the role of the Thessalian queen not only her own innate simplicity and dignity, but also an extraordinary identification with the character that sprang from the sorrow and loneliness she had experienced since her husband's death. In that subtle process whereby inner pain may be sifted, refined and ultimately converted to serve a noble purpose, her personal anguish was transmuted into the musical expression of the compassionate love of Alcestis as set forth in Gluck's sublime score. The matchless beauty of her singing, the superb clarity of her enunciation of John Gutman's English text, and the eloquent *plastique* of her acting – together with her majestic appearance in a white chiton set off by a blue train and silver-banded golden hair – lifted us out of time and place and transported us to that ideal world of truth and self-sacrificing love that she represented. As the curtain swept down at the end of Act One, leaving Flagstad a solitary figure on the stage, her face and arms uplifted to the heavens after the great apostrophe to the gods of death, we were left to marvel once again at the power of this unique artist to move our hearts and ennoble our minds.

Although their appearance on stage together as husband and wife was somewhat incongruous because of the twenty-four-year difference in their ages, Brian Sullivan and Kirsten Flagstad managed to portray convincingly the royal couple's devotion to each other and to their children. I wondered if the talented Californian tenor shared my opinion that he was singing opposite the greatest singer in the world. In my mind's eye I saw Dr Genhart, my vocal coach at the Eastman School, take him aside, look him straight in the eye, and say, 'Young man, you have the opportunity of a lifetime. You are rehearsing and performing with one of the greatest singers of all time in a masterpiece of operatic literature. Make the most of it. Exploit your opportunity to the fullest. Listen to Kirsten Flagstad, observe her, speak with her, ask her questions. Learn from her. You could not have a better model.'

As Alcestis and Admetus, reunited, stood with their children in front of the palace to receive their grateful subjects' tribute in song and dance, the curtain descended on Kirsten Flagstad's final performance on the stage of the Metropolitan Opera House. Her ovation went on for over twenty minutes, interrupted briefly while she received farewell gifts from the company. I thought of what Virgil Thomson had written at the end of his *Herald Tribune* review of the first performance on 4 March:

> [The] evening belonged in glory to Miss Flagstad; and hers were the plaudits, the repeated recalls, the full gratitude. It is of no point at so late a date in this artist's career to analyze her vocal production, to describe the beauty of her vocal sound or the strength of her expressive power. She is unique among living vocal artists; and hearing her is a privilege, as remembering her will for all our lives be a pleasure.

We drove back to Rochester overnight, taking turns at the wheel, and sleeping when we could. In order to make the trip, I had saved up my permissible absences from school for the Tuesday and Wednesday and rearranged my work schedule at the library. When we arrived on the Wednesday morning, I went home and slept soundly for hours.

Alcestis inevitably brings to mind the other great music drama of conjugal love, Beethoven's *Fidelio*. Flagstad had sung her final Leonore in New York in March 1951, with Bruno Walter conducting, just as he had for the *Fidelio* performances a decade earlier. I had listened to the broadcast of 10 March, and had been impressed by how much Flagstad had grown in the role over those years. There was greater warmth and depth of feeling in her singing. And in the Melodrama with Rocco (Dezso Ernster) in Act Two, Scene One, her speaking voice, a musical instrument in itself, had taken on a deeper, darker quality, which brought out the intense compassion of everything she said. Later in the act, after Leonore had revealed her true identity, kept the villainous Pizarro at bay with a pistol, and heard with relief the trumpet heralding the arrival of Don Fernando, her response to Florestan's 'Meine Leonore, was hast du für mich getan?' – her 'Nichts, Nichts, mein Florestan!' – as spoken by Flagstad, was intensely poignant. Then came the ecstatic duet, 'O namenlose Freude!', with Set Svanholm, and Bruno Walter's supremely dramatic reading of the Third Leonore Overture, which roused the audience to a resounding ovation.

It was this 1951 performance of *Fidelio*, heard throughout the United States and Canada, that symbolized the complete vindication of Kirsten Flagstad from the charges of Nazi collaboration levelled against her by certain Americans ever since her return to the United States in March 1947. She had endured almost four years of demonstrations, slander, libel, and threats against her life. And she had learned first-hand the bitter truth of Schiller's 'Es liebt die Welt, das Strahlende zu schwärzen,/Und das Erhab'ne in den Staub zu ziehn' ('The world loves to blacken radiance and to drag the sublime down into the dust'). But she had triumphed, and triumphed in the only way that is meaningful: by being true to herself and standing her ground, by keeping her own counsel, and by letting time give the lie to her defamers. She was a survivor.

'What matters is not to submit. What matters is constantly to bear in mind what life should be and what man can shape for himself in defiance of all that threatens to destroy him and violate him.' – these words, with which the Nobel Prize Academy summarized the philosophy of Greek poet Odysseus Elytis, recipient of the 1979 award for literature, cogently express the inner conviction that enabled Kirsten Flagstad to come victoriously through this harrowing period in her American career.

It is possible to discern in the seamless vocal scale of a great singer certain notes which, when sustained for a beat or more, have unusual communicative power. In Flagstad's voice there were two: the G and the A-flat (*not* G-sharp) above the staff. (I differentiate between A-flat and G-sharp because a musician of Flagstad's calibre hears and intones them as two distinct pitches. The G and the A-flat each took on a different vocal colour depending upon the tonality and the word context of the passage in which it occurred.) For example, the G on the first syllable of the word 'Farbenbogen' ('rainbow') in Leonore's recitative 'Abscheulicher! wo eilst du hin?' in Act One of *Fidelio*, possessed a luminosity so intense that you could *feel* the meaning of the word, and its connotation, without *knowing* what the word meant; and the A-flats on the first syllables of the words 'Herrlicher' and 'Erde' in Brünnhilde's phrases 'O Siegfried, Herrlicher! Hort der Welt!' and 'Leben der Erde, lachender Held!' in Act Three, Scene Three of *Siegfried*, had a crystalline quality that immediately transmitted the ethereal yet somehow humanly tender mood of the passage.

These two notes were the prismatic gemstones of this extraordinary vocal instrument which its possessor rightly regarded as a gift to be cherished, and which, in fulfilling that obligation, she used with such consummate skill that it retained its pristine quality until the day she died.

I completed the course work for my Master's degree in mid-May 1952, and spent the next three months completing the essay which was one of the requirements of the degree. Its subject was melodrama, the musical form which had its beginnings in ancient Greece and evolved over the centuries into the music drama shaped by Richard Wagner. The form intrigued me because it had evinced such extraordinary germinative power in the evolving history of dramatic music. The essay was accepted by the Graduate Committee, and I received my Master of Music degree in music literature in the September. I continued to study singing, and early that December I made my first appearances as a professional soloist in two performances of Bach's *Christmas Oratorio* by the New Jersey Chorale. Later in the month I sang an audition in New York for the Fulbright scholarship that I had applied for – but that I was not, in the end, to be awarded – and then I began looking for a job to keep myself busy until I heard yes or no from Washington.

In January 1953 I began working in the art and music department of the Newark Public Library, where I was able to make use of what I had learned while working for two years in the Sibley Music Library at Eastman. In the summer of 1954 I mounted an exhibition to commemorate the one hundred and fiftieth anniversary of the birth of Hector Berlioz. It was an attractive display that benefited from the revival of interest in the composer sparked by *Berlioz and the Romantic Century*, Jacques Barzun's 1950 biography.

November 1954 turned out to be opera month at the library. I had formed a small company, the Newark Chamber Opera Society, and, spurred by reports of Kirsten Flagstad's recent triumphs in *Dido and Aeneas* in London, I asked the head of my department, Marcelle Frébault, for permission to put on the Purcell opera in the fourth-floor auditorium, while a major opera exhibition, already planned, was on display in the gallery. She thought it was a great idea, but the assistant director, James E. Bryan, was clearly not so sure. 'How much will all this cost?' he asked. 'Oh, not much,' I said. 'All we'll need is a stage built at the end of the room, some lights and a piano. I'll take care of the rest.' He was nonplussed. He looked intently at me through his heavy glasses, and said, 'I'll speak to the director. You'll be hearing from me.'

John Boynton Kaiser, the director, struck me as a rather austere man who would look upon a project such as presenting an opera, live, in the library as inappropriate, if not downright frivolous. I was evidently wrong, because a few days later Miss Frébault told me to go ahead with my plans.

I prepared the opera in my own time; and at work, when I was not scheduled on a desk, I wrote to singers and opera houses around the world asking them to lend us items for the opera exhibition. Kirsten Flagstad and Kerstin Thorborg were at the top of my list. Flagstad wrote on 24 August from her home in Kristiansand, saying that she was sending me the portion of her *Götterdämmerung* score that she took with her on her travels. It was Brünnhilde's part, removed from the complete vocal score and bound separately to reduce the weight. The text was underlined in red, and scattered throughout were numerous pencil notations, mostly in Norwegian, designating breath intake, phrasing and dynamics. Thorborg sent her working score of *Tristan*. The markings in it indicated that the work habits of the two master Wagnerians were very similar.

Helen Traubel contributed brochures and programmes from her 1952 tour of Japan and Korea; Lauritz Melchior sent his Siegfried sword; and Julius Huehn sent his Kurwenal wig. Zinka Milanov, who was then at the height of her career, and who that very month received critical acclaim for her portrayal of Maddalena in the Met's new production of Giordano's *Andrea Chénier*, lent us her elaborate jewel-bedecked Turandot headdress, which we displayed in one of the lobby showcases to entice people to the fourth-floor gallery. Milanov had sung the role of the oriental princess at the Teatro Colón in Buenos Aires, but had never sung it in the United States. Rosa Ponselle, Milanov's great predecessor in the Italian dramatic soprano repertoire, sent us her vocal score of Luigi Spontini's *La Vestale*, which was staged at the Metropolitan for her in 1925 and then disappeared from the scene. In all, nine world-renowned singers, twelve opera companies, one music critic and four arts organizations sent material. The exhibition was a tremendous hit with the public and created a standing-room-only audience for the performance of *Dido and Aeneas* on 15 November.

I had asked the young American soprano Claire Watson, whom I had met through my brother, to sing Dido. Claire, who stood then at the threshold of a distinguished international career, was in her mid-twenties. She was quite tall and willowy – potential liabilities which, by calling attention to them, she had turned into assets. Her posture was regal, and she moved with ease and grace. Her voice was a lyric soprano of good size and distinctive quality, and she sang with intelligence. She often expressed warm admiration for Kirsten Flagstad; in 1958 she sang Freia in the historic recording of *Das Rheingold* in which Flagstad sang Fricka. For the role of the Sorceress, the second most important in the opera, I had chosen Elaine Bonazzi, a classmate of mine at Eastman, who in 1954 was studying in New York. Elaine, too, went on to make a name for herself as an accomplished singer and actress, particularly in the field of twentieth-century American opera. She developed into a mezzo-soprano, but in 1954 her voice was mezzo-contralto in timbre, and in the middle and lower range it took on a cavernous quality particularly appropriate to the malevolent character of the Sorceress. The Aeneas was Leonard Hooper, a young lyric baritone from Union, New Jersey, who was appearing in an opera for the first time. His voice was pleasant, but as an actor he didn't have much temperament – which suited Purcell's conception of Aeneas perfectly. It wasn't the first time an audience was left wondering why in the world a woman of fire and passion like Dido would go to pieces over such a nonentity. The other principal of the cast, Belinda, was a young soprano from Newark named Ann Columbo. She had a beautiful lyric soprano voice with just enough of the *spinto* in it to make it arresting.

During the summer I had made the acquaintance of a talented young dancer, Martina Nolan, whom I asked to choreograph and perform the Triumphing Dance in Act One, and to pose immobile as a Naiad fountain in the Grove scene of Act Two. Her fountain was so effective that people commented on how lifelike the statue looked. I recruited the chorus from the whole of northern New Jersey, and we rehearsed in my teacher's studio around the corner from the library.

The musical preparation of the production was child's play compared to the staging and costuming. The library's carpenters built the stage platform in record time, and the local Mosque Theatre agreed to lend us the necessary lights. Then the fun began. Claire Watson knew a young man named Don Manfredi whom she considered a very talented scenic designer and stage director. He was. He was also an extremely nervous and excitable individual who thought nothing of barging into an important musical rehearsal to insist upon a decision on a minor point of staging. He drove the poor carpenters crazy with his incessant demands, and acted the outraged impresario to perfection, raging at everyone and about everything. I consider it one of the major achievements of my career that by the time of the dress rehearsal I had tamed him to behave in an almost civilized manner.

I conducted from the left-stage wing, with the pianist (a friend of the family) next to me, so that the audience would have an unobstructed view of the stage, with no distractions. Here was the Wagner sunken orchestra idea in its most primitive form, but it worked. At the end, the three-hundred-strong audience gave us a lengthy ovation, and afterwards, many people asked why we weren't repeating it, so that they could see it again and bring their friends. That was certainly the reaction we had hoped for – but the opera had been planned as a special event, and that was what it remained. No one was paid, except for expenses.

This performance of *Dido and Aeneas* in the Newark Public Library in 1954 was the first time that a complete opera had been staged in a public library in the United States. It marked the beginning of my long-term efforts to make the public library the cultural centre of the community: a place where the public can go for concerts, opera, drama and dance, as well as for books, information and education.

Kirsten reminisced about the year 1953:

It was a great pleasure for me to end my singing career in my beloved Norway. My secret wish had been to sing my final performance where I had sung my first, at the National Theatre in Oslo. And, if possible, I wanted to end my career forty years to the day after my debut as an opera singer. But would the voice hold out? This was something I often asked myself. Happily, my fears turned out to be groundless.

I didn't plan any engagements in 1953 beyond those I had already accepted: I wanted to be free to fulfill my wish, if possible. At the beginning of the year I had rented the National Theatre and hired the Philharmonic Society Orchestra for the occasion, so that much was done. I went to Amalienborg, saying it was now in the lap of the gods. My hope that Else, Arthur and Sigurd would settle in Norway turned out to be a pipedream. They didn't feel comfortable in what for them were strange surroundings, and so they returned to America in the autumn of 1952, after only a few months in Norway.

It wasn't long before it became known that I would accept Norwegian engagements, and offers poured in. At the beginning of February 1953, I had a wonderful experience: I gave a concert solely for children. 'Adults not admitted!' A marvellous idea – it should happen more often.

I was introduced by Kaare Siem [the Norwegian pianist and conductor], who told the children I was almost as famous as the Christmas elf, and they shouted for joy. I love the yells, the spontaneous outbursts of joy. Children are so honest – if they like something, they say so; if they don't like it, they let you know too. If only we grown-ups were as healthy and as uncomplicated.

The year 1953 was Kirsten Flagstad's last as an opera singer. She appeared only as Dido, which was an ideal role for both her voice and her temperament, and coincided with her wish 'to take things a little easier'. The opportunity to sing the role in a Norwegian production was a high point in her post-war career. As it happened, theatre manager Axel Otto Normann of Det Nye Teater wanted to mount a Norwegian production, and it did not take a great deal of persuasion on his part to get Flagstad to work with him. On the contrary – she grasped the invitation with both hands. Thus, after many years, it came about that she stood once more on a Norwegian stage in an opera role.

Bernard Miles came from London to produce Purcell's opera, bringing with him the original sets from his own Mermaid Theatre, to make the production as authentic as possible. Ivo Cramér was the choreographer and dance director, and the small baroque ensemble was led by Øivin Fjeldstad. Kirsten remembered:

> It was a joy from first to last. We repeated it twenty-five times in all, to a full house each time. Performing with my Norwegian fellow artists was both happy and sad, for I suddenly realized what I'd missed in all the years I hadn't sung in a Norwegian production. I was sorry that it had been so seldom.
>
> Saturday 28 March 1953, the closing night in Oslo, was filled with nostalgia and gratitude. Perhaps it was only I who felt that way, because I realized that that was the last time I would

238

sing an opera role in Oslo – indeed, in Norway. The greatest joy for me has always been to sing on the Norwegian stage.

I said farewell to my career as an opera singer at the Mermaid Theatre in London. In the coronation year, 1953, Bernard Miles had rebuilt his little theatre in the City of London, at the Royal Exchange. There I sang Dido twenty-seven times, and my very last performance was on Friday 5 June 1953.

I have seldom been so shaken as I was that last evening. I didn't think I could manage to go on stage in such an emotional state – I was so overcome by the realization that this was the last time I would step out onto an opera stage. The theatre had been my life, always. It was hard to say goodbye, but I lived through it. I sang the last lines of Dido's 'Lament', turning to face the audience: 'Remember me! Remember me!' At that point, the opera singer Kirsten Flagstad became a part of history.

My opera career has given me so much. I have received back tenfold whatever I have given.

In 1953, her 'finale', as she called it, she sang her last concerts in Europe's great cities; but she also found time to sing in many small towns in her own land. Together with her accompanist, the Norwegian pianist Waldemar Alme, she sang benefit concerts for small, hard-pressed orchestras: 'I felt fortunate to be able to help where help was needed,' she said.

The Norwegian flag flew from the balcony of the National Theatre on Thursday 12 December 1953, in honour of Kirsten Flagstad who, that evening, would celebrate her fortieth anniversary as a singer. Great torches illuminated the entrances as the elegant and animated audience streamed in. Norway's great singer should have a festive farewell. No one who was fortunate enough to be present will ever forget this magnificent concert. The *Aftenposten*'s review spoke for all: 'It was a night to remember. The enormous self-control exercised by Kirsten Flagstad in her art made itself felt in a purely personal way during this poignant hour. . . . She would have nothing sentimental. She was inspired by only one wish: if possible, to sing better than ever before. Her wish was fulfilled. No singer has ever taken a nobler farewell of her public.'

After accepting the thunderous applause and floral tributes, she thanked the audience: 'I wish only to say that my heart is filled to overflowing with joy and gratitude for having been able to celebrate my fortieth anniversary here. I had my doubts that it would really come to pass, but now it has happened, and I am deeply moved. A thousand thanks.' 'This is the happiest day of my life!' she said at the midnight supper in her honour at the Grand Hotel. 'Only one thing will make me happier, and that is the day when Norway has her own Opera!'

It had been Kirsten's intention to end her public appearances after she had presented her farewell concert at the National Theatre. To the constant stream of concert offers at top fees from all over Europe she said 'no', but added, 'I didn't say I would stop singing. I will sing where it is needed, when I want to, and for my friends.' Kirsten's 'friends' were those who needed her support.

While the rest of Europe had to live on memories of her voice, it could still be heard from the south of Norway to the north. Norwegian newspapers recorded her journey: 'Sincere Gratitude for Kirsten Flagstad's Generosity', 'Artist Gives Entire Fee to the Skien Orchestra', 'In Kongsberg Church She Sang for Red Cross Fund', 'Church Concert in Kristiansand Raises 17,000 Kroner for Children's Fund', 'Kirsten Flagstad Raised 25,000 Kroner for Great Hamar Church'. Of their arrival at the northerly city of Tromsø, Waldemar Alme recalled:

> You'd think she was a queen. The train had all its signal flags flying. As we approached, people lined the bridge. It was just the same outside the church where she sang. And how secure she was as an artist. For instance, when the organ suddenly stopped as I was playing the prelude to the Beethoven 'Hymn of Praise', she went right on with the exact note at exactly the right moment. She continued without accompaniment and no one knew the difference. Of all the artists I have worked with, Kirsten Flagstad was the greatest. But even more important, she was a great human being.

The skin condition from which Kirsten suffered had now gone from bad to worse. To keep it more or less in check, she had to go into hospital for treatment at least twice a year. Immediately after one hospital stay she flew to America to visit her daughter and her family. 'I seemed to be free of pain while I was abroad,' she said. 'A trip to America and two hospital stays a year became my routine in those years.'

Kirsten was a very orderly person, very meticulous in her everyday habits. Whenever she went to visit her daughter and son-in-law, they would marvel at the way she always managed to keep all her things in apple-pie order. It was rather a traumatic time for Else before her mother arrived for a visit because, although Else was an excellent housekeeper, there was a growing boy in the house and things were not always as shipshape as Kirsten would expect them to be. So for about a week before she arrived, they would go around the house every day picking things up and putting them away, hoping that it might develop into a habit.

Then there was breakfast. As Arthur Dusenberry explained, Kirsten was a night person because of the nature of her career, so over the years she had become used to staying up very late at night and then remaining in bed until noon or after the following day. Wherever she was – at home, in a hotel or with Else and her husband – she always had her breakfast in bed. When she was visiting the Dusenberrys, this favourite meal of the day was served at about 10 a.m. And needless to say, everything had to be just so: the eggs cooked just right, and so on. It was Else's responsibility to preside over this morning ritual. She would prepare the food, set it on a tray, and carry it out to her mother in the little cottage that she stayed in when she was visiting them. After breakfast, Kirsten would spend the rest of the morning in bed knitting. Practically everyone she knew at all well had a sweater or a scarf or a pair of mittens beautifully knitted by her. Another major event of the day was the preparation of the dinner menu. Kirsten loved good food, and once when visiting her daughter and son-in-law she enthused at length about a dish that she said was called Finnan Haddie del Monaco. On this particular occasion she had just arrived from Boston, and it was there that she had been served this delicacy. After listening to her mother describe it several times, Else was able to prepare the dish from scratch so expertly that Kirsten was very impressed. Thereafter Else would prepare it almost every time her mother came to visit.

In December 1954, she was preparing to travel to America. A month or so before, she had received a tentative letter from McArthur, written on behalf of the Symphony of the Air, the former NBC Symphony Orchestra, in which he inquired whether she might possibly consider helping the orchestra out of its dire financial straits. They hoped to regain their fiscal health by presenting a Wagner concert with Kirsten Flagstad as soloist. She wrote back that she could not give an answer until she arrived in America, and, together with McArthur, had decided in the first place whether she still had voice enough to sing Wagner. One rehearsal proved to both of them that she had more than enough, even for Wagner, so she agreed to appear in concert with the orchestra on Sunday 20 March 1955. McArthur was invited to conduct.

As soon as it was known in New York that Kirsten Flagstad's voice would once more be heard in Carnegie Hall, there was a race to secure tickets. Many were disappointed and had to be turned away. 'All the tickets gone in a day?' she asked, amazed. 'Then we'll give another concert, which will mean more money for the orchestra.' The second concert, on 22 March, was Flagstad's last appearance in America. She said later:

> If I had known how strenuous those two concerts would be for me, I doubt I would have said yes. The rehearsal, especially, was a trial because I was so out of practice. It was all I could do to make my way back to the hotel, where I fell into a chair and threw off my shoes. I sat there for I don't know how long. My friend Caryl Beckwith was concerned about my fatigue and wondered how in the world I could get through two concerts. But I managed. The voice seemed all right, but the strain of producing it was tremendous. I knew then that I had stopped at the right time, for even the last concert of a busy season, and a concert with a demanding programme at that, had seemed quite effortless a few years before.

Ten of us attended that first all-Wagner concert in Carnegie Hall by the Symphony of the Air on 20 March 1955.

When Flagstad walked on stage after a performance of the overture to *Der fliegende Holländer* by the orchestra, the audience rose in a body and greeted her with an ovation. She was wearing a becoming midnight-blue velvet gown with a centre insert of pale-blue silk crepe, and her customary two-strand necklace of pearls and teardrop pearl earrings. She was heavier, and there was more grey in her hair, but there was a light in her eyes, and her smile was as warm as ever. She could still manage with grace the quick, short curtsy which had so endeared her to the public when she first sang in America. As the applause subsided and the audience settled down, her body assumed that characteristic posture of poised tension that meant she was ready to sing. With her opening selection she harked back to her American debut twenty years before, singing Sieglinde's 'Schläfst du Gast? . . . Der Männer Sippe' and 'Du bist der Lenz' from *Die Walküre*. Later came the *Wesendonck Lieder*, the 'Liebestod' and the 'Immolation'.

Here was a woman four months short of her sixtieth birthday singing with the technical security, tonal splendour and musical command of a great dramatic soprano in her absolute prime. Only the vocally discerning could detect the extra effort it now cost her to establish and maintain the vital connection between voice and body. The power in the voice, that incredible arching up and over of golden tone that set her apart from all other singers, was still there. She remained supreme.

Nineteen fifty-five was a busy singing year for me. The most important events were a United Nations Day concert in the Mosque Theatre in Newark with the New Jersey Symphony Orchestra conducted by Samuel Antek, in which I was baritone soloist in the finale of Beethoven's Ninth Symphony, and a performance of Schubert's song cycle *Die schöne Müllerin* in the library auditorium. The Schubert evening was the first of many Lieder concerts I gave with an excellent pianist, Suzanne Loeb, who had been born, brought up and educated in Germany, and had fled to the United States with her parents to escape the Nazi scourge. Her knowledge and understanding of the German song literature was keen, and I learned a great deal from her about the subtleties of the German language. We worked well together, principally because we both believed in letting the music and the text tell their own story through the voice and the piano, without our underlining and thereby overstating every sentiment, as was becoming the fashion in Lieder singing. The composer indicates what he wants in his setting of the poem, and either the singer and the pianist have the talent, technical proficiency and artistic insight to transmit his intention, or they do not. No amount of posturing, crooning, sighing or pedalling, passed off as 'interpretation', can substitute for that. Indeed, a reliance on special effects and a neglect of the basics have led many music lovers to believe that Lieder singers are

243

very sensitive people without voices. This is a pity, for it is far more difficult to sing, for example, Schumann's *Dichterliebe* well than it is to sing and act well on stage an entire major operatic role; and it is far more difficult to play the *Dichterliebe* on the piano than it is to perform the Schumann Piano Concerto with orchestra.

Suzanne preferred Flagstad's singing of *Frauenliebe und -leben* to Ferrier's because she found it more straightforward, but she valued Lotte Lehmann's performance more than both because, as she put it, 'of the three, Lehmann is the born Lieder singer. The expressive quality of her voice, her personal warmth and her outstanding ability to communicate mood without resorting to artifice, are unmatched. And her voice itself doesn't stand in the way; it doesn't captivate you by its sound alone.'

I found renditions of the Schumann cycle by all three artists persuasive in different ways: Flagstad sang it as though she was reliving the events in her mind, Ferrier as though she was actually experiencing them at the moment, and Lehmann as though she was telling a cherished story. A very important factor, often overlooked, was that each of these three singers was most eloquent in the songs and poetic language of her homeland: Flagstad in the songs of Grieg and Alnaes, with Norwegian texts; Ferrier in the songs of Purcell and Maurice Greene and in folk-songs, with English texts, and Lehmann in the songs of Schubert and Schumann, with German texts. All singers, no matter how proficient they may be in the music and language of another culture, have a natural affinity with their native musical idiom and tongue. Take Flagstad's singing of 'Det første møde' ('The First Meeting'), a poem by Bjørnstjerne Bjørnson set to music by Edvard Grieg. It is one of Grieg's most magical compositions, and one that is thoroughly Norwegian in character. In its original form as a song with piano accompaniment, it is a haunting evocation of young love, with the characteristic moods of exaltation and melancholy masterfully woven into its lyrical fabric. It is a miniature work of art, as are many other little-known songs by Grieg. Their greatness is apparent, however, only when they are sung in Norwegian.

Flagstad's voice when she sang this song took on a communicative quality we did not hear, for instance, in her singing of Schubert's 'Frühlingsglaube', which is similar in musical style and poetic imagery. In the Grieg, Flagstad's voice sounded completely at home, as though it came from the very core of her being, while in the Schubert there was a certain angularity to her delivery.

She recorded both of those songs, and there is also a Flagstad recording of 'Det første møde' with orchestra (orchestration by Arvid Kleven, a promising Norwegian composer who died in 1929 at the age of thirty). A comparison of the two performances is revealing. In the original version, with piano accompaniment, the voice modulates itself effortlessly to the intimately ecstatic mood of the song. There is no sense whatever of the singer saying to herself, 'Now, this is a reflective song with piano, so I must be careful not to sing too loud.' The accommodation is obviously the intuitive one of the born musician. And the vocal rendering of the text confirms the singer's sensitivity to the colouristic beauties of the poem. The same musical intelligence is at work in the orchestrated version: the voice is, as it were, intuitively turned up in volume to blend with the larger accompanying force, and – what is most remarkable – it takes on a range of colour consonant not only with the text but with the instrumentation as well. This is musicianship of a high order indeed.

The brilliance of Flagstad's voice, and memories of its full glory in Wagner, disposed audiences to undervalue her ability as a recitalist. Here, her voice did militate against her. And her natural reserve, coupled with her abhorrence of 'special effects', was interpreted by many as coldness and detachment. In fact, when a singer friend of mine once used the word 'detached' to describe Flagstad's singing of Lieder, I argued that what he felt as 'detachment' was really the absence of emoting, not of emotion. To support my position, I read to him several paragraphs of Virgil Thomson's review of her concert of 8 November 1940 at Carnegie Hall. In this review, entitled 'Correct and Beautiful', which appeared in the *New York Herald Tribune* on 9 November, Thomson writes:

Straightforwardness on the concert platform is something rarely encountered except on the part of children and of the very greatest artists. Straightforwardness in musical execution is met with practically only on the part of great artists. Madame Flagstad is straightforward in her platform manner and in her musical interpretations.

She is not, for that, an unsubtle musician. Nor is her

splendidly majestic voice an unsubtle instrument. All the shading is there that one might wish and all the refinement of expression that lieder repertory requires, which is much. But such an assured mistress is she of her voice, and so clear is her comprehension of the songs she sings, that she is not constrained to seek to please her listeners by any trick of willful charm or cuteness or feigned emotion.

In consequence, she can afford the highest luxury of the concert stage, which is to sing the songs of Brahms and Grieg and Hugo Wolf and of our American song-writers as simply and as candidly as Miss Helen Hayes, say, might read Shakespeare's sonnets in a drawing-room. No intonation is false, no word unclear, no sentiment either under- or over-stated. By eschewing exploitation of her personality, she warms all hearts to that personality. By not feeling obliged to give her operatic all to every tender melody, she offers us each song as if it were a living and a fragile thing in our hands, like a bird.

Our century has known great mistresses of vocalism and many intelligent interpreters of songs. I doubt if there has existed within the memory of living musicians another singer so gifted as to voice, so satisfying as to taste, and withal such mistress of her vocal instrument as Madame Flagstad.

My friend remained unconvinced. And there are many other people who feel the same way. But I am confident enough of my own musical judgement to maintain that Flagstad was generally underrated as a song recitalist.

All of this is not to say that she was perfect. She herself would have been the first to laugh at such an idea. She had the voice, the technique and the interpretative ability to sing many things she never sang. Her repertoire was limited, both in opera and in song. Had she been more flexible in her approach to the Italian bel canto style in the early years of her American career, she could have sung Norma to a fare-thee-well without in the least compromising her exemplary musical standards. Her unerring musicality would have prevented her from indulging in any excessive vocal ornament-ation, and in time she would have found her own way to a memorable stylistic account of the great role. Time, of course, was one of the problems. She was always working under tremendous pressure – partly because of her laudable but possibly unwise determination to fulfil the exorbitant demands on her prodigious talent, and partly because of her unswerving devotion to the highest standards of her art. Nevertheless, in many ways she was made for the Bellini role. Her noble head and commanding figure, her charismatic presence and her striking ability, already noted, to convey emotion without moving, would all have been reckoned rare assets had she portrayed the Druid priestess on the stage. She would also have sung a superb Amelia in Verdi's *Un Ballo in Maschera*, and an unforgettable Elisabetta in his *Don Carlo*. She had in fact sung the *Ballo* role in 1921, when she was twenty-five. She said herself, during an interview in December 1961, that there were three roles she wished she had sung on the stage: the Countess in *Le Nozze di Figaro*, the Marschallin in *Der Rosenkavalier*, and Elektra in the Strauss opera.

I think, too, that she would have been a very fine exponent of French song literature. She liked the French, and she had an aptitude for languages that would have enabled her to sing as persuasively in French – notoriously the most difficult language for a foreigner to sing in – as she did in English. She was sensitive to nature and to mood, which would have made her performances of, say, Fauré's 'Dans les ruines d'une abbaye', or Duparc's 'Lamento', with its subtle Wagnerian overtones, something to remember. Her somewhat unbending stance in certain matters of style probably sprang from a fundamental component of her character – namely, her stubbornness, which, in its most acute negative form, was tantamount to a well-nigh obsessive rigidity – and this was definitely a contributing factor in many of her professional disputes and personal misfortunes. And it may very well have been this trait that underlay what some felt in her singing as a detachment bordering on coldness. In its positive form, her stubbornness stood her in good stead: without it, and without the indomitable spirit that it engendered, she never would have survived the nightmare of the first post-war years. Virtue and defect were two sides of the same coin.

My one reservation about Kirsten Flagstad's vocal delivery – and it is a minor one – was what struck me as her tendency to clip the endings of some words, especially in German, when they were set to short notes, giving more stress to final consonants than to the vowels which preceded them. I attributed this to a characteristic of her native language.

In the autumn of 1956 I left the Newark Public Library to accept a position as instructor and music librarian at Northern Illinois University at DeKalb, about sixty miles west of Chicago. I remained there for five years, presenting a recital each year, and hosting a weekly radio programme called 'Invitation to Listening' on the university's FM station, WNIC. In 1954, while in Newark, I had decided to enroll as a part-time student in the newly established Graduate School of Library Service at Rutgers University. I returned to New Jersey in the summers of 1958 and 1959 to complete the Master of Library Service degree, before being appointed an assistant professor at the university.

The Lyric Opera of Chicago, which celebrated its thirtieth anniversary in 1984, was just two years old when I went to DeKalb. This enterprising company staged many excellent productions during the five autumn seasons that I was in the Chicago area.

I heard the Swedish dramatic soprano, Birgit Nilsson, for the first time in October 1956 as Brünnhilde in *Die Walküre*, conducted by Georg Solti, with Inge Borkh as Sieglinde, Ludwig Suthaus as Siegmund and Paul Schoeffler as Wotan.

Nilsson was Flagstad's worthy successor, the only dramatic soprano of the next generation who could legitimately wear the Flagstad crown. Their careers have been remarkably similar, although Nilsson is the more versatile artist. Like most Scandi-navians, she is essentially reserved, but she is more informal on the concert platform than Flagstad was. I remember her, dressed in flowing black chiffon, waltzing around the piano while singing the lilting refrain of Rudolf Sieczynski's 'Wien, du Stadt meiner Träume', as an encore following a marvellous recital in New York's Philharmonic Hall in April 1973. The primary difference between the Flagstad and Nilsson voices lies in their projection. In Wagner, for instance, Flagstad's voice soared over the orchestra or shone through it, whereas Nilsson's gleams above the orchestra or, like a ray of light, pierces it. I think of gold when I hear Flagstad and silver when I hear Nilsson. Andrew Porter, music critic of the *New Yorker*, put it in a similar way when he wrote in his 19 November 1979 review of Nilsson's return to the Met on Sunday the 4th: 'Where

Flagstad shone like the sun, generously, warmly, Nilsson's radiance is on a narrower beam, its lustre that of burnished gunmetal.'

The finest production of *Die Walküre* I have ever heard or seen was the one staged by the Lyric Opera of Chicago during its 1960 season. The conductor was Lovro von Matačić, the Yugoslav maestro, and Christopher West, from London's Covent Garden, was the imaginative stage director. The cast was one of the greatest that could be assembled at that time: Nilsson was Brünnhilde; Hans Hotter, Wotan; Jon Vickers and Gré Brouwenstijn, the Dutch soprano, were Siegmund and Sieglinde; Christa Ludwig sang Fricka; William Wildermann was Hunding; and Brünnhilde's eight Valkyrie sisters were a well matched group of excellent singers. The production had obviously been prepared and rehearsed with care, and in performance everything came together to give the audience an inspiring night in the theatre.

Other outstanding productions in that five-year period were the 1957 *Otello* conducted by Tullio Serafin, with Mario Del Monaco, Renata Tebaldi, Tito Gobbi, Leslie Chabay (Cassio) and Andrea Velis (Roderigo); *Falstaff* led by Serafin, with Gobbi, Cornell MacNeil (Ford), Tebaldi (Mistress Ford), Annamaria Canali (Mistress Page), Giulietta Simionato (Dame Quickly), Anna Moffo (Nannetta) and Alvinio Misciano (Fenton); *Tristan und Isolde* conducted by Artur Rodzinski, with Nilsson, Karl Liebl (Tristan), Grace Hoffman (Brangäne), Walter Cassel (Kurwenal) and Wilder-mann (Marke) in 1958; Janáček's *Jenůfa*, in English, in 1959, with Matačić conducting, Christopher West in his American debut as stage director, Brouwenstijn in the title role, and Sylvia Fisher, the British soprano, as Kostelnička; and *Le Nozze di Figaro* in 1960, conducted by Josef Krips, with West again the stage director, Walter Berry (Figaro), Rita Streich (Susanna), Elisabeth Schwarz-kopf (Countess Almaviva), Eberhard Waechter (Count Almaviva), Ludwig (Cherubino) and Fernando Corena (Bartolo).

There were also some memorable individual performances in those years: Dimitri Mitropoulos conducting Puccini's *La Fanciulla del West*, and Eleanor Steber as Minnie; Gobbi as Scarpia, Rigoletto, Simon Boccanegra, and De Siriex in Giordano's *Fedora*; Boris Christoff as Filippo II in *Don Carlo*, and in the title role of *Boris Godounov*, in Russian; Nilsson as Turandot, Amelia and Senta; Bjoerling as Radames; Schwarzkopf as Fiordiligi and Ludwig as

Dorabella in *Così fan Tutte*; Leontyne Price as Thaïs; Tebaldi as Fedora. Then and later, Chicago far surpassed New York in presenting singers of international stature in some of their most challenging roles.

One of my most rewarding experiences while I was in DeKalb was my involvement in the establishment of a local arts programme for children. Raya Garbousova, the renowned cellist, lived in town, and for years she had dreamed of developing a cultural programme for children in the area. She found, in 1960, that there were enough interested people around to get the project off the ground, so a benefit concert was planned for 19 May that year, featuring Raya as soloist with the Northern Illinois University Symphony Orchestra. The concert was the social and cultural event of the season, and the $3,200 in proceeds got the newly organized Children's Community Theater off to a good start. (It is still going strong today, twenty-five years later.)

Raya Garbousova is a charming, vivacious person with an expressive low-pitched speaking voice and an infectious laugh, which reflect both her Russian heritage and her cosmopolitan background. She has a marvellous sense of humour and a gift for telling musical anecdotes with the flair of the born actress. Her home is a meeting-place for distinguished musicians, especially instrumentalists, who are in the Chicago area for concerts. She has added a delightful touch of European *savoir-faire* to the life of the essentially rural farming community. When Suzanne Loeb visited DeKalb in April 1960 to perform Schubert's *Die schöne Müllerin* with me at the university, Raya invited us to rehearse in her spacious two-storey-high living-room. I wish we could have presented the concert there, for it was acoustically far superior to the library auditorium.

I resigned from my position at the university in June 1961 and returned to New York to study singing with Sebastian Engelberg. He was the last, and the best, teacher of singing with whom I worked. My brother had been studying with him for about a year, and I was impressed when I heard the quite remarkable improvement in his singing. I was at home for the Christmas holidays in 1960, so I went one day with my brother to one of his lessons; in the course of that hour, I realized that Sebastian, who was a bass, had worked out for himself and mastered the technique of singing that Gillis Bratt had taught to Kirsten Flagstad. He knew how to explain and demonstrate the fundamental principle of good singing: the physical relationship between body and tone. I studied with him regularly for the next six years, and during that time a warm friendship developed between us which lasted until his death in June 1979. I'm glad to say that before he died he had the satisfaction of knowing that one of his pupils, Frederica Von Stade, had achieved international recognition.

In order to pay for two lessons a week, maintain my apartment in New York, and eat, I knew I would have to look for a part-time job. The last weekend in August, while I was visiting my parents in New Jersey, I picked up the classified section of the *New York Times* and saw a small advertisement for a professional librarian. The library in question turned out to be the Bloomfield Public Library. I took to the atmosphere there immediately. During a friendly interview with the director, Kenneth McPherson, I agreed to work three days a week, beginning on 1 November. In a way it was like coming home, because I had lived in Bloomfield during the first eight years of my life. I liked the library so much, and my work was so congenial, that in December I agreed to work there full time, beginning the next month. Thus began my association with the Bloomfield Public Library.

9

The Norwegian Opera

Towards the end of 1955, the Norwegian Broadcasting Company asked Kirsten Flagstad if she would sing the *Götterdämmerung* Brünnhilde for a broadcast performance and complete recording of the opera. Remembering what a tremendous physical strain the two New York concerts the year before had been, she was ready to reply that she could not undergo such exertion again. But on second thoughts she realized that a broadcast, without an audience and spanning a longer period, would be nowhere near as exhausting as a concert. She sat down at the piano and played and sang through the demanding role to find out if her voice could still stand the intense pressure. She decided it could, and said yes to the project: 'I must say I was as amazed as anyone that I could do it. And I was really pleased to be taking part in this *Götterdämmerung*, which would be preserved for posterity. Besides, I was looking forward to working with Norwegian singers. As the time for the recording drew near, I found myself elated and overjoyed to be setting to work on an opera again.'

When she went to the first rehearsal in the University Auditorium, where the recording was to be made from 2 to 10 January 1956, she told the conductor, Øivin Fjeldstad, that it would be wonderful to sing out full-voice again. She was present at every rehearsal. When she was not singing, she sat in the hall and followed everything with interest. 'Let me know,' she told the young singers, 'if I can help you in any way. Don't misunderstand – I don't say it presumptuously. But since I've worked in so many productions, perhaps I know a little more about opera than they do here at home.'

The soprano Ingrid Bjoner, who at that time stood at the threshold of her career, was cast as Gutrune and the Third Norn. She related how she seized the opportunity to ask Flagstad questions about everything connected with opera.

It was fantastic for us young singers to work with the sovereign singer of Wagner. I asked her directly if she would be our teacher and give us lessons. She laughed and said, 'How could I give lessons when I don't fully understand myself how I sing?' I replied that I wasn't referring to singing but to how she built up an opera role. Madame Flagstad put her arm around me and said warmly, 'My dear child, that I can teach you anytime. Come to Kristiansand with me when we are finished here. Stay as long as you want to. Then we can go through the parts you are interested in. Call me Kirsten. We are, after all, colleagues.'

Unfortunately, I had an engagement in Germany and couldn't accept this generous offer. But every day, as long as she was in Oslo, she worked with me in her hotel suite, instructing me in her method of work, teaching me how to develop a role both musically and psychologically. We concentrated on Elsa in *Lohengrin*. I remember that she said, 'It's not enough, Ingrid, to know the words and the music. You must also know the bases for Elsa's actions. Think about what lies behind every note, every gesture. While you work on your own part, you must also try to discover and understand the thoughts and feelings of the other characters. A person's actions are to a large extent determined by his relationships to those around him.'

What Madame Flagstad taught me has been invaluable. As time went on, I learned at first hand that when I step onto a world-famous opera stage I have to know my part inside out, and even be able to go on without a rehearsal. That is when I send up to Madame Flagstad a prayer of thanks for taking the time to explain and demonstrate to me her manner of working. One of the last things she said to me before we parted was, 'Now don't go off and develop nerves!' 'Don't develop nerves?' I exclaimed. 'The problem is how *not* to be nervous. How do I solve that?' She put her hands on my shoulders, looked me right in the eyes, and said solemnly, 'By knowing your part perfectly'.

I personally think that that was one of the secrets of her phenomenal career. She was always fully prepared.

Flagstad always emphasized that text and music are indissolubly bound together:

My teachers impressed upon me from the beginning that I must always sing with words, even when I was singing exercises. And I had to sing not just isolated words without meaning, but a narrative text.

I owe my teachers an enormous debt of gratitude for teaching me respect for words. We singers have a tendency to consider the music the most essential thing, and to pay little attention to the words. But it is the words, after all, that have inspired the composers. We must try to imagine and convey the composers' feelings and moods when they read the poems. Only then is it apparent that the words and the music are of equal importance.

I am also particular about the spoken word. I don't like slipshod speech or slang. One should speak one's rich language as beautifully as possible, be it Norwegian, a foreign tongue or a dialect. I myself love to sing the resonant Norwegian dialects. For me, Garborg's *Haugtussa*, which Grieg set to music, is in a class by itself, and so are Grieg's lovely songs composed to Aasmund Vinje's texts. No matter where on this earth I have sung, some of these songs have been listed on my programmes.

It was a matter of course that I would participate in the convocation in the city hall auditorium to celebrate the golden anniversary of the Riksmål [Official Language] Federation on Sunday 2 June 1957. Those who took part, except for me, were all poets, writers and actors. It was heartening to see so many out supporting the federation on a beautiful summer day when they could have been enjoying themselves in the country.

It was not easy for Flagstad to adhere to her intention not to sing in public any more. Everyone wanted to hear her. Had she said yes to one group and no to another, there would have been hurt feelings, so she appeared only when it seemed appropriate. On 10 August 1957 she sang at a concert in Molde honouring Bjørnstjerne Bjørnson, the poet laureate of Norway, on the one hundred and twenty-fifth anniversary of his birth. For the occasion she wore a colourful traditional Vest-Agder costume, which she had obtained especially for the outdoor event. More than five thousand people attended the celebration. Pictures of Flagstad appeared in the

London press, giving Sir Malcolm Sargent the idea of asking her to appear in Norwegian costume on 7 September in London, at a memorial concert for Edvard Grieg on the fiftieth anniversary of his death. She commented:

> It goes without saying that I would want to take part in a concert honouring Edvard Grieg, whose music meant so much to me. Grieg's songs had a special place in my repertoire. It had been a very pleasant surprise to me that the American public loved his music so much: I always had to sing one or more of his songs as encores. And the Grieg song they asked for more than any other was 'With a Waterlily'.
>
> I sang nine Grieg songs at the memorial concert in the Albert Hall. As an encore, I purposely chose 'I Love You'. With it I wanted to express my affection for Edvard Grieg, and for my concert public, to whom I was now saying goodbye for good. This concert marked the end of my singing career abroad.
>
> The rest of 1957 was taken up completing the series of church concerts that had been planned. On this concert journey, we mainly drove, Waldemar Alme and I: we were able to see so much of Norway that way. And we met so many wonderful people in our travels. A church concert was always a moving experience for me. The mood, the stillness, the sound of the organ affected me greatly. Between my groups, Alme always played an organ solo. How I enjoyed listening to the sound of the organ as it filled all the vaults of the church.
>
> Many of my listeners had heard me only on the radio. One little girl cried out when she saw me, 'Mamma, is that Mrs Ronderne?' I smiled when I recalled that, in request programmes, Grieg's 'Ved Ronderne' was asked for more than many of his other songs.
>
> When I had sung my last church concert, I was as happy as a child to be going home, without a thing in the world to do, at least for the present. I was finally free!

At last she could do what she wanted to do: read, play the piano, embroider or play patience. Kirsten liked to plan her day, even at home. Awake at the same time every morning, she took her meals at regular hours and went to bed at a set time. The time of day she liked best was the morning, which she spent in bed. After an egg and a cup of coffee, she would read the newspaper from first page to last, and then take up one of the many pieces of embroidery that she was always working on. She would listen to a morning concert on the radio while she did the finest petit-point. Just how many cushions and chair seats she had made, she herself had no idea. She had given most of them to family and friends. But in the music room at Amalienborg stood a complete suite of rococo furniture upholstered in her own fine petit-point.

At the turn of 1957–8, the outlook for a permanent opera in Oslo was being discussed in the press. It seemed that the years of planning and effort to establish a national opera stage would finally be crowned with success. Kirsten followed everything that was written with the most lively interest: throughout her singing years she had championed the cause of a Norwegian opera company. Now that it was to become a reality, she thought she might like to be a member of the Opera Board. But she kept her thoughts to herself.

One evening in late January 1958, when she was sitting as usual after dinner in the music room enjoying coffee, Berit Stabben, the housekeeper, came in to tell her that theatre manager Axel Otto Normann was on the telephone from Oslo.

The Norwegian Opera Board had been constituted in the autumn of 1957. At one of the early board meetings, Rolf Stranger had mentioned Kirsten Flagstad as a possible general manager. The board had agreed that it was a bold suggestion, but chose first to discuss the candidates who were seeking the post. When they had gone through the applications without settling on any of the candidates, the board chairman, Olav Lid, sought the advice of Normann. Normann, also, suggested Kirsten Flagstad, and offered to phone her to find out if she would consider accepting the position.

Kirsten was dumbfounded. It had never occurred to her that she might be asked to be the general manager of the Norwegian Opera. She asked for time to think it over before the board chairman called to tell her what the position would involve in the way of day-to-day work. She remembered later:

> It was a great honour, and I was both proud and happy to have been thought worthy. But did I dare to accept such a responsible position? To manage an opera company would be both new and strange for me, although I was familiar with

many details from my singing years. And did I have the stamina to stand up to the daily routine? I felt very well, except for the skin disease which came and went, and the pain in my hip which also came sporadically. I called my doctor, who assured me that I need not hesitate to accept.

I decided that if the Norwegian Opera felt it needed me, it was my duty to put myself at its disposal, even though it would interfere with my private life and would mean a complete change from the peaceful existence I had planned to lead for the rest of my days. The more I thought about it, the more I wanted to help build the Norwegian Opera from the ground up. When Olav Lid called later in the day and assured me that I would be ably assisted, I decided to travel to Oslo to personally confer with the board.

It would be a great advantage to have a general manager with a world-famous name: with Kirsten Flagstad as its head, everything connected with the Norwegian Opera would be followed with interest throughout the world. But this was not the board's main reason for asking her to accept the post: they asked her because they felt that she had the qualifications necessary to lead an opera company.

Professor Olav Lid described the meeting:

There were three of us board members at the meeting with Madame Flagstad and Leif Stake in the Grand Hotel the same evening she arrived from Kristiansand. During the discussion, I said that we had a very limited budget, and I mentioned what salary we had agreed upon for the general manager. This she accepted at once. That was the only time we ever discussed her salary, because she really wasn't concerned about it.

When the board met to adopt a formal resolution appointing Madame Flagstad, we were all so elated that we sent an announcement of the appointment to the Norwegian Telegraph Bureau. It isn't every day one takes part in something one knows will be news the world over – and we knew that would be the case the minute Kirsten Flagstad's name was mentioned. This was perhaps what made me first realize what a great gift we had received. Later we were to see much tangible evidence of this.

The news was announced on 3 February 1958, and bulletins circled the globe the same day. The next day her picture appeared on the front pages of European and American newspapers, and the bold headlines were followed by complete summaries of her singing career.

Kirsten had asked to be the first to tell the news to her mother, who was in a private nursing home in Oslo – Maja had not been feeling well, and was there to recuperate. The board had bound Kirsten to silence until the news was sent out by the Norwegian Telegraph Bureau, but when she visited Maja the next day, she found her lying there with an open newspaper on the covers. She smiled proudly as Kirsten came alongside the bed; then she took her daughter's hands in hers and whispered, 'Opera chief! Opera chief!' 'Yes – now you must hurry up and get well, Mother, so you can help me,' said Kirsten. 'You know so much about opera.'

Kirsten Flagstad's diary tells of meetings, interviews, conferences and telephone conversations from early morning till late afternoon, every day for weeks on end, after she became general manager. When she had retired from the stage and the concert hall, she had decided to refuse all interviews. But now she welcomed them, 'because now it's not I but the Opera that's being talked about, and about the Opera there can't be too much talk,' she said with a smile.

Some time before this new career had even been mentioned, she had signed a contract to make some recordings with the London Philharmonic Orchestra in London; then from London she was to fly direct to America to visit Else and her family. The board thought it would be best if she did both before her work with the Opera went into top gear.

Before the trip, Kirsten visited her mother to say goodbye. Maja appeared much improved. Several days later, Karen Marie went to see her mother and mentioned that she was planning to take a holiday in the mountains. 'Yes, by all means, my dear,' commented Maja. 'But you will come back for the funeral, won't you?'

'What funeral are you talking about?' asked Karen Marie.

'Mine, of course,' said Maja calmly.

'But surely you're going to get well and help Kirsten with the Opera?'

'No, I'm going to die,' Maja said simply.

Kirsten was notified that her mother was becoming steadily weaker. She wanted to return home immediately, but she received word that Maja did not want her to break a contract that involved not only herself but many other musicians. A few days before Maja died, Berit Stabben visited her. She lay almost in a coma and did not recognize Berit. When Berit said she was Kirsten's housekeeper, Maja smiled happily, and murmured, 'Opera Chief, yes. That's all I remember now. That child of mine has never brought me anything but joy.'

Late on the evening of Tuesday 18 February 1958, Kirsten received a telephone call from Oslo: her mother had died.

As the newly appointed head of the Opera, Kirsten had been interviewed several times by a representative of the Norwegian Broadcasting Company. The interviews had been taped for future broadcasting. On one occasion in the studio, she learned that some of the hymns she had sung earlier in Riis Church, with Sigvart Fotland at the organ, would be broadcast on 21 February. 'I wish I could hear them, but I'll be flying to Los Angeles then,' she had said. By a strange coincidence, Maja Flagstad's funeral service took place on the same day. It was a poignant experience for the family to hear Kirsten singing hymns over the radio on the day her mother was buried. They knew how distressed Kirsten was that she could not be present at the funeral.

When she stepped off the plane at Los Angeles, she was besieged by reporters. As head of the Norwegian Opera, she was again front-page news in the American papers. Since there had earlier been anything but a cordial relationship between her and the press, the reporters were surprised to find her both gracious and cooperative. But now she was the Opera's 'chief spokesman', as she put it, and that made all the difference. She was willing, in fact eager, to answer all their questions.

From Los Angeles she flew direct to Phoenix, Arizona, to visit Else, Arthur and Sigurd. They met her at the airport. Sigurd was now a tall, slim boy of eleven, with a young American's charming self-confidence. It was not long before the two of them had re-established the special relationship that had always existed between them. He was obviously proud of Mormor's new title; for her part, Kirsten was overjoyed to find her dear ones healthy and happy.

On her way back to Oslo, she stopped in New York to see if the theatres were offering anything that might be considered for the Norwegian Opera.

I've always been interested in acting and dramatic art, and I've gone to the theatre and the opera as often as possible. But it was a new experience for me to sit and evaluate performances from a professional standpoint. I found it both interesting and instructive. The Metropolitan put tickets at my disposal whenever I wanted to attend. The same was true of the Broadway theatres. I saw several musicals. To my surprise, I discovered that I was no longer shy and embarrassed when I was recognized and greeted by strangers. On the contrary, I enjoyed attracting a certain amount of attention. To me it made a big difference to be recognized as the head of the Opera, and not as an opera singer.

In Arthur Dusenberry's opinion, Kirsten considered this the crowning achievement of her career. She was a true Norwegian, and the appointment was an honour of which she was very proud. She talked a great deal about her work with the company. It was a new experience for her to be in the office and not on the stage, and it was not long before she began to realize how complex the role of an administrator can be. For the first time she had to deal personally with production problems, and with all the petty squabbles and backstage jealousies that crop up in any artistic organization.

The Opera had no house of its own to move into. If any project merited the designation 'castle in the air', it must surely have been Christoffer Hannevig's Norwegian Opera. The opera house that the Norwegian shipping tycoon had so generously 'given' to Kristiania in 1917 had never left the drawing-board; nor had the sum of money he had offered towards the building of it ever been received. His offer had been sincere enough, but the post-First World War years of economic crisis had buried his plans so completely that almost forty years passed before they were revived.

The Norwegian Opera of which Kirsten Flagstad became the head was to come into official being on 1 September 1958, but that did not mean that she and her associates did not have their hands full throughout the preceding spring and summer. Kirsten had never had a secretary in her life, and she continued to work without one for her first few months as general manager:

I hadn't signed my name as many times in my whole singing career as I did in those first months as head of the Opera. I wrote more than six hundred letters by hand at the Grand

Hotel and at Amalienborg. I scribbled away to those at home and abroad, and felt for the first time that it was fun to write letters. Before, it had always been a chore for me to answer all the letters that piled up.

But it was very inconvenient for us that we had no place to call our own. The administrative director, Gunnar Brunvoll, shuttled between his little hole-in-the-wall up in Keyser Street and the Grand Hotel, where I lived before I took a flat in Oslo. We also had our board meetings at the Grand. We longed for the day when we would all be together in the Folketeater building in which the Norwegian Opera, in the first years, would share the stage with the Folketeatret [the resident theatre company]. My first day at that office was Monday 18 August 1958. That was a happy day: we who were responsible for the day-to-day operation were together at last under the same roof. We also had a secretary, Rigmor Ottho, a pleasant and capable woman.

On 1 September the entire staff met in the general manager's office for a press conference. 'This is one of the most important days of my life,' said Flagstad. 'But not only for me. It is a milestone in the musical history of Norway. We must show ourselves worthy, put our backs into it, sacrifice, and work towards that great day when the Opera moves into its own home. I hope for your friendly cooperation and loyalty.'

'Are there many obstacles ahead?' the press inquired of her.

'A whole host,' she replied, 'but it will be interesting to try to solve them. It's a new world to me. I've always been used to a fixed role, only appearing on stage to sing. Now I am becoming acquainted with the work behind the scenes, and the administration of such a large operation. And good heavens, it's so interesting! Not that we won't have our share of problems to contend with.'

One of the problems was the limited budget that forced the Opera to begin on a small scale – much too small, many thought. There should be splendour and festivity at the grand opening, with one of opera's 'pearls' on the stage. No one wanted that more than the general manager, but she neither could nor would disregard the budget allocated. Gunnar Brunvoll, the administrative director, wondered whether Flagstad was qualified to manage the company;

it had been intimated in the press that she was, in all likelihood, only a figurehead. Brunvoll said later:

I must say I had my doubts. You see, a general manager must be strong and independent, and very courageous. It soon became apparent that Madame Flagstad was authoritative, purposeful and firm. No one could dictate anything to her when it concerned her independence in artistic matters. I admit that I met her with scepticism. But I very soon became a great admirer of hers, as a person and also as head of the Opera. In my opinion, she had without question all the qualifications needed to fill the post. She was fond of her staff, but she could not be influenced by anyone's wishes.

I have never met a human being as honest as Kirsten Flagstad. It made working with her so much easier. She was not unfriendly, but she could perhaps seem a little severe now and then. I can well believe that those who didn't know her became a bit frightened when they saw her like that. But really, there was more firmness than severity in her manner, and I always felt that behind it all lay warmth and humanity. She had no problems with authority – she treated everyone on an equal basis. No doubt she stepped on some toes. She must certainly have been tempted now and then to skirt the issue – and that would also have been more diplomatic. But she never did. She stood fast, and that was of decisive importance, especially in the Opera's first days.

Madame Flagstad prepared the repertory in close co-operation with her chief conductor, Øivin Fjeldstad. Both of them, independently, chose d'Albert's *Lavlandet (Tiefland)* as the opening opera, partly because it demanded no chorus. Indeed, we had no chorus – nor our own orchestra either, for that matter. We had to start from the bottom, with almost nothing. The general manager contributed money of her own as she felt it was needed. She herself paid to have her office decorated, up to and including the purchase of a new piano, so that the office could be used in the afternoons as a rehearsal studio. Four or five young singers whom she had faith in, but who could not be hired because of budget restrictions, she employed as student apprentices out of her own salary. I'm breaking a confidence, for Madame Flagstad never wanted that to be known – but it's really no secret, so I'm glad to say it now. Later some of these young singers fulfilled expectations, and have become permanent members of the company: something they also can thank Kirsten Flagstad for.

The general manager's eye for the economical was harshly criticized in the press and by the man in the street. Some, in the belief that the deficit would have been covered, observed that she should have exceeded the budget. They reasoned that once the Norwegian Opera was established, it would not be possible to close it down. Brunvoll commented:

> I'm not at all sure that such an argument would have stood up. There were very many at that time who felt they could get along very well without opera. If it became too expensive, it would have to be discontinued. *Now* we have come so far that no one would think of shutting down the Opera. What Madame Flagstad should have credit for is that she laid a sound foundation. She developed two things: a fine ensemble, because we had a permanently employed group, and a healthy financial base.
>
> I am pleased to have the opportunity to talk about working with Madame Flagstad. It meant a great deal to me. One of her outstanding qualities was that she openly acknowledged to her colleagues that there were many things about management she didn't know. 'You mustn't think that I'm all-knowing and can manage an opera company just because I've been an opera singer,' she constantly reminded us. She was eager to learn, and was always willing to listen to advice. As general manager, she was serious, but always lively and imaginative. It was certainly no prima donna we had put in the manager's chair, but, as gradually became apparent, a splendid organizer who was a joy to work with.

After all the intense preparation to establish the Norwegian Opera, the day of the first public performance arrived. A ballet production in Hamar on Sunday 2 November 1958 marked the official opening. Immediately there was criticism: the Opera should have opened in Oslo, not in some small town! Those who criticized the choice of Hamar for the opening quite overlooked the fact that it was the *Norwegian* Opera, established for all the land – for all its cities, large and small. Kirsten Flagstad felt strongly about this, and so did the board; while preparations for the Oslo opening were under way, the out-of-town production was quite in order.

The red carpet was rolled out in front of the Folketeater when the Opera opened in Oslo on Monday 16 February 1959 with d'Albert's *Lavlandet*. The curious crowded around the entrance to the foyer, where General Manager Kirsten Flagstad and Chairman of the Board, Professor Olav Lid, stood waiting for King Olav v and his party. Inside, the auditorium shone with white shirtfronts, medals and jewels. Representatives of the Norwegian government and cultural organizations were present, together with foreign guests. The rest of the twelve hundred persons who filled the theatre were opera enthusiasts of all ages who wanted to bid welcome to a permanent Norwegian opera. It was a truly festive occasion, with prologue and speeches.

National and local dignitaries greeted the Opera, and promised it their support. Then the general manager addressed the audience: 'The Norwegian Opera! The name sounds good. It is a proud name, and that puts us under an obligation. For years, many have worked for a permanent opera in Norway, and now that we have it, we must remember with gratitude all those who with their enthusiasm and with their work have contributed to the fulfilment of our dream. . . .'

The curtain rose on the opening performance. Already the next day there was criticism in the press – some of it sound and objective, some of it sour and petty. Criticism was to constantly attend those in charge of the Opera. The weight of it fell on General Manager Kirsten Flagstad and her plans, but she took it all in her stride.

Board Chairman Olav Lid told it this way:

What I most admired about Madame Flagstad was the personal courage and strength of character she showed. Personal courage is rare, but Madame Flagstad had it in abundance. Time after time she said, 'Put the blame on me!' She was criticized for much that others had done. I think she saw it as a duty to *sacrifice* something for the Opera. And to her that meant, among other things, that she could go ahead and take the blame for things that others, through thoughtlessness, had done in the first difficult days.

She was able to do that, *able* to take criticism on herself and not mention it to anyone. For the Opera, that was a tremendous help. It was also a help for us that she was so generous. At many a board meeting I received a note under the table saying, 'I will pay for it', when we needed extra musicians or chorus members that fell outside the scope of the budget.

I regret that she was so criticized here at home, often unjustly. It must have hurt her, especially since she knew she was being unfairly treated.

Kirsten Flagstad had hoped to remain as general manager for five years, and then to hand over her chair to another. Illness put a stop to her plans. Already in her first year as manager, the hip pain came back, more severe and longer-lasting than earlier. When she sat, the pain was not so severe, but when she stood or walked, it could be excruciating. When she was not in pain, she felt as strong and healthy as before.

She would arrive at her office each morning eager to begin work. She was interested in everything pertaining to the Opera. When she did not feel up to supervising a production herself, she followed rehearsals with keen attention. She tried to get her office work out of the way so that she would have time to attend rehearsals. 'I think it's important for a general manager to have personal contact with the creative work going on in the house,' she said. She made tours around the house to keep in touch with those who worked in the paint shop, the costume shop and the carpentry shop. Her visits were looked forward to with pleasure; she always had a friendly word to say, and a warm smile to go with it.

When she was appointed general manager, she was asked if people could also expect to hear her voice from the Norwegian Opera stage. 'No, that is the only place in the house where I will not appear,' she answered. 'Let the young ones have a chance now: my singing days are over.'

Kirsten had decided that her voice would be heard for the last time in her birthplace, Hamar. After a church concert there on 22 October 1958, she would sing no more in public. Such was not to be the case, however. Twice more her voice was heard from a platform, both times from the stage in the main studio of Broadcasting House. The manager of the Folketeatret, Jens Gunderssen, invited her on to his programme 'Guests in the Main Studio', on 18

January 1959; she was 'weak enough to let herself be persuaded', as she put it. When she had sung, Gunderssen complimented her, adding, 'Thank you for coming. You're a good girl, Kirsten!'

One day in October of the same year, she received a telephone call from Lennart Hyland, who was in charge of short-wave broadcasts. Would Madame Flagstad give him and his listeners the pleasure of hearing her on one of the programmes? 'Unfortunately, Lennart Hyland, I really can't,' answered Kirsten. 'In the first place, I don't sing any more in public; in the second, I have enough to take care of here at the Opera; and in addition to that, I have a terrible cold. So you will understand why I have to say no.' 'Then we will just have to postpone the programme until the general manager has recovered from her cold,' said the irrepressible Hyland.

On 21 November Kirsten Flagstad sang on a shortwave programme. She came onto the stage in the main studio in her black velvet gown with the white lace collar, smiling and apparently in good humour. The audience greeted her with enthusiasm. After Hyland had introduced her to them, and to the listeners in Sweden and Norway, he said that he had asked Madame Flagstad to sing the first song she had ever sung in public: 'When was that, and what did the general manager sing?' he asked.

'I believe it was "Toward Evening", by Agathe Backer Grøndahl, which I sang in the old Chat Noir of Bokken Lasson in 1912,' answered Kirsten.

'And shall we hear it here this evening?'

'I thought so, but when I tried it, it was like a bassoon trying to be a flute; so I've chosen another song I also sang in my youth, "Blåbærli" from *Haugtussa* of Edvard Grieg.'

Did those in the auditorium and the thousands of radio listeners who heard her sing 'Blåbærli' that evening, with the glorious voice intact, suspect that what they were hearing marked the end of one of the greatest singing careers of all time? Flagstad's last public appearance as a singer was just as she wished it to be: she had sung to help and please a colleague. Only her closest friends knew that she had terrible pain in her hip while she sang.

The pain eased again, and she felt well enough to fly to Arizona to spend Christmas with Else, Arthur and Sigurd. But the long flight and the change of climate had an adverse effect on her illness: the pain returned, more intense than ever. She spent the entire holiday in bed, hardly able to move. Alarmed at seeing her mother in such a wretched state, Else wanted to call the doctor, but Kirsten assured her that it was only arthritis and that the pain would certainly go away again, as it had before. She was under the care of Norwegian doctors in whom she had full confidence; there was no reason for anxiety.

It was not Kirsten's intention to keep her daughter in the dark. At that time, she herself believed absolutely that the pain was rheumatic; that it would come and go, and perhaps completely disappear if only she had time to undergo treatment. 'I have been so fortunate to be healthy all my life,' she said to Else, as cheerfully as she could. 'It is not unreasonable that I should have a few aches and pains with age, just like everyone else.'

But her illness had taken a serious turn. When there was no improvement, she flew back to Oslo early in January. A few days later, she had to enter hospital. Her doctors, who were of the opinion that this attack could be a prolonged one, advised her to request leave of absence from the Opera. On 19 January it was announced through the press that Odd Grüner-Hegge, the conductor of the Philharmonic Society Orchestra for many years, had been appointed temporary general manager.

Kirsten Flagstad's diary reveals what a difficult year 1960 was for her: she was in hospital for treatment no less than eight times. After the first stay, which lasted a month, she was permitted to go home for a few weeks. But the pain was so intense that she asked to be readmitted: she was better off there, she said. Various tests were made to determine the cause of the pain; little by little, the doctors became convinced of the seriousness of the illness. But Kirsten did not inquire: she continued to believe that it was severe rheumatism, and left it to the doctors to do what they thought best.

There was a change for the better in the summer of that year. She was able to resume her work at the Opera – for a short time, at any rate. Gunnar Brunvoll recalled:

At the Opera, Madame Flagstad tried to conceal the fact that she was in constant pain, but she and I worked so closely together that I was aware of how much she was suffering. She was a fighter and had fantastic willpower. In meetings and conferences, she appeared outwardly so well that no one realized what agony she was in. It was unbelievable how long she managed to keep going. But in the end she *had* to give up.

When the pain became acute, she informed the board that she had to offer her resignation as general manager for reasons of health. It is conceivable that people who did not know the situation believed that Madame Flagstad withdrew because she had been under criticism, or that she felt obliged to resign, or that the Opera board had asked her to resign. Let me make it quite clear that there is no basis for such thinking. All of us who worked with Madame Flagstad at the Norwegian Opera were very distressed that she had to give up on account of her health. Her illness was indeed much more serious than any of us realized. The board received her letter of resignation as general manager, and announced it on 17 October 1960.

Odd Grüner-Hegge was officially appointed general manager of the Opera.

When Kirsten felt up to it, she took part eagerly in everything that concerned the Opera. From her reserved seat in the auditorium, she watched as many performances as she could. If asked, she willingly offered advice. The Opera was her 'child', which, to the end, she nurtured and loved, and to which she gave financial support when it was needed. Every time she did this, she said sternly: 'Not a word to anyone. That is a condition.'

While she was general manager, she lived in a furnished flat in Oslo. Later, she divided her time between Amalienborg and the Hotel Bristol in Oslo. If the pain was tolerably moderate, she could take part in whatever she wished:

> I even sang a few times after my retirement from the Opera, but not in public. I am thinking of the evenings I spent with the old people in Vågsbygd, *my* home ground. Getting together with them at the home for the elderly was one of my most enjoyable experiences. They were so touchingly grateful and so easy to get to know. I wrote out the programmes myself. They especially liked to hear Norwegian songs and hymns. When I arrived, I would sit down at the piano and announce one at a time what I was going to sing and play. Memories of my own Mother became vivid whenever I was with the old people in Vågsbygd.
>
> It came as a complete surprise when I received a telephone call one day from Waldemar Alme, who told me that it had

been decided to present a painting of me to the Norwegian Opera. Alme asked me to get in touch with Per Krohg, who was to paint the portrait. At the start, I wondered if I'd have the strength to pose, but it went remarkably well. Those were happy times we had while he painted me as Isolde.

Kirsten was there when the painting was presented to the Norwegian Opera and unveiled in the foyer, on Sunday 3 September 1961. Per Krohg wrote:

Kirsten Flagstad – an idea was born, like a spirit, in the minds of two human beings: 'A portrait of Kirsten Flagstad must be painted and given to the Norwegian Opera!' None who know them will be surprised that it was the thoughtful Waldemar Alme and his wife who had the idea. Immediately they went into action, and it was I who received this honoured assignment. So she came, that warm and generous human being. I must say, they were enjoyable sessions. To the accompaniment of recordings of *Tristan und Isolde*, she stood and posed. She was again Isolde, completely involved in the role. As I sketched, sparks seemed to fly from the pen! She talked about her performances, so that the painting would have the right colours. This has been a great adventure for my wife, for me and for our house. I give thanks that I was asked to paint the world's greatest singer.

At about the same time, Kirsten noted:

As always when I felt well, I longed for Else, Arthur and Sigurd. My doctor said I could travel to America. With horror, I remembered my last flight, and wondered if I should go by ship. But that would take too long, so I took a chance and flew over in March 1961. It went fine. Some of my friends had been so disappointed at not seeing me the last time when I had been sick in bed at Else's, that now I had to make up for lost time.

But first I had to see Sigurd. Every year I looked forward eagerly to seeing him again. He grew so fast. It didn't seem possible that he was fourteen years old – almost a man. Why, it was only yesterday, I thought, that I was sitting next to his crib singing lullabies. Sigurd once thought that I wanted him to be a musician. He tried hard to learn to play and sing, but he wasn't very successful – fortunately, I'm tempted to say! For there is one life I certainly do not wish for my daughter's son, and that is a musician's. Now I understand why Mother did what she could to make us four children go in for a middle-class profession. I don't want Sigurd to experience the drudgery that goes with being a professional musician.

Now the Americans finally understood that I came only as a tourist to their country. I was also left alone by reporters, now that I was no longer general manager. In short, I no longer had to worry about appearing in public. I could travel around as I wished, comparatively unknown. I travelled as Mrs K. Johansen, and who could figure out who was hiding behind that name?

Katharine Cornell, the great American actress, was one of Kirsten's closest friends. On this trip, she found time for a ten-day visit to that delightful place, Martha's Vineyard, in Massachusetts, where Katharine lived with another of Kirsten's good friends, Nancy Hamilton. Kirsten brought with her tapes of all the songs she had recorded as a gift for Miss Hamilton, who regretted that she understood only the English texts. 'Then I'll translate the Norwegian and German texts into English and send them to you,' promised Kirsten. No sooner was she back in Norway than she began the hard work of translating the Norwegian and German song texts into English, just to please her friend Nancy Hamilton. 'I thought I was so fluent in English,' she said, 'but there were certainly many language "nuts" to crack. It was all lyric poetry. I made prose translations so that she could follow along with the songs as the tape was played. When I had finished, I wrote out the translations by hand and sent them to Nancy.'

Nancy Hamilton was overwhelmed when she received the translations. She had thought that Kirsten, in her weakened condition, would never manage to complete the work.

But we were really not surprised: neither that Kirsten had accomplished such a feat, nor that she had the ability to maintain the poetic mood of a verse in her prose translation. With her neat handwriting, and in near-perfect English, she had set down translations full of beauty and poetry. Katharine Cornell has recorded them, and it is our hope that sometime we can have a record made with Kirsten's singing, and her translations interpolated by Katharine. Several artists have heard this combination, and have been inspired and amazed. We who know how Kirsten worked, methodically and meticulously, are likewise inspired, but not so amazed.

Here in America we love her. As an artist she was unsurpassed; as a friend, unequalled. She was great in every way. We who had the good fortune to be her friends will never forget her.

In 1961, whenever she had the time and was more or less free of pain, Kirsten worked on her scrapbooks. She sorted, trimmed and pasted in the hundreds of clippings relating to her career that had accumulated since her return to the concert platform and the opera stage after the war. In the end, the scrapbooks contained a complete record of her career, from the first small notice in the *Eidsvoll Blad*, in which she received praise for her skill at the piano, to the reviews of her last recording, which appeared in the spring of 1959. As she worked with the clippings, she marvelled at all the lavish praise that had been showered on her. Had she really been so outstanding? 'I myself knew that my singing was of a certain standard,' she said, 'but other than that, I considered myself just an average person.' She recalled a conversation with Caryl Beckwith one day in New York, when she had been annoyed by a man who had been almost servile in her presence. 'Why can't people treat me the way they treat everybody else?' she had asked.

'Because you're not "everybody else",' answered Caryl, 'and you can't blame people if they go overboard when they suddenly discover who you are.'

'But I'm only doing the same thing you are, working to support myself. You teach, I sing. Is there any difference?'

Now she realized that all through her public years she had been fighting a hopeless battle against the prevailing image of her person. When people read what the press had to say about her, they must have had the impression that she was unique. Once or twice she had found the excessive worship almost humorous, as when a cab driver had asked for her autograph to please his son. 'How old is your son?' she had asked, very pleased. 'Three months,' answered the proud father.

While most people were looking forward to the Christmas holidays, Kirsten was getting ready to spend Christmas 1961 back in the hospital. For the third time that year she had to undergo treatment for her skin disease. 'This skin ailment is nothing; when it flares up, I'm not in pain,' she said. During this particular hospital stay, Kirsten and Aslaug Rein had long discussions about the biography in Norwegian that Miss Rein planned to write. As Kirsten began to reach back into her memory, details she had forgotten gradually came to mind; she seemed to enjoy immersing herself in the memories of her eventful life. They agreed that Aslaug should take all of Kirsten's material with her and go through it, until they could meet again at Easter, at Amalienborg, to continue their work together.

During their last conversation before she left Oslo, Kirsten said suddenly: 'I have such pain in my hip again. I hope it's only a strain. Don't mention it. I don't want anyone to worry unnecessarily.' Unfortunately, the pain did not come from a strain. The fatal disease in the bone marrow had flared up again, and there were no further extended remissions. For a whole year she fought against the pain. Occasionally she had better days, when she could still take joy in life. But the 'good' spells became shorter and fewer.

Kirsten Flagstad was never more heroic than during her illness. She tried to pretend that nothing was wrong. She read books, embroidered, made notes for the biography, and answered the letters that streamed in. One night she called Aslaug Rein from Kristiansand: 'I've received a letter I think you should include in the book – as an example of what I'm asked,' she said with a laugh. 'A little girl of eleven asks if I would advise her to become a Wagnerian singer because she has such a big chest. What does one answer to that? If I can bring myself to do it, I'll write and say that she should wait until she is sixteen to see if she can sing.'

Kirsten never gave in. If she suspected that her illness might be fatal, she never mentioned it. Only now and then did she disclose what she imagined when she was despondent. One afternoon during Easter, when she had had an exceptionally painful day, she said suddenly to Aslaug: 'If I become an invalid, I'll lock myself in here at Amalienborg and refuse to see anyone. I won't greet anyone from a wheelchair or on crutches.' Suddenly aware of what she had blurted out, she quickly pulled herself together, lifted her glass and said, 'But why borrow trouble? Let's say Skål instead!'

Immediately after Easter she asked to be readmitted to the hospital again, where she lay until the middle of August. Then she was given permission to spend a short time in her home. In the car with her this time were both wheelchair and crutches, and a nurse. To make it as pleasant as possible for her, she was made comfortable in a hospital bed next to the music room (it was no longer possible for her to walk upstairs to her own room). The wheelchair was not used during those few weeks that she stayed for the last time in the home she loved. She could not leave her bed. She was taken in an ambulance back to the hospital, where she was to remain for the time she had left to live. She did not want to worry those closest to her, especially Else who was so far away. Else wanted to come, and Kirsten's family wanted her to come, but Kirsten said no. There was no hurry. Else, Arthur and Sigurd should come for Christmas as they had planned earlier, she said.

In mid-November, Else Dusenberry received a telegram saying that her father, Sigurd Hall, was dead. He had been ill for some time, but the news of his death came nevertheless as a shock. Else took the next plane to Oslo to be present at his funeral service. When she visited her mother in the hospital, she realized immediately that she was dying. She reproached herself for not coming sooner, but she had always respected her mother's wishes.

One day when Kirsten felt somewhat better, mother and daughter talked for over an hour: 'I know this is the end, Else, but you mustn't be sad. It is best so. You must be a brave, strong girl and take it calmly and naturally.' That same day Kirsten asked to speak with her faithful friend, Leif Stake. She wanted to say goodbye to him and to thank him for what he had done for her through the years. Stake began to cry, but Kirsten, with something of the old spirit in her voice, said, 'No, you mustn't cry. You must be strong like Else. There's nothing to cry about. I have sung my song.' After that, she slipped gradually into a coma. She died on the night of Friday 7 December 1962.

She had not wanted the news of her death to appear until after she was buried. With her name and fame, this was an impossibility: her death became known in Oslo the same night. The next day the whole world knew it. Her picture, with a black border around it, appeared on the front pages of foreign as well as Norwegian newspapers. Numerous tributes told readers what she had meant to the world of music and what a debt opera stages the world over owed her.

Her wish for a private funeral was respected. Only her family and close friends were present at the service, on Friday 14 December.

Beautiful flowers had arrived from people and institutions at home and abroad who wanted to express their gratitude that she had lived. On the white coffin lay only a small bouquet of pink roses. Wreaths, sprays and bouquets of flowers in colourful profusion surrounded and crowned the catafalque, with the king's wreath of white lilies and chrysanthemums a striking centrepiece. A wreath of deep red roses, decorated with a flowing ribbon in the national colours, was on the right: it was from her 'little family', Else, Arthur and Sigurd. On the left was a wreath of red and white carnations, with a ribbon in the same (Danish) colours and inscribed in gold, 'To Isolde from Tristan'. It was a last greeting from Lauritz Melchior, her good friend and colleague of earlier days.

Pastor Lars Johan Danbolt, who officiated at the service, took as his text the words of the Prophet Isaiah: 'In quietness and in confidence shall be your strength.' 'In this quiet moment we must stop and dwell upon something that is greater than being a great artist,' he said. 'Kirsten Flagstad was also a great human being, a great human being who poured out upon us her genius and her rich humanity. She preserved her childhood faith, read in her Bible every day, and there received strength for her great calling.'

No gleaming marble monument with her name engraved in gold marks the place where the ashes of Kirsten Flagstad lie. Her resting place is unknown – that was her wish. Leif Stake was the only person who knew what became of Kirsten's ashes, and when he died, some three years after she did, that knowledge died with him. Arthur Dusenberry told me that her feelings with regard to her death were very much in character. She believed that death was a private part of one's life and that this privacy should remain inviolate. She felt no disillusionment with the world or desire to obliterate her name; Kirsten was much too intelligent, perceptive and realistic a person to believe that her legend and fame would die with her. For all her innate simplicity, she had a healthy appreciation of her own worth and of her pre-eminence as a singer.

In the spring of 1962, having decided to take up a long-standing invitation from Kerstin Thorborg to visit her at her home in Hedemora, Sweden, I had made plans for a three-week trip to Scandinavia in July and August. I wrote to Kirsten Flagstad in Kristiansand, asking if I might pay her a visit. There was no reply before I left New York on 21 July, but when I arrived at Thorborg's on the 22nd, she handed me a letter postmarked Oslo. It was from Leif Stake: Flagstad was in hospital, and she regretted that she would not be able to see me.

The week-long stay with Kerstin Thorborg was a joy. We had not seen each other since 1950, when she and her husband, Gustav Bergman, had returned to Sweden. He had died in 1952, and Kerstin's brother, Carl, had taken up residence with her in 'Björkhagen' (Valley of the Birches), her red villa just outside the town. The evening of my arrival, after supper, we rowed across the lake at the foot of the garden to a small island where we walked for hours in the summer twilight, through meadows aglow with marsh marigolds, reminiscing about days gone by. Later in the week, we sang for each other and for her friends. I said goodbye to her on the 28th, and although we continued to correspond regularly after that, we never saw each other again. Kerstin Thorborg died in Falun, Sweden, on 12 April 1970. She would have been seventy-four on 19 May.

After leaving Thorborg's, I spent two days in Stockholm, during which I made the short trip to Uppsala to visit Dag Hammarskjöld's grave. The gravestone had been strewn with flowers: I looked at it closely and saw that the day before had been his birthday.

On the morning of the 31st, I boarded the train for Oslo, arriving at the Bristol Hotel some time after 7 p.m. I was concerned about Kirsten Flagstad, and since I couldn't get in touch with her, I decided to send her a memento. I walked across the street to the Forum, a lovely shop specializing in handmade Norwegian products, and there my eyes lit on a pair of small, rectangular, blue and white porcelain vases. I bought both of them. I sent one to Kirsten Flagstad with best wishes for her speedy recovery, and the other I later brought home.

On 3 August I left Oslo and began a six-day trip by coach to Bergen. We travelled through some of the most spectacularly beautiful countryside I have ever seen; I pondered on how perfectly the music of Edvard Grieg and the voice of Kirsten Flagstad captured the unique spirit of their homeland, mirroring the calm majesty of its snow-capped mountains, broad valleys, swift-flowing streams and deep, silent fjords.

I spent the Saturday and Sunday nights at the Hotel Alexandra in Loen, on the Nordfjord. After supper on the Saturday I sang some

English folk-songs, among them 'The Keel Row', in remembrance of Kathleen Ferrier, and 'Because I Were Shy', for the three hundred guests assembled in the hotel's Viking Hall. There was much applause, and shouts for more. I obliged with as many as I could remember. The next day I wrote to Kirsten Flagstad about it, telling her how much I had enjoyed singing for some of her countrymen, in her own fair land.

When I arrived back in New York on 13 August, to be met at the airport by my brother and my aunt Alice, I could tell by their demeanour that something was wrong. I soon found out that my father had been in hospital while I was away, and that although he was home again, he was, unknown to him, fatally ill.

Soon after I returned to work on 15 August, Kenneth McPherson, the director of the Bloomfield Public Library, asked me if I would be interested in becoming assistant director. The board had applied to the state for area library status, which, if it was granted, would mean a major building programme, the expansion of the collections and a much larger staff. It didn't take me long to make up my mind. I felt completely at home in the library, I got along well with the staff, and I enjoyed helping the public. In addition, I was given every opportunity to use my musical background to plan special programmes and exhibits.

When I arrived home at my New York apartment after work on 21 September, there was a letter in my postbox postmarked Kristiansand. I opened the letter, and read:

15 September 1962

Dear Mr Vogt

I am sorry I am so late in writing you to thank you for the lovely vase which pleased me very much. It is really very fine.

I am home now but still in bed, but I am improving.

Kindest regards.

Yours sincerely

Kirsten Flagstad

I began to wonder just what was wrong, and I suddenly recalled Thorborg, one day when we were talking about Flagstad, referring to her as 'poor one!'. I didn't attach any special significance to it at the time, assuming that she was referring to all that Flagstad had gone through after the war. But now it struck me that she must have meant something quite different.

I moved to Bloomfield in the November. On 8 December, as I was getting ready to leave for a lesson with my teacher, Sebastian Engleberg, at his home in Bergenfield, I turned on the radio to catch the news. The first words I heard were, 'last night in Oslo at the age of sixty-seven', and I knew what had already been announced. On my way to the bus, I picked up a copy of the *Newark News*: there was her picture on the front page.

I decided to give the twin vase I had brought home from Norway to my brother for Christmas. I looked upon it as a memento of the many unforgettable hours we had spent together in the opera house and in the concert hall listening to the greatest singer of our time.

10

'Remember Me'

In January 1963 I began a series of five monthly lectures on the life and works of Richard Wagner in observance of the hundred and fiftieth anniversary of his birth. The third programme, on *Tristan und Isolde*, was dedicated to the memory of Kirsten Flagstad. The series ended on 22 May, the anniversary date, and there was a major Wagner exhibition in the library throughout that month. It included priceless scores on special loan from the Treasure Room of the Sibley Music Library at the Eastman School of Music.

The following year, I decided to prepare a six-part lecture series on *Tristan und Isolde* for presentation in 1965, with the sixth programme to take place on 10 June, the one hundredth anniversary of the opera's first performance. To illustrate the musical points, I used both the private recording of *Tristan* made from the 2 January 1937 Met broadcast performance conducted by Bodanzky, with Flagstad, Melchior, Thorborg, Huehn and Ludwig Hofmann, and the complete commercial recording made in June 1952, with Furtwängler conducting the Philharmonia Orchestra, and Flagstad, Suthaus, Blanche Thebom, Dietrich Fischer-Dieskau and Josef Greindl in the leading roles. The series was very well received. On 10 June we had a special guest, Kirsten Flagstad's niece, Sigrid Johansen Daley, the daughter of Henry Johansen's brother, Alfred. Kirsten had first met the family soon after her arrival in New York in January 1935. In 1965 Sigrid was living with her husband in Wanamassa, New Jersey. I had invited them both to attend the final anniversary programme. The evening was dedicated to the memory of Kirsten Flagstad, and in honour of Lauritz Melchior, who had celebrated his seventy-fifth birthday on 20 March. Again, a major exhibition occupied the library's main floor.

The ground-breaking ceremony for a major addition to the

Bloomfield Public Library took place on 26 December 1965, and less than two years later, on 5 September 1967, the building was opened to the public. It housed the books and other resources for adults that had occupied the main floor of the original building, where we had continued to work and to serve the public while the construction was going on. The children's and young people's departments, which had formerly occupied the lower floor, were moved to the main floor, and the two downstairs rooms were converted into a meeting room and staff room.

At about that time, Ken McPherson was offered the position of director of the Morris County Library, which he accepted. So the board of trustees of the Bloomfield Public Library was suddenly faced with the task of selecting a new director. I asked to be considered as a candidate, and in November five people, including myself, were interviewed by the board. When my turn came, I was asked what I would do, if appointed, to build upon the solid foundation of high-quality library service that had been established by the three previous directors. Having said that I would seek to make the library the cultural centre of the community, I then proceeded to outline a comprehensive cultural programme, including book reviewing, public seminars on topics of current interest, a wide range of activities for children, film programmes, lectures, plays, concerts and opera performances. With the exception of the president, who was aware of my work, the board looked either sceptical or nonplussed. I didn't blame them: the concept was so far removed from what they thought of as a library service that they had difficulty taking it in. They asked me to clarify many points, including the crucial one of how I would go about obtaining financial support for such a project. I had spent many hours thinking about all aspects of the plan, and I was ready and willing to tell them. In the end, they must have thought it was worth a try: I was appointed library director, starting 1 January 1968.

I founded the Bloomfield Opera Theatre, under the aegis of the library board, in 1969. The company was established primarily to give talented singers in the area the opportunity to appear in fully staged operatic productions. From the outset, the aim was to achieve a professional standard of performance. A grant of $5,600 from the state library enabled us to get the project under way. The meeting room was made into a theatre, a director was engaged, auditions were held, and the first public performance took place in May. From then until the end of 1984 the company presented numerous performances of eleven operas, from Mozart to Menotti. We initiated an annual concert series in 1970, the year of the Beethoven bicentennial. Ernest Goldman, an accomplished pianist who had studied in Vienna with Richard Robert, teacher of Rudolf Serkin, and who lived in the town, presented a series of Beethoven sonata recitals. The concert season ran from late September to early May, with a performance almost every Sunday afternoon. Unfortunately, both opera and concert performances were discontinued at the end of 1984, when I retired.

In November 1973 I devoted the first half of a song recital in the theatre to ten songs by Edvard Grieg. I sang them in Norwegian, and in memory of Kirsten Flagstad. I had made a rudimentary study of the language in 1957, while planning the programme for my first recital at Northern Illinois University. I wanted to include three songs composed by Grieg to texts by Vinje, and I was determined to sing them in the language in which they were meant to be sung – not in barely passable English translations, and certainly not in German, which, contrary to belief and practice, is completely out of tune with Grieg's mature musical idiom. Thereafter, I listened attentively over and over again to Kirsten Flagstad's recordings of songs by Norwegian composers, until my ear became attuned to the characteristic sounds of the language and I could reproduce them with a fair degree of accuracy. Grieg's settings of his compatriots' poems I found to be uncommonly sensitive and evocative; they are unique in the song literature.

The eightieth anniversary of Kirsten Flagstad's birth was observed in Oslo in 1975. From 6 to 13 July an exhibition of Flagstad memorabilia occupied rooms in the Norwegian Music Collection Library, a division of the Royal University Library, and programmes were scheduled throughout the week. Unable to be in Oslo at that time, I set up a small commemorative exhibition at the Bloomfield Public Library. It was supposed to be on display just during July and August, but the public's interest in it led us to extend it to the end of October.

My research for this book began when I was in San Francisco in late June and early July of that year, representing the New Jersey Library Association at the annual conference of the American Library Association. I had found time between conference meetings to visit Schubert Hall, the Library of the California Historical Society, and had examined parts of the Kirsten Flagstad Memorial Collection established there in 1964 by Caroline Esberg, Flagstad's closest friend in America. Then, on 7 July 1976 I flew to London on the first leg of a three-and-a-half-week trip to Europe undertaken expressly to continue research for the book. I spent over a week in Oslo poring over the vast amount of material in the Norwegian Music Collection, housed in the former University Observatory building. On the twelfth I was privileged to join Øystein Gaukstad, the music librarian, and the members of his staff, in a delightful informal celebration of Kirsten Flagstad's eighty-first birthday anniversary. Berit Stabben, her former housekeeper, who lived nearby, arrived with her sister Karen to take part in the festivities, bringing with her a birthday cake and the last known recording of Flagstad's voice, made when she had sung Grieg's 'Blåbærli' on a radio programme on 21 November 1959. How poignant it was to listen to that superb voice, as fresh and clear as ever, and to realize that it had been captured then for perhaps the last time.

Berit and her sister offered to show me the house at 6 Tidemand Street in Oslo, where Kirsten and her husband had lived. I walked the short distance with them and took a photograph of them in front of the house, which is now the Belgian Embassy. Later in the year I received a letter from Berit, in which she had enclosed copies of some treasured personal photographs of her beloved Fru Flagstad.

The day after the party, I took the train to Kristiansand to visit Amalienborg, Kirsten's former home there, which is now an office for Henry Johansen Ltd. It was hard to believe that this forlorn building had once been the lively home of one of the world's greatest musicians. Not far from the house is a street named 'Kirsten Flagstads Vei'.

The next day I took the afternoon train back to Oslo.

During the ten days I was in London after my trip to Norway, I drove down to Glyndebourne with Ed Willson, my old Eastman classmate now living in London, for a performance of *Le Nozze di Figaro*; I was impressed with the voice of the young Swedish soprano, Helena Döse, who sang the Countess, whom I could imagine developing into a dramatic soprano of the Wagnerian class. Most of my time in London was spent in the archives of the

Royal Opera House, Covent Garden, where Boris Skidelsky, the archivist, and Margaret Nicholson, in the adjacent office of the Friends of Covent Garden, were very helpful to me in my research on Kirsten Flagstad. Boris brought out the costume she had worn in Act One of *Tristan* at Covent Garden, and Margaret modelled it so that I could take a colour photograph. Before leaving for Paris, I made arrangements to return to London in the October to continue my research, and to attend the second *Ring* cycle at Covent Garden, to be conducted by Colin Davis and directed by Götz Friedrich.

In Paris I enjoyed a reunion with Suzanne Loeb, my former accompanist, who had gone to France in 1972 to marry the composer Rudolph Goehr, brother of the late conductor Walter Goehr. I spent several hours in the Musée de l'Opéra going through the material there on Flagstad, and on Wagnerian productions at the Opéra. I also heard Mozart's *Entführung* and *Figaro* at the Opéra: Christiane Eda-Pierre (Konstanze), Norma Burrowes (Blondchen) and Kurt Moll (Osmin) were delightful in *Entführung*, and Margaret Price (Countess) and Gabriel Bacquier (Count) were outstanding in *Figaro*.

The performance of the *Ring* at Covent Garden in October was distinguished by the fine playing of the orchestra under Davis, and the performances of the German tenor, Peter Hofmann, in his Covent Garden debut as Siegmund in *Die Walküre*, and Berit Lindholm, the Swedish soprano, as Brünnhilde in *Götter-dämmerung*. Hofmann was an ardent, virile Siegmund, lithe of figure and poetic of face, whose voice gave promise of a significant career ahead, and Lindholm was an impressive and dramatically eloquent Brünnhilde. Stepping in at short notice for another singer, she sang Isolde in a concert performance of *Tristan* at Carnegie Hall on 31 December 1978, performing the arduous role very well. In appearance and gait, she reminded me of Kerstin Thorborg. I left the auditorium wanting to hear and see her as Isolde on the stage. Why hasn't she sung the role at the Metropolitan? *Tristan und Isolde* was revived at the Metropolitan on 9 January 1981, after an absence of six seasons – which, for a company that regards itself as the best in the world, is inexcusable. The title roles were sung by Spas Wenkoff, the Bulgarian tenor, in his Met debut, and Gwyneth Jones, the Welsh soprano. James Levine conducted *Tristan* for the first time on this occasion. The score was performed in its entirety, without cuts.

Wenkoff, an intelligent singer, acquitted himself well, both musically and histrionically. Vocally, however, he was defeated by the size of the auditorium, and his overall portrayal lacked the measure of passionate intensity that the role demands, especially in the third act. Gwyneth Jones, on the other hand, had voice enough and to spare, though she has yet to perfect her vocal technique: breath control, intonation and phrasing. In her portrayal of Isolde she came so close to being exceptional: it is not difficult to envisage her very soon taking up her rightful place of pre-eminence among today's Wagnerian sopranos. She has everything going for her: a potentially great voice, a commanding presence on the stage, striking good looks and a natural dramatic instinct. She *could* be today's great Isolde.

The finest performance of the evening was given by the other debut artist, Matti Salminen, the Finnish bass, as King Marke. He was eloquent in voice and noble in action; indeed, his portrayal of the grieved Cornish monarch moved the audience deeply. When he appeared before the curtain after the second act, he was greeted with an ovation. The orchestra played well for Levine, but the young conductor naturally needs experience with the score to bring out the dramatic sweep which is such a vital part of its musical architecture. I attended two subsequent performances with the same cast, and the third, on 13 February 1981, was by far the best, primarily because of Levine's surer hand at the helm.

I flew from London to Oslo on 12 October 1976 to meet Aslaug Rein and Karen Marie Flagstad, Kirsten's sister. We had a marvellous dinner at Blom's, Oslo's famous artists' restaurant, on the 13th, and the next day, braving the first snowstorm of the season, I met Karen Marie at the Music Library to go through some photographs of her sister. When we parted, she overwhelmed me by presenting to me Kirsten Flagstad's personal bound copy of Grieg songs and her copy of Schubert's *Wanderer Fantasie* for piano, which she had studied in 1956 with her brother Lasse, who was a concert pianist.

Before leaving for Europe, I had done some preliminary work on a five-part lecture series, scheduled for presentation in November and early December, on Wagner's *Der Ring des Nibelungen*, to commemorate the hundredth anniversary of the Bayreuth Festival and the first complete performance of the *Ring*. The series was

283

planned as a benefit for the performing arts fund of the Bloomfield Public Library. For musical illustration, I used the special-edition recording of the March–April 1950 La Scala performance of the *Ring*, released in 1976 by the Bruno Walter Society and Sound Archive, with Wilhelm Furtwängler conducting a distinguished cast headed by Kirsten Flagstad as Brünnhilde. The series netted $820 for the fund.

This book is published in the 1980s, a decade of special significance for those who loved and admired Kirsten Flagstad. The second of February 1985 was the fiftieth anniversary of her Metropolitan Opera debut; 22 March of that year was the thirtieth anniversary of her last public appearance in the United States, and 12 July was the ninetieth anniversary of her birth; 18 May 1986 was the fiftieth anniversary of her London debut at Covent Garden (where Francesca Franchi, archivist of the Royal Opera House, set up an exhibition to commemorate the occasion), and 12 December 1988 will be the seventy-fifth anniversary of her debut as a professional singer. Kirsten Flagstad's voice is preserved more or less faithfully on records. But the total, unsurpassable impact of a Flagstad performance is recorded only in the memories of those who heard her and saw her on the stage.

On one of his television interview shows in America, Dick Cavett had as his guest the eminent theatre critic of the *New Republic*, Stanley Kauffmann. In answer to a question from Cavett as to what defines 'great artists', Kauffmann said simply, 'They transform our lives.' That is what Kirsten Flagstad did for hundreds of thousands of people throughout the world.

When I am asked whether any soprano I have heard in recent years reminds me of Kirsten Flagstad in quality of voice and musicianship, I reply, 'Yes. Jessye Norman'. I am always struck by the unusual timbre and evocative power of her voice, and by the sensitivity with which she uses her voice throughout its wide range. She sings with the assurance, *élan* and insight of a master.

Select Bibliography

Biography and Autobiography

Benestad, Finn og Schjelderup-Ebbe, Dag. *Edvard Grieg: mennesket og kunstneren*. Oslo: H. Aschehoug, 1980

Biancolli, Louis. *The Flagstad Manuscript*. New York: G. P. Putnam's Sons, 1952

Bing, Sir Rudolf. *5000 Nights at the Opera*. Garden City, NY: Doubleday, 1972

Geissmar, Berta. *Two Worlds of Music*. New York: Creative Age Press, 1946

Gunnarson, Torstein. *Sannheten om Kirsten Flagstad*. Oslo: Flagstad-selskapet, 1985

Leider, Frida. *Playing My Part*. Translated from the German by Charles Osborne. London: Calder and Boyars, 1966

Leinsdorf, Erich. *Cadenza: A Musical Career*. Boston: Houghton Mifflin, 1976

McArthur, Edwin. *Flagstad: A Personal Memoir*. New York: Alfred A. Knopf, 1965

Newton, Ivor. *At the Piano – Ivor Newton: The World of an Accompanist*. Boston: Crescendo Publishing, 1966

Pleasants, Henry. *The Great Singers, from the Dawn of Opera to Our Own Time*. New York: Simon and Schuster, 1970

Rasponi, Lanfranco. *The Last Prima Donnas*. New York: Alfred A. Knopf, 1982

Rein, Aslaug. *Kirsten Flagstad*. Oslo: Ernst G. Mortensens Forlag, 1967

Sheean, Vincent. *First and Last Love*. New York: Random House, 1956

Select Bibliography

Music, Opera and Operatic History

Bloomfield, Arthur. *The San Francisco Opera, 1922–1978*. Sausalito, California: Comstock Editions, 1978

Briggs, John. *Requiem for a Yellow Brick Brewery: A History of the Metropolitan Opera*. Boston: Little, Brown, 1969

Culshaw, John. *Ring Resounding: The Recording in Stereo of Der Ring des Nibelungen*. London: Secker & Warburg, 1967

Davis, Ronald L. *Opera in Chicago*. New York: Appleton-Century, 1966

Eaton, Quaintance. *Opera Caravan: Adventures of the Metropolitan on Tour, 1883–1956*. New York: Da Capo Press, 1978

Furlong, William Barry. *Season with Solti: A Year in the Life of the Chicago Symphony*. New York: Macmillan, 1974

Gilman, Lawrence. *Wagner's Operas*. New York: Farrar & Rinehart, 1937

Grinde, Nils. *Norsk Musikk Historie*. Rev. edn. Oslo: Universitetsforlaget, 1975

Jaques-Dalcroze, Emile. *Rhythm, Music and Education*. Translated from the French by Harold F. Rubinstein. London: Chatto & Windus, 1921

Kolodin, Irving. *The Metropolitan Opera, 1883–1966: A Candid History*. 4th edn. New York: Afred A. Knopf, 1966

Lange, Kristian. *Norwegian Music: A Survey*. Oslo: Johan Grundt Tanum Forlag, 1971

Rosenthal, Harold. *Opera at Covent Garden: A Short History*. London: Victor Gollancz, 1967

Seltsam, William H., compiler. *Metropolitan Opera Annals: A Chronicle of Artists and Performances*. New York: H. W. Wilson, 1947

Norway and the Second World War

Andenæs, Johs., Riste, O. and Skodvin, M. *Norway and the Second World War*. Oslo: Johan Grundt Tanum Forlag, 1974

Gjelsvik, Tore. *Norwegian Resistance, 1940–1945*. Translated from the Norwegian by Thomas Kingston Derry. Montreal: McGill-Queen's University Press, 1979

Petrow, Richard. *The Bitter Years: The Invasion and Occupation of*

Denmark and Norway, April 1940–May 1945. New York: William Morrow, 1974

Riste, Olav and Nökleby, Berit. *Norway 1940–45: The Resistance Movement.* 2nd edn. Oslo: Johan Grundt Tanum Forlag, 1973

Opera and Operetta Roles Sung
by Kirsten Flagstad

Work and Composer	Role	First appearance	Total career performances
Tiefland (Eugene d'Albert)	Nuri	12.12.1913	20
The Bells of Corneville (Robert Planquette)	Germaine	autumn 1914	7
Mountain Story (Waldemar Thrane)	Aagot	summer 1915	26
Die Fledermaus (Johann Strauss)	Rosalinde	summer 1915	89
Holy Night (Gerhard Schjelderup)	Angel	31.8.1915	8
Spring Night (Gerhard Schjelderup)	Emilie	31.8.1915	8
Der Evangelimann (Wilhelm Kienzl)	Martha	16.1.1919	6
The Gypsy Baron (Johann Strauss)	Arsena	1.3.1919	24
Pagliacci (Ruggiero Leoncavallo)	Nedda	23.3.1919	13
The Beautiful Galatea (Franz von Suppé)	Ganymed	25.3.1919	17
The Nürnberg Doll (Adolphe Adam)	Bertha	1.4.1919	7
Abu Hassan (Carl Maria von Weber)	Fatima	24.4.1919	5
Die lustigen Weiber von Windsor (Otto Nicolai)	Anna	10.5.1919	7
La Belle Hélène (Jacques Offenbach)	Orestes	28.8.1919	10
The Little Lark (Franz Lehár)	Margit	5.10.1919	16
Gypsy Love (Franz Lehár)	Zorika	26.12.1920	10
Die Zauberflöte (W. A. Mozart)	Erste Dame	18.1.1921	6
	Pamina (?)	26.1.1921	19
Otello (Giuseppe Verdi)	Desdemona		
Un Ballo in Maschera (Giuseppe Verdi)	Amelia	20.2.1921	9
Das höllisch Gold (Julius Bittner)	Die Frau	17.4.1921	3

Opera and Operetta Roles

Work and Composer	Role	First appearance	Total career performances
La Fanciulla del West (Giacomo Puccini)	Minnie	5.5.1921	18
Tosca (Giacomo Puccini)	Shepherd	9.5.1921	2
Orpheus in the Underworld (Jacques Offenbach)	Diana	1.6.1922	2
	Eurydice	5.6.1922	8
Phi-Phi (Henri Christiné)	Phi-Phi	13.6.1922	11
The Lady in Ermine (Jean Gilbert)	Marianne	15.7.1922	35
The Girl from Holland (Emmerich Kálmán)	Helena Maria	10.11.1922	71
When Love Awakens (Eduard Künnecke)	Countess	12.9.1923	?
Die Bajadere (Emmerich Kálmán)	Odette Darimond	30.9.1923	141
Boccaccio (Franz von Suppé)	Fiametta	22.1.1924	27
The Dollar Princess (Leo Fall)	Alise	21.2.1924	37
The Queen of the Movies (Jean Gilbert)	Delia Gill	12.4.1924	36
Lucullus (Jean Gilbert)	Melissa	4.8.1924	16
Carmen (Georges Bizet)	Micaëla	22.11.1924	47
You-You (?)	You-You	2.6.1925	?
Les Brigands (Jacques Offenbach)	Fiorella	6.10.1925	?
Gri-Gri (Paul Lincke)	Yvonne	30.10.1925	47
The Sailor's Bride (Sigwardt Aspestrand)	Ragnhild	12.12.1925	9
The Queen of the Carnival (Emmerich Kálmán)	Alexandra Maria	3.1.1926	141
The Cousin from Batavia (Eduard Künnecke)	Julia	4.6.1926	?
The Circus Princess (Emmerich Kálmán)	Princess	11.11.1926	79
Faust (Charles Gounod)	Marguerite	7.12.1926	41
Alexandra (Albert Szirmai)	Alexandra	7.5.1927	63
Orfeo ed Euridice (Christoph Willibald Gluck)	Euridice	6.7.1927	11
Orloff (Bruno Granichstädten)	Nadia	11.10.1927	?
Her Excellency (Richard Heuberger)	Duchess	17.6.1928	25
The Orange Duchess (?)	Duchess	10.7.1928	16
Countess Maritza (Emmerich Kálmán)	Maritza	26.7.1928	25

Work and Composer	Role	First appearance	Total career performances
Der Freischütz (Carl Maria von Weber)	Agathe	4.10.1928	28
Saul and David (Carl Nielsen)	Mikal	29.11.1928	15
The Girl Friend (Richard Rodgers)	Mollie Farrell	25.1.1929	31
Aïda (Giuseppe Verdi)	Aïda	7.3.1929	27
La Bohème (Giacomo Puccini)	Mimi	11.4.1929	6
Tosca (Giacomo Puccini)	Floria Tosca	19.4.1929	21
Lohengrin (Richard Wagner)	Elsa	14.6.1929	40
La Rondine (Giacomo Puccini)	Magda	4.10.1929	7
L'Enfant prodigue (André Wormser)	Mother	4.10.1929	7
Die grosse Unbekannte (*Donna Juanita*) (Franz von Suppé)	Lucie	17.10.1929	1
Die Meistersinger von Nürnberg (Richard Wagner)	Eva	18.2.1930	21
Jonny spielt auf (Ernst Křenek)	Anita	10.4.1930	6
Švanda the Bagpiper (Jaromir Weinberger)	Dorota	3.12.1931	14
Rodelinda (George Frideric Handel)	Rodelinda	16.2.1932	7
Tristan und Isolde (Richard Wagner)	Isolde	29.6.1932	182
Die Walküre (Wagner)	Ortlinde	25.7.1933	2
Götterdämmerung (Wagner)	Dritte Norn	28.7.1933	2
Die Walküre (Wagner)	Sieglinde	24.5.1934	14
Götterdämmerung (Wagner)	Gutrune	6.7.1934	3
Tannhäuser (Wagner)	Elisabeth	5.10.1934	35
Fidelio (Ludwig van Beethoven)	Leonore	10.12.1934	37
Die Walküre (Richard Wagner)	Brünnhilde	15.2.1935	77
Götterdämmerung (Wagner)	Brünnhilde	28.2.1935	47
Parsifal (Wagner)	Kundry	17.4.1935	39
Siegfried (Wagner)	Brünnhilde	6.11.1935	31
Der fliegende Holländer (Wagner)	Senta	7.1.1937	11
Oberon (Carl Maria von Weber)	Rezia	30.5.1942	2
Alceste/Alcestis (Christoph Willibald Gluck)	Alceste/ Alcestis	29.5.1943	9
Dido and Aeneas (Henry Purcell)	Dido	9.9.1951	111

Index

KF = Kirsten Flagstad

291

Index

Index

Index

Index

Index